A Mile in My Own Shoes

Sarah Louise Rosmond

INTRODUCTION...

This book is part 2 of my story, and it explains some of the hardest parts of my life, how I have found my way to accept my past and finally found a way to move on.

At the sweet age of seventeen, I moved out of my parents' home to take on the world by myself. In my still very childish mind, I thought moving out of the house I shared with my paedophile Dad would be the end to my misery, and in some ways it did, for a while anyway. Follow me on my journey from teenager to young adult and visit all the twists and turns I encountered on the way. Nothing has ever been easy for me really, but I stick to my saying that 'everything happens for a reason.'

I may not be proud of every decision I have made in my life, but I am proud of what I have been through and at no point have I given up hope that life can get better, not only for me, no but also my children and the other people I hold dear who had entered my life and stuck by me when I needed them the most. I have surprised both myself and my friends with the determination and strength I have shown until now, and long may that continue. Just because we have a terrible start in life, doesn't mean that we can't break that cycle and create a life we truly want. The best advice I can give anyone is always stay true to who you are, no matter what –

Sarah Rosmond xox

ACKNOWLEDGMENTS

Like before, I would like to thank my Mother who since realizing the depth of what I went through as a child, has been my rock in this chapter of my life, and I don't give her as much credit as she deserves.

My cousin Jody, who you will meet again in this book, is my best friend and has supported me through this full process and continues to encourage me to this day.

Lastly, I would like to thank Ryan Traill who created the perfect imagery for this book; I look forward to working with him again in the future. The man is fantastic at capturing the detail needed in an image.

Other titles now available:

Part 1 of the Sarah Rosmond Story – My Life in His Hands

Part 3- Where will my journey end?

Contents

LEAVING HOME…

No sexual abuse happened after the last night my dad had been watching his pornography, I think I am too old for him now. A paedophile likes the control they have over younger children, and I think my dad could see he was losing the hold he had on me. Since Wayne, the cousin who drug raped me and got away with it, my attitude had changed completely. No more was the timid young girl that you met before, now I was older, angrier, and more determined to take control of my own life. I had started to argue more, resulting in more beatings, but I had gotten used to it, and in any situation, once you get too used to it, it becomes repetitive and boring. I was no longer scared of my dad, and I didn't care what he would do to me anymore. To make sure he didn't have the chance I spent all day, every day out, only returning home to get a bite to eat and going out again.

I had a full-time job working at a local factory making chocolate; it sounds a lot more glamorous than it was. I hated the job itself but loved the freedom it gave me, and the wages at the end of the week. Not that I saw most of my wages, with Mum and especially my Dad still heavily addicted to crack cocaine, most of my money was taken off me to feed their dirty drug habit. So, I took a second job working in the evenings at the hotel where I had done my work experience in the year before. I enjoyed my job, but it was demanding work, the hours almost killed me after working all day in a hot factory, but I was trying my hardest to put money away for my big escape. I had convinced myself I needed money to move, so I started saving in a tub underneath my bed. I must have saved over two hundred pounds when I returned home one day to find the container rolling around the floor outside my front door, I ran over to pick it up, but it was empty, all my money had gone.

I stormed into the house shouting about my finding, and my dad told me it was my own fault that I should have put it in my bank, he then started to question where I had the money from in the first place. When I told him though, I could tell he thought I was lying. I had asked if he knew where the money had gone, and he looked down at his crack pipe.

'Doesn't go far' he said smirking at me.

I was ready to explode and stormed back out of the house. I made my way to the other end of the estate to where my cousin Katie was chilling with a few of our mates. She was seeing a boy called Deane. He was an ugly looking thing with a balding head and eyes that looked far too big for his tiny head, but who was I to talk. I had been flirty with Simon all night. I had known him for over a year, but as he was almost ten years older than me I never looked twice at him, but I knew he really fancied me, so I played along with it. I had told him previously about my crack head parents, so it was no surprise when I turned up angry that my Dad had stolen my money. He then commented on me moving in with him and his cousin Vicky, I didn't get on with Victoria, but the idea tempted me. We sat and had smoke and about nine o'clock that evening they had walked me home.

Once we got the end of my street we stopped, and I said my goodbyes. 'I was serious by the way.'

Simon said as I was walking away. I turned back round to face him, walking backward and almost losing my footing.

'What do you mean? '

He smiled and said, 'You are welcome to move into mine, we have plenty of room.'

I wasn't sure if he was serious, so I just replied, 'Oh don't tempt me,' and laughed as I walked away.

Dad was asleep when I got home, so I said goodnight to my Mum who was lying down on the sofa with the TV on low and the lights off. She had slept on the couch most nights since my little brother had been born, at the start it was so the baby didn't disturb the rest of the house, but it had turned into a regular thing now. Even though my little brother now slept upstairs, Mum would stay downstairs and relax on the sofa with a small blanket that barely covered her.

The next morning, I got up for work as usual, Dad had asked what time I was due home, and if I had work at the hotel that evening. I told him I was home for about six and no I didn't work at the hotel on a Thursday night. He then tried to tell me that I was staying in that evening. I wasn't going to be staying in at all, by this point I was seventeen and I knew I had more control over my life, so after work instead of going home, I had decided to go straight round to Si's. I knew he was in because he was a lazy bum who didn't work, lived off benefits and smoked weed all day. I knocked on the door, and he answered with a big grin on his face.

'Were you being serious when you said I could stay?' I asked,

'Of course, I was you daft mare, I would do anything to see that smile back on your face,' was his reply, so with that I smiled at him and walked through into the living room.

Our mate Leachy was being weird, sat in the middle of the room with incense burning around him, he believed he was a vampire and convinced himself that he could do spells and stuff.

'He is trying to control the candle,' Si whispered.

So, we left Leachy to it and went upstairs where the rest of the crew were skinning up and listening to music. To be honest, I hated all the heavy metal stuff they were listening to but the more I sat in the room, the more I got used to the screams of Cradle of Filth's frontman. So, that day it was decided that I was to move in and have the spare room. Simon knew I worked but said he didn't want my money and that I was just to put a tenner in the electric once a week and buy my food. So, with everything sorted I just needed to find the right time to tell my parents I was moving out, which I wasn't looking forward to.

The moment to tell my parents came a few days later, it was the weekend, and I had returned home to get my dinner like planned, as soon as I walked in through the door my Dad had started bitching at me,

'You use this fucking house like a hotel,' he snapped.

'Start spending more time at home, or you can move out.'

I just looked at him in disbelief and replied,

'I want to move out anyway,' he just laughed at me.

'And how do you expect to do that?' he asked.

I had sat down and explained where I was moving to, and Dad thought it was funny. He said I wouldn't last five minutes without my Mum doing everything for me and that I wasn't allowed to come running back when it all went wrong, he said I was on my own and never to ask them for help again.

This suited me as I was glad that I was finally able to get away from all this shit I had to cope with at home. I wasn't thinking about anyone but myself, not even my brothers, the way I saw it was this was the chance I had to get away, and I was taking it no matter what.

Mum tried, that evening, to talk me out of it, but I had made up my mind. I was finally moving out and was excited about the idea of overseeing my own life, and I was convinced that things would be a lot easier from this moment on. I left the kitchen and went up to my room to pack some things, I only took stuff I needed for a few days, clean underwear, clothes and toiletries.

Dad was still shouting abuse up the stairs, but I had switched off, the only comment I remember him yelling was that I am a traitor for leaving the family. I was moving ten minutes away, it wasn't as if I was moving to a new country, but I think if that if option were offered at that point I would have taken it. When I finished packing, I made my way back down the stairs and into the kitchen where my Dad was sat at the table with his head in his hands as usual.

'I can go tonight if you want,' I said.

'Yeah, fuck off!' Dad snapped, 'you will be back in a few days, I guarantee you, and you can't even cook for fucks sake. If it weren't for your mother doing everything for you, you wouldn't do shit.'

I shook my head at him. 'I can cook, by the way, it's just that you never let me,' I said sarcastically.

'Oh, just fuck off, you have an answer for everything.'

So, I did just that. I hugged my Mum and told her I would see her soon and grabbed my bag. I noticed one of my brothers had walked into the kitchen, he was meant to be in bed with a sickness bug but had overheard the argument downstairs.

'Where are you going?' he asked,

'Just to my friends for a bit, I will see you tomorrow dude,' I said kissing him on the forehead before walking out of the front door.

I had stuck to my word and returned to my parent's house every day that first week, it was awkward at first, the atmosphere could have been cut with a knife, but this time it was on my terms, and a part of me loved the control. If my Dad had started bitching or ranting I could just say I had to go home and I was out of the situation.

TIMES ARE CHANGING...

Life seemed easy at Simon's house; we always managed to have a house full which at the start suited me just fine, I was out working all hours during the day, and when I got home most evenings Si would cook us all dinner. My only issue was Vicky: Si's cousin, who apparently hated me, and it seemed to me that she had no valid reason for the spitefulness she showed me, she was also a bit too clingy with her cousin, and after a few weeks of living with them, the penny finally dropped. We were all sitting in the living room when I noticed the lingering looks between the two of them. I had waited till Vicky had left the room, to go and make us a drink and I moved over to the other side of the room and sat down on the sofa beside Simon; he had a massive cheesy grin on his face.

'You okay?' He asked, I just nodded and smiled back. Nessa, who was his younger sister, was huffing and puffing, so Simon had asked her what was wrong.

'You know,' she replied.

'No, I clearly don't, that's why I am asking!' He said sarcastically.

Ness stood up 'You are meant to be with Vicky, but you are flirting with her,' she said pointing at me.

'Hey, leave me out of this!' I snapped 'And no offense Simon, but that's your fucking cousin, its sick.'

'I agree with Sarah, its wrong on so many levels,' my cousin Katie butted in.

'It's not as if he has many offers!' Leachy said laughing to himself.

I looked over at Si and shook my head, 'You still don't need to sleep with a family member for fucks sake.'

He just shrugged his shoulders. Feeling annoyed I got up and walked out of the living room.

I overheard Simon asking why it was such a big deal to me and then I could hear them all chatting among themselves, but I couldn't make out what had been said. I made my way outside and sat on the wall out the front of Si's house just looking up at the sky, it had started to get overcast, and the sun was slowly setting at the back of the Moors, which was the big mountain you could see throughout the whole of Crosby.

I must have been outside for a good twenty minutes when Simon finally appeared in the doorway.

'Kate told me about your cousin I am so sorry to hear about it,' he said with a grim look on his face.

'Well, she had no right!' I snapped back.

Then he walked over and sat down beside me, and I found myself opening to him about the whole ordeal. Wayne was my cousin who at the time was almost twice my age. Si knew a little about the rape but never knew the full extent of what had happened, as I spoke to him I felt sick that I had not been strong enough to stop it happening and the tears streamed down my face making a wet puddle in the palm of my hand. He placed his arms on my shoulders and told me that everything was going to be okay. Although I couldn't see how, I decided to trust him and we sat outside for over an hour, every now and again we would notice silhouette's in the kitchen windows as everyone else in the house wanted to know what was going on including Victoria.

Part of me loved that she was getting annoyed because I was getting all his attention and she wasn't. Now, Simon wasn't a good looking guy by any means; he had a stupid mullet haircut which was short on top and shoulder length at the back and sides, and with his hair being dark mousy blonde it always looked greasy, and his dress sense was almost as wicked as his hairstyle. Old oil stained dark blue jeans that hung from his skeleton frame and a worn out Metallica band t-shirt to cover his wafer-thin arms. But behind the looks was a very caring sensitive man, almost straight away I knew I could trust him, which for me was a breakthrough by any means.

I decided then that this man could not be in a relationship with his flesh and blood. So, my mind was set on making sure I could stop it and getting one over on Vicky just made me even more determined to get what I wanted. Even if I wasn't a hundred percent sure about what I wanted, I knew what I didn't. Simon would be mine, even if it were to get him to realize he could do a lot better than he was settling for.

When we returned to the living room, both Vicky and Ness had gone upstairs in a huff. I was secretly glad, but at the same time, I felt guilty that I had pushed Ness away. Simon had gone upstairs to try and keep the peace, but that almost seemed to feed the fire as I could hear him and his cousin shouting at each other over the heavy metal music playing beside me. I sat beside Katie 1 and asked her why she told everyone about my past and she informed me that it was the only way he could understand why I was so disgusted in his own chosen relationship, I had understood where she was coming from and didn't mention it again.

Mini Victory...

Weeks turned into months, Simon and I had started to get closer, and it helped that Vicky had gone back to Basingstoke to move back in with her parents. Simon and I had started sharing the same bed. Most of the time we just slept as I wasn't ready for anything else, not that it would stop him trying most evenings, but he knew that no meant no and he would eventually give in and stop trying. I could tell it was frustrating him, but I wasn't going to do anything until I felt a hundred percent comfortable with him.

'Just lying here beside you is good enough for me,' he would tell me all too often, but from the growth in his trousers, I knew deep down he wanted a whole lot more.

So, after a few weeks of sleeping in the same bed I finally gave in to his advances, he was so loving and gentle that it made me feel uncomfortable and I had to tell him straight.

'I am not a fragile ornament, you won't break me y'know!' and with that, we became more passionate.

Oral sex was good even though it was the part that scared me the most, Si had a way of making me feel a little more comfortable, and we finally slept together. Afterwards, he held me so lovely that I had started to forget about my past and really thought he might be the one. After that first night, we were inseparable from each other, I even quit my jobs, so I could spend all day with him, and we got on brilliantly.

Even Ness could see the difference in her brother, and she told me a few times that I made him happy. I could honestly say at that point in my life, I felt the same.

So, after a couple of months, we decided to have my name added to the tenancy, and that gave me the security I had been craving. I had finally felt safe in my own home, something that was new to me as a young adult.

That afternoon I had gone to see my Mum and Dad and told my Mum that I was in a relationship with Simon. She wasn't over the moon and made it clear to me that I could do a lot better than 'that tramp' but I didn't listen and told her that if she got to know him, she might even like him.

'I just don't want you to rush into anything and to get hurt,' she said.

Getting hurt was not on my list of things to do I assured her.

After my hour long visit which seemed to last the entire day I set about going back to Si's house, on the way I bumped into a small chubby girl with streaked shoulder-length hair, she stopped me in my tracks.

'You're Sarah,' she said pointing in my direction.

'I am,' I replied as she walked off, it seemed weird as I didn't know her, but for some reason, she had seemed familiar.

The rest of the ten-minute walk home I couldn't help but think how strange the encounter was. How did that girl know my name and why did she just walk away when I told her who I was?

I was still baffled by the whole thing when I got home, and in my own little daydream, I hadn't even realized Simon was placing his arms around me, as he had missed me. It wasn't until he kissed my face that I realized I was standing in the hallway to his large four bedroomed rented home. The house was dark and in desperate need of decoration, but with none of us the house working since I gave up my job, there was no way we could afford to do anything. The house may have been unkept, but it was now my home and the only place I felt safe. I could feel Simon squeeze me and at that moment, it dawned on me, that all I had ever wanted was to be appropriately loved for who I was and not what sick sexual games could be used against me.

I knew I could trust him, and I could feel the warmth and love baring into my soul, I had hoped one day I would feel the same about him, but I wasn't going to rush anything, it would be if it were meant to be, is what I kept telling myself.

It was a Friday morning and Si was due to sign on at the job centre, I was going with him, and we were going to make a joint claim, that was a statement that we were both in a relationship. It was the proof my troubled little mind needed at the time.

When we were called to the desk, a small middle-aged friendly looking woman handed us both some forms and said we had to fill them out together.

'I hate these bloody forms,' he sighed.

He had been on benefits for years and didn't seem fussed about finding a job, which to me sounded odd, but who was I to say anything, I had myself not long quit my job, so I was as bad as him. After filling out the forms we handed them back to the lady at the desk, she scanned the forms to make sure we had filled out all the parts needed on them and then she looked at me.

'Miss Rosmond, can you confirm your date of birth please?' so I told her my date of birth.

'I am sorry, but you cannot claim benefits just yet,' she said.

I looked at up at Simon, as he asked her why, she continued, 'you must be at least eighteen to receive benefits, you are not eighteen for a few more weeks, is that right?' she asked, and I nodded.

For the first time since I had moved out of my parent's house, I had felt like a child again, and it hurt me.

All the way home I was bitching, at my age, I could buy cigarettes, gives birth to a child; yet I couldn't apply for benefits.

I was annoyed, but Simon tried to reassure me that we could make a claim next month when I turned eighteen.

EIGHTEEN...

The day of my birthday arrived and most people turning eighteen might have been excited and over the moon, but my birthday this year fell on Father's Day, Sunday was a shit day to have a party, but Simon was adamant that he was going to throw me a small get together.

'What time you are seeing your Mum and Dad?' he asked. I hadn't thought about it, but I knew I would be going up at some point.

'Not sure why?' I replied.

'I've got to see my Dad this morning; I will bring Ness back with me and get this place cleaned up for your party later if you want to go out then, we can have it ready when you get back.' He said.

I agreed even though I wasn't in the partying mood, I knew Si had been waiting to have a big get together, and I didn't want to let him down.

'Why don't you get your lot to come down?' he asked as he was walking out the room, I followed him into the hall where he was putting his shoes on.

'My parents won't come you got to be joking, and if I invite the kids I will be looking after them for the whole night, not my idea of fun love,' I said grinning at him.

Si had just left when there was a knock at the door, it was only nine-twenty, so I guessed it might be the postman for a second till I realized it was Sunday morning. When I answered the door and man introduced himself to me as Mr. Thomas from the council. He waved his identity card in my face and asked to come in for a moment.

'It is Sunday morning!' I snapped.

I felt a little on edge that was starting to be normal nowadays when strange men were near me; I felt the hairs on my arms stand on end and a horrible shudder up my spine,

'I know, sorry miss, but it is important, I won't take up much of your time I promise,' he said. Part of me wanted to slam the door, but I ignored my feelings and moved from the doorway to let the man in.

'Is Mr. Simon Davis in?' he asked.

'No, sorry you have just missed him; do you want me to give him a message?'

Mr. Thomas shook his head and reached into his bag to produce a letter. 'Can you just give him this please and ask him to contact me as soon as he can, and again sorry to bother you at the weekend but it is urgent that I speak with Mr. Davis'.

I took the letter and saw the man out; once I closed the door my legs felt like they wanted to give way, I slid my body down the wall and sat in a heap on the floor squeezing the letter in my hand till it almost ripped.

'Get a grip,' I told myself.

It was apparent to me why this strange man had made me feel uncomfortable, after the childhood I had, had it been only normal, but I knew that I had coped and got out of the situation, so I didn't need to worry anymore. I still worried though, who wouldn't after spending years being sexually abused by family members and other men I should have been able to trust. I was due to go up and see the worst of all later that day, so I needed to sort my head out, and quick. I ran myself a bath and made a cup of tea and a joint, I knew after a relaxing bath and smoke I would be fine, and I was.

Smoking cannabis was my one way of taking my mind off things; it dawned on me that it was Tom's fault I had ever started. Tom was my boyfriend in Belfast, we were together for a while, and I had lost my virginity to him just after my fifteenth birthday. It was a big deal to me because at the time I was in complete control, and I knew I was young, but it seemed the most normal thing to do at the time and after learning how to suck Daddy's penis from the age of nine, losing my virginity at fifteen seemed normal.

I had promised Tom that when I was old enough, I would move back to Belfast to be with him, but we hadn't spoken for almost three years and I was sure he had moved on with his life, just as I had with mine.

I made another joint to walk up to my parent's house with and picked up the Father's Day card for my Dad, it was warm outside, and I have done myself no favors by wearing black most of the time. I got accused of being a Goth, but I didn't see it like that, I just liked to wear black, and I had a few farfetched beliefs, but I was never a Goth.

As I was approaching the front door of my old house, I put the joint out, even though my Dad had smoked it my whole life and never hid the fact that he took hard drugs I still had a stupid thing called respect, and I didn't want to smoke it in front of them. I knocked the door, and my little brother answered.

'Why did you knock silly?' I smiled at him and walked in. Dad, as usual, was sat at the kitchen table with his newspaper, smoking a joint in one hand and a bottle of Budweiser in the other. He looked up for a whole two seconds and then looked back down at what he was reading. I pulled a chair out and sat at the table; Mum would have walked into the kitchen by now, so I guessed she was asleep or out.

'I got you a card, happy Father's Day,' I said passing him the card.

'Thanks,' was his reply still not lifting his head from his paper.

'Your Mother will be back in a minute, she is just round your Nans, Happy Birthday by the way,' he said, finally closing and folding his paper up.

'Thank you, it doesn't feel like my birthday,' I said smiling. '

'That's what happens as you get older, birthdays become less important,' he replied.

I was eighteen, surely that was important enough; I had guessed that if I were getting a present or anything I would have had it by now. I got up to go to the toilet which was right beside the front door. I didn't need to use the bathroom, but I just needed a reason to get out of the kitchen and compose myself.

As I was sitting there for a few minutes, I heard my Mum and the kids walk in through the front door, so I flushed the toilet and washed my hands.

'Oh hello, happy eighteenth birthday,' mum said all cheerily.

I smiled, and she turned to the kettle to make a hot drink 'have you had your card yet?' Mum asked.

'No, didn't know I had one,' I replied.

'Of course, you have a card; it's your birthday!' Mum reached into the cupboard above the kettle and pulled out a card and passed it to me. Inside the card was a twenty-pound note. She apologized for it not being more, but she had no need to, my parents thought I was stupid, but I had seen them waste all my Mum's weekly wages on crack cocaine. So, I knew why she couldn't afford this much really, but I decided to place the note in the back pocket of my tight black hipster jeans, complete with the trendy scuffed knees.

'It's more than enough Mum, thank you,' I said leaning in for a kiss on her cheek.

We were never the normal affectionate family anyway. Hugs for me usually meant the monster in my Father's mental head was probably about to appear. Just the thought sent a shiver down my spine.

Mum offered me a cup of tea, and I sat myself down on the table opposite my Dad.

'Well, now you are eighteen you can sit and have a joint with your Dad,' my Dad said smiling.

'My tin is the top drawer if you want to pass it too me,' he continued.

I went to the kitchen drawer and opened it wide to see the tin my Dad had kept his cannabis in; I should have known really, that as soon as I open the drawer, the dreaded Wilkinson Sword knife would be in there, staring straight at me, to remind me I was lucky to be here, celebrating my birthday. I just couldn't help staring at it for a few seconds, and I hated the knotting feeling in my stomach that was left behind after I had sat back down.

It happened every time I saw the stupid knife; I was angry at the way the sight of it still made me feel. Ironically the blade has a lifetime guarantee, I think that meant a lifetime of bad memories and not only now but for the past seven years, I was being reminded of the afternoon that same knife was placed against my throat.

Seven years ago, seems like a long time ago but to me, it felt like it was yesterday.

I stayed at my parent's house for just over an hour; Dad was pleasant the whole time to be fair to him, and Mum seemed in a good mood too, I left feeling quite happy and grown up. I know in the real world, sitting having a joint with your dad seems outrageous, but not to our family.

To us that was the most normal thing we could do, ultimately sit and take drugs together. At one point when I was about sixteen, my Dad had said to me that if I ever wanted to try drugs to do it with him as he had been taking almost everything for so long, he knew the effects of most drugs. I can gladly say apart from smoking a bit of pot now and again with him I never had the need to take him up on his offer. Also, I knew if I ever did experiment it wouldn't be in the company of the monster I knew as my Father.

When I got back to mine, Si had already gathered a few of our friends and family, and the house was already lively and buzzing. Luckily for me, Katie oversaw the music, so our friends didn't need to cope with stupid death metal.

Si saw me walk in through the back door and told me I wasn't allowed to go into the kitchen as there was a surprise for me, so I found a seat by Katie and made myself a joint. My Aunt Kath was giving me the evils, but I just ignored her, after all, I was an adult now. The party got into full swing, and Si had finally let me know what my surprise was, he had baked me a cake which I thought was sweet. His fruitcake was excellent too; his Mum had taught him how to make it when he was younger, so it was like the family recipe. After we had all eaten the cake, Si had asked for the music to be turned down as he had something to say. I felt nervous as I hated being the centre of attention and he knew it. Just then he did the worst thing possible, he got down on one knee and produced a silver and onyx ring and asked me if I would marry him.

What I wanted to say was no I am far too young, but I saw everyone looking at me, I paused, and Simon took hold of my hand, he continued to tell me and the whole room how much he loved me, so I felt compelled to say yes.

I was saying yes to the engagement, but I didn't think it would go further than that. That evening after most of our guests had gone home; he had told me how happy he was that I said yes, I was delighted because I felt wanted. The fact that I made him content was good, but I knew deep down that nothing would come of it.

Settling down…

Simon and I had been together for a year when we decided to move to Kent, to be nearer his family. I was excited about living somewhere where I had no horrible memories, and we set about making plans for our new life by the sea.

I had spoken to his Mum on the phone a few times, and I was nervous to be finally meeting her in person, I always worried what people would think of me, the Mother of your boyfriend must be the scariest out of them all.

Diane seemed lovely and from first impressions we seemed to get on well, but I can honestly say living with Si's family was quite testing. Simon had a younger brother who was almost the spit of him; Christopher was a few years younger than Si and worked as a chef in the local arcade.

Kay, on the other hand, looked nothing like her brother and her and Si clashed on an almost daily basis. This caused most of the atmosphere in the house, after a month of siblings bickering all the time Diane had honestly had enough and asked her son and me to move out as soon as possible. Of course, he took loads of offense and threatened to fall out with his mother, but I could see exactly where she was coming from.

So, within a few weeks, we had found ourselves a room in a large Victorian townhouse just twenty-minute bus ride from his Mother's house. The rent on the place was more than the local council was willing to pay, so I had agreed with the landlord to tidy both our large house share and the other two similar houses he owned across the road from us. All I needed to do was hoover the communal areas and clean the shared bathrooms twice a week, so I didn't mind. I did think Simon should help me with the cleaning, but I knew he wouldn't, he had a heart of gold, but he was the laziest person I had ever met.

A few months into living in Kent I had started to feel ill, and the local doctor did some tests on me. I was sent to Margate hospital to have some more tests, it was a horrible time, and after weeks of tests I was told by the doctor that it was a high possibility that I would never be able to conceive. I was eighteen and told that I needed hormone treatment to increase the chances of carrying a child in the future. Simon was a mess and couldn't understand why I was okay with it. The way I saw it was if there was a chance I would never have kids it was for a reason, like with everything in my life, it must all have a reason behind it. After all, if there wasn't, then what was the point to it all?

He didn't share my beliefs, and even though we had never talked about kids, it was evident that it was something he wanted.

'Hey, don't be sad,' I said to him. 'Hormone treatment might mean I will finally have boobs!' I joked.

'I love you the way you are,' he replied.

'Well then, why rush for kids anyway? I am still young myself, and I don't want a family for ages yet,' was my response.

'I thought I was your family?' He snapped and with that walked out of our room down the stairs and straight out of the front door.

So, Simon wanted to start a family and marry me within a year of us being together, and I didn't want that at all. Yes, I did like him, but I couldn't see him being the man I wanted to spend the rest of my life with, I was only eighteen.

The next few weeks passed and being cooped up in a rented room with Simon was starting to get to me. I had been talking to my Mum and my cousin on the phone, and I had told them that I was planning on leaving him and moving back home as soon as I could afford the travel. I felt guilty, but the bottom line was that I didn't feel for him the way he did towards me. I liked him a lot, but I knew deep down that I would never be in love with him, so what was the point in drawing out the inevitable.

It was the start of February, and the weather was as depressing as my relationship. I had gone out to do some shopping while Si had a lie in at home. Just as I walked into Asda my phone started ringing, it was Katie, 'Oh am I glad you answered,' she said.

'What's up?' I asked concerned.

She had recently had a baby boy, so I was worried for her. 'You need to do a test,' she said.

'What sort of test? If you mean a pregnancy test, then there is no point because I was told a few weeks ago, I cannot conceive.' I explained.

'Well, I think they are wrong. Honestly, I don't know why but I feel like I am pregnant, and I can tell you no man has got near me since Leon was born. I know it isn't me, which leads me to believe you are pregnant!' she said all matter of a fact.

So, while I was out I decided to pop into the chemist and buy a pregnancy test just to prove a point, I made my way to the public toilet as I was desperate for a wee anyway and knew I wouldn't make it home on time. I removed the test from the box and followed the instructions on the box.

I waited for a few moments and almost broke into tears when realized that two lines meant I was defiantly pregnant. Oh, my God, she was right. Simon was going to get his wish after all, and I was going to be a young Mum. This was all too much to take in at once, so I decided to stay out longer.

Just gone midday my phone rang again, this time it was Si, but I decided to ignore the call, I was beginning to get hungry so started to walk up the seafront to a little café I had been into a few times since living in Margate. The owners were lovely people, and they took the time to remember their customers so much so that even though I had only been there a few times, I knew they would cook my bacon sandwich perfectly if the fat wasn't crispy I wouldn't eat it at all. A few minutes later my phone rang again, and again so, in the end I answered it.

'Yes?' I said abruptly.

'Where are you? I have been ringing for ages,' he sounded stressed out, and I wasn't in the mood.

'I just needed to clear my head, Si, I am going back home, and I won't change my mind this time!' I snapped.

'Where the hell are you? I will come and meet you; my shoes are on, please we need to talk,' he begged.

'At the café,' I said as I hung up the phone.

Within ten minutes he was sat opposite me trying to convince me to stay, but I was a stubborn cow, and nothing would change my mind. Even the fact the test had come back positive, I didn't want to believe it so as he was sitting there begging me to give him another chance, all I could think of doing was running away as fast as possible.

That evening I had started packing my bags, and I had planned to leave the following Thursday as that was the day our benefits were paid into the bank. I was placing the last little bits in my bag when suddenly the strain took its toll, my knees buckled underneath me, and Si came running to my side.

'Been smoking weed again?' He asked. I told him I hadn't, but he kept on at me,

'Why are you dizzy then? What have you eaten today?' eventually, I snapped back at him.

'I'm fucking pregnant you stupid dick, I did a test, and it came back positive!' wow, admitting it made it seem so real and after the shock of what I had just said removed itself from his face as he started to laugh.

I didn't understand what he thought was so god damn funny and it infuriated me. Still lightheaded I stood up to walk out of the door, and he darted towards it first to stop me in my tracks.

'You aren't going anywhere,' he snapped and stood with his pigeon chest sticking out.

'You can't stop me!' I shouted back.

That was our first proper argument, he was demanding that I was carrying his child and he wasn't going to let me leave, the biggest mistake he made was trying to control me, and I wasn't putting up with it. That night we went to bed without talking to one another, and the next morning things were still as awkward between us, but I only had to cope with him for one more night and the next day couldn't come soon enough.

Goodbye, I'm going home...

Thursday morning came, and even though Simon had excepted that I was going he still hoped I would have changed my mind. The fact that I didn't really hurt him so I told him if he wanted to be part of our baby's life then he would have to move back as well. I didn't expect him to run out of the house and I guessed he had gone off in a huff. My train was due to leave Margate station in a few hours, so I went off to try and find him, but he was nowhere to be seen. I rummaged through my bag to find my mobile but noticed he had taken it with him.

'You think taking my phone will stop me you silly man?' I said out loud.

I was getting the last of my things into the hall and was waiting on my taxi, as he had stolen my phone I just used one of the other tenant's phones. I had decided that Simon must have run off to his Mums as he was gone for over two hours. I was angry and upset that he wasn't even willing to say goodbye to me as if the past fifteen months was nothing to him, and the fact that I had said I was carrying his baby, I was sure he would be there to say goodbye. As my taxi arrived a massive surge of guilt washed over me. How evil could I be? I have just told a man I am carrying his baby, and then I tell him I am moving three hundred miles away from him. I had to think of myself, and I refused to change my mind. We had a conversation about him moving back with me, but he said he hated Crosby. So that was that, or so I thought.

Once I had arrived at the train station, the guilt had started to be replaced with excitement; I was pissed off that Simon had my phone as I was sure my cousin would be ringing me by now to see what time I was due. You see it had been planned for the past week that I was moving back, and she had offered to put me up even though she had just had a baby. Family comes first, she would always say, and even though we had times where we didn't see each other for months, it made no difference to the bond we had shared.

Katie was nine months older than me, and when we were younger and both living in Crosby, we were joined at the hip, doing almost everything together. I think that's how she knew I was pregnant before I even did.

I was still scared at the thought of being a Mum and with the doctors saying I wouldn't conceive I was worried I would lose the baby. So, I couldn't get excited, and that's why part of me wished I hadn't told Simon. I put my rucksack on my back and pulled my suitcase on wheels behind me and made my way to the platform.

My train wasn't due for twenty minutes, but I had a feeling something would go wrong, I was feeling sick and weak, so I decided to take the lift rather than walking down the stairs. The elevator was grubby and smelt like a urinal; I was heaving trying my hardest to hold my breath for a few more seconds. I stood still for a few moments once I got onto my platform to compose myself and to breathe in the air that was a little fresher than the urine stench I had experienced a few seconds before.

Once I sorted my hair back into the bobble, I made my way around the corner to find a seat. I was shocked to see Simon waiting for me; I was shaking, I am not sure if it was seeing him and worrying that he was there to stop me or if it was the morning sickness starting to set in.

'Don't try and stop me Simon, I have made up my mind,' I said.

'I don't care because I am coming with you,' he smiled.

I just looked at him confused, and he took the heavy bag from my back.

'I decided that if I can't make you stay here with me, then I would have to come back with you and our baby,' he said touching my stomach.

He continued 'I have spoken to Kate, and she said we could have her spare room.'

'But we are splitting up,' I reminded him.

Simon had this thing where he thought he was in charge of me or something, just because he was nine years older than me didn't give him the right to control me and I would remind him of this anytime I felt restrained.

Right at this point, I felt I needed to take the control back, so I snapped at him.

'You can't decide if I stay with you or not, you don't own me!' he looked at me and sighed.

'I didn't say I own you; I just think we need to try for our baby's sake, don't you?' he asked.

'I suppose,' I said shrugging my shoulders.

The train journey lasted over four hours and in this time, we had come to a truce, we would see if we could make it work for the sake of our unborn child, and you never know I might fall in love with him one day, but I thought it was doubtful.

We had started to settle into my cousin's house quite well; I had my first appointment with the doctors after having done three more tests and all coming up with a positive two lines. I had aired my concerns about miscarrying with both Si and Katie, and they both shared my worry, so they decided they would come to my first appointment with me.

I was nervous, but I had no reason to be, the doctor just asked me to do another test and said I would have my results back later that day, so my cousin headed back home, and I walked up to my Mum and Dads with Simon while we waited on the call.

We knew the answer anyway, but we had to go through the motions. The phone call came, and I was given an appointment for my first scan for two weeks later to find out how far gone I was. I couldn't let myself get excited about being a Mum until I had passed the twelve-week mark, under twelve weeks is classed as the danger months. The first three months of pregnancy were the most worrisome as that was the time you were almost four times more likely to miscarry, and after the news I had had a few months before, at Margate hospital I was convinced there would be something wrong.

I never let on too much to anyone about how I felt really; I had, after all spent my whole childhood painting a happy picture of family life. Where really, I was living in a nightmare. So, if I could convince everyone back then I was coping, and everything was fine I was confident I could do it now.

FAMILY MATTERS...

My first scan was amazing, seeing our baby floating around on the screen, I was now looking forward to my twenty week scan where we were also hoping to find out the sex of our baby. I did have a few complications during the previous month.

I was born with a hole in my heart, and the doctors worried that the strain on my body would affect my heart murmur, so I had to have more frequent antenatal appointments. I was glad though in a way because it meant we could have piece of mind in some respects and we knew our baby was okay, but the extra appointments did make me worry. You hear about women dying during childbirth and I was scared shitless, but I obviously didn't tell anyone my fears.

Simon and I were still bickering almost on a daily basis, and I had had enough. We split up the week before my second scan. It was all too much, and I didn't need the extra stress. Simon cried like a baby, and the guilt got to me, but I told myself I wasn't going to change my mind this time. I walked out and made my way to my Mum and

Dads, they only lived a few minutes away, and as I made my way up the path I could still hear him sobbing. I was glad to get away for a few hours, and my Mum agreed with me that I couldn't stay with someone I was growing to dislike just for the sake of our unborn child.

When I returned to Katie's, Simon had calmed down, but I think he had hoped I would have changed my mind, he should have known how stubborn I could be. We sat down, and I explained that I didn't want to end up hating him and that if he didn't just accept what I was saying that I would just leave entirely. I know I couldn't have done that to him, but I needed him to realize that what I was saying was final. As expected he stormed out of the living room and shut himself away in the bedroom we were sharing.

'I think you are doing the right thing if it helps,' Katie whispered low enough, so Si wouldn't overhear.

'I know,' I said, 'I just feel awful for hurting him that's all,' Katie scrunched her mouth and nodded. 'Sometimes you need to be cruel, to be kind. No point if you don't love him, but that's just my opinion.' she said.

The next week went by awkwardly; the atmosphere was so thick you could have cut it with a knife. Si was in a mood all day, every day and I was getting sick of it, my scan was booked for the next day, and I asked him if he was still coming with me.

'Of course, I am, can't believe you even felt the need to ask me!' he snapped.

Well, how was I meant to know, I wasn't a mind reader, and he had hardly spoken two words to me since I had split up with him.

The morning of my scan came, and Simon was in an okay mood, he was excited to find out the sex of our baby, but I did explain that they might not be able to tell us if they can't see properly. He just dismissed every word I had said and didn't acknowledge I was there.

The second scan was so clear; I could hardly believe that this baby was growing inside me. I was excited but felt sick at the same time, Simon was beaming with pride bless him, he smiled through the whole scan, and I realized how much he wanted our baby, maybe he even wanted all this more than me.

'Your baby boy is looking very healthy and growing at the speed we should expect,' the midwife said,

'Baby boy, did you say?' I asked.

'Yes,' she replied pointing to the screen to show us a white mark on the screen 'defiantly a boy.'

I looked at Simon's big grin, and he held my hand. 'We are having a little boy,' he said as if I was dumb and couldn't understand what the midwife has just said.

That afternoon we started looking at blue items for our new arrival, and now I could begin to get excited. We had started to get on well by this point, but that made him think that we were going to get back together. It wasn't until a few weeks later when he had asked me again if I would marry him again. The last thing I wanted to do was hurt his feelings, but I told him that I didn't mind giving things another go, for the sake of our child, but that I was no longer in love with him, and I couldn't pretend that I was.

After giving birth to our son things didn't improve, and after a month of always bitching at each other I decided to move into my Mum and Dads while I got myself sorted, Simon stayed in our rented property even though he was willing to move out, I knew I needed a fresh start. Things were weird, to say the least, but I grinned and bared it.

Luckily, my Dad had been okay with me too, which made me even more determined that my childhood happened because I was a child, now I was looking older and had a child I was no longer of use, which was good for me.

After a few days, there was a knock on my parent's door, I am not sure where my Dad was, but my Mum was in the toilet. She shouted down to me to answer the door, and I knew it wasn't Simon as he had headed home earlier that day, as I opened the door I was shocked to see a small ginger haired girl at the door, she looked a mess, and frantic.

'Oh my god, you haven't changed one bit!' she said in a broad Belfast accent, then it clicked who she was. She was my cousin Jody. 'What the hell are you doing here?' I asked all shocked 'I didn't know you were coming.'

Jody was my Uncle Derek's daughter. She went on to tell me that she had been kicked out and that her Mum had given her my parent's address. My Mum made her way downstairs and shouted into the kitchen asking who was at the door. She was shocked to see Jody stood in the kitchen. 'Oh, what brings you here?' she asked her.

Jody looked shifty; her bright red dyed hair covering most of her face as she looked down at the floor. Then she told us that she was homeless and had nowhere to go, she had travelled over from Belfast a few days before and said that she was given our address, from her Mother before she left.

'I have nowhere else to go.'

'Well, we won't see you on the street don't you worry,' was my Mum's reply.

That was until Dad walked through the door, he was livid to see her sat in our living room even if he tried not to show it.

Mum and Dad were bickering in the kitchen, Dad was adamant that Jody should be put into a hostel, but my

Mum was standing her ground and stating that she was family, so that wasn't going to happen.

'Are they arguing about me?' Jody asked me.

'They argue about everything, don't worry this is normal' I said with a big smile on my face, and then I was called into the kitchen.

Dad had the idea that Jody could go and live with my ex Simon, I decided after a few minutes debate that it was probably the best option, so I rang Si and explained the situation.

He was more than willing to help, so we called my cousin into the kitchen. She was worried that she didn't know this man, even though I had told her about him, she said she didn't feel comfortable being on her own.

In the end, I moved back into my house with our son, it was decided that she would have the small bedroom. Simon was happy that I was home, but I told him we needed to take thing slowly. Not that he took too much notice as we were sharing a bed that same evening.

LITTLE CHANGES...

Living back with Simon was easier than I thought and it was kind of nice having Jody staying with us. That was until she informed us that her ex-boyfriend from Ireland had got the boat over and wanted to see her. Jody was a bit vague when Simon and I had asked about him, so we were a little apprehensive about him arranging to see her in our home. 'Who are we to stand in the way of love?' I joked.

Jody's ex Tommy was probably nice enough, but I took a dislike to him, I had no reason to dislike him really, but I just got a strong feeling he was bad news and after he left I expressed my concerns with Simon and my cousin. It turned out that he had been known to be heavy handed and Jody went on to tell us that he was on the run from the police because an old girlfriend of his had accused him of rape and that Jody was in two minds whether to believe him. As soon as she said that I put my foot down and said he was never welcome to set foot through my door again. My cousin was upset, but she understood at the same time.

A few weeks had passed, and Jody had started to worry that she might be pregnant. She was scared stiff to do a test but admitted she hadn't had a period in two months. I told her she had to do the test sooner rather than later, but she kept refusing. In the end, I went to the chemist and bought her a test, but still she refused.

So that was it as far as I was concerned, I couldn't force her after all. I was having a coffee at my Mums when Jody walked in with the test; she wanted to get advice off my Mum, I had already told my Mum that she had refused to do a test, so I wasn't surprised when she started the whole scared animal routine with my Mum.

My son was asleep in the buggy, so I asked Mum to watch him while I popped to the shops with Jody. While out, I bought another test, and I was going to force her to do the bloody test because I was sick of hearing about it. When I got back to my Mums it was agreed that I would do a test too, just to show her that it was nothing scary.

Jody used the downstairs toilet while I used the bathroom, I peed on the stick and left it on the sink to check back on it a few minutes later. Downstairs Jody was still locked in the toilet, so I knocked the door. 'You okay in there?' I asked, but all I could hear was a quiet sobbing.

'Jody, are you okay? 'The door unlocked and a moment later she emerged with her test in her hand.

'I'm going to be a mummy,' she said with a big cheesy grin on her face.

I was happy for her, and gave her a big squeeze, though I hadn't noticed my Mum going up the stairs and she must have heard Jody's news because she hurried down the stairs and informed me that I was also pregnant.

'I am fucking what?' I asked stocked to the core.

'But I can't be, I have only slept with Si twice since Mark has been born,' I explained.

'Sometimes it can only take one-time love,' was my Mums reassuring words.

'I've got to ring him now, for fucks sake, how the hell? this isn't the way it was meant to be,' I laughed a nervous laugh as I left the room to make my phone call.

Simon, as expected, was as shocked as me, but you could tell he was excited. I was scared, and our son was only six months old himself, so it all seemed to be happening again far too quick for my liking. The next day I got Si to look after our son, I went to have a smoke with my Dad, just to get out for a bit. My Dad and I were sat in the back garden, and he piped up about me being pregnant again.

'You are crazy if you keep the baby love, I'm not saying it to be harsh, but you don't want to be tied down to that idiot for the rest of your life, it is bad enough you already have one kid with him for fucks sake. To have two kids by the man is just stupid,' he ranted.

'Stupid maybe, but I won't get rid of the baby, I just can't do that,' I said defending myself.

The atmosphere changed instantly, and I could tell Dad was angry I had disagreed with him, but I was almost twenty one, and I wasn't going to let him determine my life in any way, that is why I had moved out years before. The good thing about moving back in with Simon was that I could make my excuses to my Dad and leave his company anytime I wanted.

A few months later, Jody and I had a falling out, and she was asked to move out, even though I wasn't that bothered about Si if I was honest with myself I was jealous of their friendship. I had good reason to be as one evening I caught them both in an embrace in the kitchen. I had been ill in bed but heard my son crying, so I had got up to see to him. The kitchen door was closed which was strange because we always had it wedged open, so I walked down the small flight of stairs to investigate, with my son in my arms I quietly opened the door, and they were kissing with hands all over each other. Jody told me that Si had made a pass for her, and it was either she goes, or I would leave for good, so Simon agreed, of course, to kick her out.

It was the last thing I needed; my pregnancy was hard enough anyway this time around without the added stress. I had complications through my pregnancy. We had found out I was carrying a baby girl, but towards the end of my pregnancy my baby had stopped growing.

I did everything right, I quit smoking and ate better than I did in my previous pregnancy, but my daughter still struggled to grow. Within a few weeks of Jody moving out the pains in my stomach worsened.

I had been in and out of the hospital a lot in the last few months, and by the time I was thirty-six weeks gone, I was booked into the hospital to be induced. I was told there was a chance that if they didn't induce me that she could die, so I just let them do what they needed to do.

Anyone who has been induced will tell you the pain hits you suddenly, but the nurses kept an eye on me and said they didn't think I would be in full labour until the next day. Simon was told he might as well go home, but luckily for me, he slept in the waiting room as I was taken down to the delivery suite just after five in the morning. I was able to ask the midwife to get Si for me. My labour lasted for just over five hours, and our baby girl was small but perfectly formed, I heard her tiny cry and knew she was okay.

I was so shattered that I was drifting in and out of sleep. When I woke up I saw my daughter in an incubator beside me, Si was nowhere to be seen, so I lay there staring at my tiny little girl and soon fell back to sleep with a smile on my face.

ENOUGH WAS ENOUGH...

I had been with Simon for just over three years; things were getting on top of us with having two young children and Si being so addicted to cannabis, meant I was doing most of the work in our home. I was looking after our children, cooking, and cleaning, while he just sat playing on his play station with his mates.

Naturally, this led to lots of arguments between us and one day I just snapped. 'I think we need to separate; I can't cope with this anymore!' I shouted.

'You can't take my kids away from me,' he screamed back at me.

I took a step back as he walked towards me begging me not to leave him, but it wasn't as if he didn't have enough warnings since our daughter was born two months previously, I had told him things needed to change. We had a blazing row at least once a week, and I wasn't going to live like that. I had dreams and aspirations about my future. I wanted to have my own gift shop, and even though Si and I had spoken about this, he was just too lazy to do anything about it.

I had had enough and no matter what I wasn't going to back down this time. He was still shouting so I walked out of the room.

'You are going to wake the kids up if you keep shouting,' I said in a calm tone, but he continued to shout.

'Shhh for fucks sake!' I snapped.

'I will stop shouting when you tell me why you are leaving me, found someone else have we?' he asked.

'No, I haven't, I just don't want to be with you. I don't love you Si, and I can't pretend I do, enough is enough.' I replied.

'Lucy is only a few months old; things are bound to be tough, but we can make this work.' he pleaded.

'No, I can't, I have tried for years, but I refuse to keep trying, I'm sorry.'

He snapped at me, 'You're not sorry, you probably love this!'

I hated hurting him, and part of me must have loved him to stay for so long. He was kind and caring, but that wasn't enough anymore. I wanted a life, and it didn't involve Simon in any way, as harsh as that sounded I needed to concentrate on myself and my kids.

We had agreed that I wouldn't kick him out on the street; I couldn't do that to him, so he had our daughter's bedroom and she stayed in my room with me. It was tough, but we made it work the best we could for the children.

GREGORY...

Simon was still living with me, but we had barely spoken two words to each other in the past few months. He was arduous work to live with at the best of times, and the atmosphere was getting worst. Eventually I sat him down, and he agreed to move out as soon as he could afford to.

After that conversation, he spent most days in his bedroom on the computer. I didn't mind because it made my days more comfortable. I had cooked us Sunday dinner and called Si down the stairs a few times, when he didn't respond I went upstairs thinking that he couldn't hear me.

'I have been calling you for dinner,' I explained.

'Yeah, just one minute I am busy.' He said in a moody tone, so I peered over his shoulder to be nosey and see what he was doing online, and he was chatting up girls on the internet, it didn't bother me in the slightest, and I saw it as a good thing because he was moving on.

I made my way back downstairs, and as we were eating dinner in front of the TV, he started to tell me about some of the girls he had spoken to online. They all seemed nice enough, but he let slip the ages of the females he was chatting up, and that disturbed me to the core. Bear in mind Simon was thirty two and chatting up sixteen year old girls, he went on to explain how he was due to meet one little blonde girl, who he was attracted to because of her gothic style and petite frame. All sounded good until he told me she has just celebrated her sixteenth which in anyone's eyes was wrong. I explained why I thought it was a bad idea, but he just accused me of being jealous.

'I am not jealous at all, but she is a kid, and you are an adult, what happens when our daughter is sixteen, you going to date all her friends?' I snapped.

'You are sick and twisted, just because it happened in your life; don't mean it will happen in every other fucker's life!' I looked at him stunned, had he really just spoken to me like that?

My blood started to boil, 'I am sick, you are the one wanted to get in bed with a fucking child,' he told me to fuck off and stated she is old enough.

I don't think I had ever been so angry with him. Simon was always kind-hearted and loving, but this day he just seemed to be wanted to stick the knife in.

'You know about my past, and especially about what my cousin did, I just didn't expect that from you that's all,' I said, walking out of the living room to put my plate into the kitchen sink.

He soon followed me, still shouting that I must be jealous, so I told him that I was over him and had planned to go out the following weekend. Si tried to say that I wasn't allowed to go out while he was still living with me. I told him he was unreasonable and that if he didn't move out real soon, then I would take the kids and move away for good, I wouldn't have been so nasty, but I was angry and hurt by his sudden outburst that I wanted to hurt him back. It worked too; he then set about trying to gather his things and start to pack his stuff.

It was agreed that I would at least give him till the end of the month to find somewhere, and he had sold his computer to the local loan shark because he said he couldn't take it with him. It was also agreed that Simon would look after the kids while Jody and I went out to the local pub that Friday night. I was looking forward to going out, and I had even bought a dress especially.

Friday evening came, and the kids were settled in bed, I was in my bedroom getting ready, and Julie was due round within the hour. Si was downstairs and had turned the music on, the sound of Metallica echoed up the stairs. I was angry, and it was obvious that the music was far too loud. I quickly put my dress on and quietly but as quick as I could, ran down the stairs to turn the music down, the last thing I needed was the kids waking up just as I was going out.

I lent down towards the stereo and next thing I knew; Si had walked up behind me a grabbed my waist, pulling me closer to him. He was aroused, and it was evident as he pulled my hips tightly towards him. Still gripping me by the waist, he removed his right arm and moved my hair from my neck and started kissing me gently all over my neck and shoulder.

See, he knew precisely how to get my attention. 'Excuse me, but we are not together anymore,' I said.

'So, does that mean we can't have a bit of fun?' he stated, while still kissing my neck. By this point his hand was lifting the bottom of my dress.

'Simon, I am going out,' I said pushing myself away from his grip, but he just pulled me closer and whispered in my ear, 'You are only going out if I stay here and have our kids Sarah.'

'Are you kidding me?' I replied, 'Going to play that card, are we?' I asked.

He then turned me towards him and started kissing me, I knew it was probably a bad idea, but I went weak and gave into him, a quickie over the coffee table kept him happy and meant I could still go out, so it was a win, win situation. I hated every minute of it though, and I felt like I was letting myself be used, by yet another man who pretended to care just to get his own way.

Back upstairs I was getting ready when Jody knocked on the door, I shouted downstairs that I wouldn't be long and finished getting ready; twenty minutes later we had left and made our way to the local karaoke. I told Jody that I had slept with Si before she turned up and she said she was pregnant and planning to find a man that evening to be a Daddy for her unborn.

I thought she was joking and thought no more of it till later in the evening. We got to the karaoke just after nine and walked straight over to the bar, and she pointed out that two guys were looking over at us. I tried not to look over, but curiosity took over, as I turned around I realized that I knew one of the men.

'That's John; he knows my Mum,' I told her.

'Who's the other guy?' she asked.

'I don't know, do you want to go over and say hello?' I said grinning at her.

'Nah, let's leave it for a while, maybe in a bit.' she said, so we grabbed our drinks and sat at the table opposite the two men.

I decided to get up and sing. I knew I was going to sing Zombie by the Cranberries because that was a song I always sang, and I knew it suited my voice. Jody would sing but she didn't have much confidence to sing on her own, so we would love to belt out a song or two together.

I went to the toilet after singing Zombie, and when I got back, Jody wasn't on our table, and my drink had been moved, then I noticed she was sitting with John and his friend. I walked over to them confidently and sat in the spare chair.

'John,' I nodded.

'Sarah isn't it?' he nodded back.

John was a friend of the family, or should I say, my Mum, he was buying his pills and base from my parent's house, so I would see him quite often while I was visiting them.

'This is my mate Greg,' he pointed.

'Pleased to meet you,' I said shaking his hand.

'Very formal,' Greg joked.

We chatted most of the evening and just before we were getting ready to go John had insisted on walking us girls back home, so Jody and I agreed. We popped to the toilet before heading off, but in the bathroom, Jody had mentioned sleeping with Greg to trick him into being her baby's Dad. I told her I disagreed and that if she did it I would have to tell the poor lad her plan, she went a little moody for a few seconds but said she understood what I meant and that I was right.

I was usually right about most things, but I knew for a fact that this was wrong, and Jody would be caught out in the end, I refused to have any part of it.

We were walking back in the pitch-black darkness and bitter winds and then it started to rain.

'Just great,' I thought to myself.

I had planned to bring my coat when we had left the house earlier that evening, but I just wanted to get out, get away from Simon and I had forgotten to pick it up. I was regretting it by now, as the cold chills made me shiver. Jody was just behind me talking to Greg and John was trying his hardest to flirt with me, he seemed nice enough, but I wasn't attracted to him in any way. John was a big man, and I made a joke saying my Mum always told me never to date a man with bigger boobs than me, the fact that I was flat chested meant not many men would fall into the datable category. John asked if I was cold, and I just looked at him as if to say really? do you need to ask that question? Then I felt an arm on my shoulder, Greg had taken off his coat and placed it around my shoulders.

'I'm fine,' I snapped, but he just put it back around me.

'I don't need your coat, but thanks anyway,' I said as I flung it off my shoulders onto the floor.

'Feisty, are we?' Greg asked smirking at me with a half-tilted smile.

We had got to the front of my house and Jody was staying over, so we said goodnight to the boys, but she had other ideas and invited them in.

'They did just walk us all the way home, least we can do is offer them a beer,' she said.

'Simon is in the house, don't think he will be too impressed if I turn up with two strange men,' I stated.

'Oi, less of the strange!' Greg piped up.

So, I went into the house to warn Simon that we had visitors, surprisingly he was fine and didn't mind.

The first thing Greg noticed was the Guitar I had brought for Simon in the year before, it was sat up against the wall so, he had asked if he could have a play and Simon agreed and started to tune it in for him. Greg then asked me if I could play the guitar. Simon told him I couldn't, but I did write my own songs. I was then asked to get my songbook, which I didn't get out in front of people, I gave Simon a knowing look as if to say, thanks a lot. For some reason, I felt embarrassed.

Greg started to strum the guitar and tried to put some chords to the words in the book. I could tell my cousin was getting a little jealous, she had sat beside Greg and was flirting like mad with him, but he didn't seem to notice her, which made me feel a bit bad for her. After an hour, I had to call it a night, I said my goodbyes and had swapped numbers with Greg, we agreed to meet up again very soon.

A week had passed, and I didn't get any messages so guessed he wasn't all that interested, just as I had given up on the idea of meeting back up with him, he had sent me a text.

'Hey sexy, I have been thinking about you all week, I am back from my holiday at the weekend and would love to meet up with you xx.'

I replied telling him I couldn't get a babysitter, but he sent a message back asking if he could chill round mine instead. I did explain that Simon still lived with me and that I would have to clear it with him first. Si had agreed, and soon enough Greg was coming around most evenings after work.

BRUTAL BEGINNINGS...

Everything seemed to be going well between Greg and me, we had been together for a month when I had to ask Simon to move out, and we had been single for six months by this point, so I had no choice but to demand he found somewhere. That afternoon he packed his things and moved in with his dad, who only lived ten minutes away. Greg had already moved in at this point which meant us having our space, and we could be together. I knew I was hurting Si's feelings and it was necessary to me that he didn't have my new relationship rubbed in his face. Little did I know things would change so quickly.

So, Simon had been at his Dad's for just over a week when he finally popped round to see the kids. Greg was at work until one in the afternoon, and when he got home and noticed Si sat in the living room he was jealous and moody, and he wasn't afraid to show it. The atmosphere was horrible, and Si made his excuses to leave. As Greg closed the front door my heart rate increased, and my palms got clammy, I was waiting for him to start but expected just a bitch fit. I wasn't expecting him to walk straight past me and sit on the settee; he refused to speak, just scowled to himself so I sat down on the other end and didn't make eye contact. After about ten minutes of silence, he finally spoke to me.

'So, you don't think it is wrong to have your ex here when I am out, is that what you are saying?' he said calmly.

'I didn't say anything,' I replied.

'That's the fucking problem, makes me think you want to be a little slag, getting that trampy bastard here when I am out, you think I was born yesterday?'

He scowled looking at me with his piercing blue eyes, eyes that seemed to glaze over when he was getting more aggravated, eyes that reminded me of my Dad.

'He is the father of my kids and has a right to see his children,' I explained.

'And I am your boyfriend or is that not important to you? What's the matter, do you want him back or something?' he said raising his voice.

'Don't be stupid!' I snapped.

Just then Greg stood up and towered over me, screaming at me, I could feel his alcohol soaked breath against my face and his saliva spraying all over me. His wicked tongue carried on insulting me, and he was reminding me of my Dad. Of course, I made the mistake of saying that to him, which only led to him see red and dragging me off the sofa onto the floor, by my hair.

He repeatedly kicked me in the side of my body and my head. My son must have heard what was happening as he ran down the stairs calling me. Greg saw him at the bottom of the stairs and stopped. He told me to get rid of the little brat, or he would be next but as I tried to move off the floor I had a dull ache all over the side of my body, and my face was burning hot and throbbing with my increased heart rate.

I managed to get onto my feet and took him back upstairs. I explained to Mark that Greg was angry, and he had to stay upstairs, he agreed and climbed back into bed while I stayed at the end of his bed for a few minutes. I heard the front door slam downstairs so listened out to see if I could still hear that drunken mess downstairs.

When Greg returned home later that evening I was in bed, I didn't hear him come in, but when I took the kids downstairs the next morning, he was asleep on the sofa with Fosters cans all around him and on the floor.

I didn't dare to wake him so took the kids back upstairs and put the little DVD player on in Mark's room. I kept a listen out for him stirring and he didn't for ages, so I decided to get the kids dressed so I could take them out to my Mum and Dads. I opened the bedroom door to collect Lucy's clothes, Mark followed me into the other room, and then we went back into his bedroom to get dressed I was shaking and knew this wasn't right, feeling like this in my own home isn't the way I expected myself or my children to live. I closed the bedroom door again to block out some of the noise to avoid waking Greg up, the last thing I needed was another telling off by that man. Lucy had started to moan as I changed her nappy I was beginning to panic even more, my heart rate increased instantly, but she soon settled once she was sat in front of the TV again. I listened out to the closed bedroom door but still couldn't hear anything, so I let out a sigh of relief. I needed the toilet, so I told the kids to stay where they were until I got back.

When I opened the bedroom door, I jumped straight out of my skin. Greg was stood the other side of the door waiting for me, his stare was cold, and it sent shivers down my spine.

'Good fucking morning, did you sleep well?' he asked.

'Not bad,' I replied looking at the floor.

'Oh, good for you, well I can tell you I won't be sleeping on that sofa again, next time you can fucking sleep there. Do you understand?' he snapped?

'Do you fucking understand?' he then screamed in my face walking closer to me.

'Yes, I understand Greg, now if you don't mind I am going to my Mum and Dads with the kids, I will see you later,' I said picking Lucy up from her bouncer.

The toilet could wait, I just wanted to get out of the house as quickly as I could now.

'You will see me later, yes you will. Won't you?' he replied before walking into the bedroom and slamming the door.

Mark had started to cry, but I managed to calm him down before I placed him and his sister into the double buggy. As we were about to set out to my parent's house, I had decided I was going to spend most of the day there, so I didn't need to rush home too quickly. With that in mind, I had packed more than I needed in my bag.

Once we arrived at my parents, both the kids were flat out in their buggy, so I left them under the veranda in the garden, the back gate was locked, so I knew they would be safe. I was glad my son was asleep at least; it gave me a bit more time before I had to explain how he had the big bruise on his head. Neither my Mum or Dad had taken to Greg anyway, they both got on well with Simon in the end but understood why I left him, but still, I think part of them had wished I stayed with Si, rather than this new man.

My Dad had made a joint and saved me half of it.

'Your Mum has left me,' he said as he got up to make a cup of tea, 'she is moving out so expect her to ask you if she can stay at yours.'

I was surprised. 'Really, what happened?' I asked even though I knew I didn't need the answers.

'She's been having an affair for ages, but now she tells me she is pregnant, and I know it can't be mine, do you know what I am saying?' he replied.

I didn't know what to say or do; my parents should have split up years ago and didn't. At the same time, I felt a little sorry for him, he had been with my Mum since they were teenagers and apart from his brief marriage, all he had ever known was my Mother.

'What about the kids?' I asked.

'She didn't think about them when she was getting her dirty hole filled, did she?' he snapped.

'Sorry, I don't know. Your brother says he will stay with me, but we will wait and see won't we?' I guessed my brothers would stay with my Dad anyway, just because they were boys.

'Well, I hope he does, you can't be on your own Dad,' I said worrying about what his frame of mind might be.

Not only was my Dad a diagnosed paranoid schizophrenic, but he had also been addicted to crack cocaine for several years, amongst other drugs and alcohol. The night he held me at knife point when I was younger was just one of the psychotic episodes which had involved my Mum having an affair, so for it to be real this time and not in his head was quite a scary thought.

In a more normal family, if your Dad were this upset in front of you, surely you would hug them and tell them everything would be okay, but for me, the thought of first being a hypocrite, by hugging him, and secondly having to feel his hands anywhere near me still repulsed me. All I could do was look down at the table and build another joint to share with him. I couldn't even look him in the eyes, not that I looked many people in the eyes anyway, I just didn't want to let myself feel sorry for him, not after the way he had treated all of us, for so many years. I was glad that my Mum was finally going to get away from him; I also worried what would happen with the kids and think I needed the smoke, as much as he did.

My children had slept the whole time I was with my Dad and didn't wake up till I got home. I was waiting on Greg starting on me as soon as I walked through the door, and I had built myself up on the walk home. I needed to stick up for myself and not let him treat my kids or me the way he had done earlier in the day. As I got to the front of my house though, it was in complete darkness; he must be asleep I thought to myself as I opened the front door quietly as not to disturb him. I wheeled the kids straight into the living room and put the kid's channel on for them, I placed my daughter in her car seat in front of the TV, and Mark on the sofa. I then checked the kitchen, before heading upstairs. Greg was nowhere to be seen, his stuff was still in my room, but he was out.

I got my phone out to text him and noticed I had a missed call and text myself. The missed call was off Greg, I ignored it and looked at my message, it was also from him, and it read,

'I am sorry for the way I have been the past few days. I am scared to lose you, I have decided to stay at my Grandparents for a while, so if you want me you know where I am, I am sorry, Love Gregory xx PS, don't bring your kids with you.'

'Cheeky bastard!' I said out loud.

My kids were due to go to their Dads that weekend anyway, so I decided a few days away from each other would do us all a world of good. Little did I know how much I would miss him.

THE MIDDLE OF A STORM...

It was Saturday morning, and I had been up to town to drop the kids off with their Dad. It was still early, and I didn't want to knock on Greg's Grandparent's door till at least eleven, so I got Si to make me a cup of tea.

'How's this thing going between you and him?' he asked.

'As in him, I guess you mean Greg?' I replied.

'Yeah, you knew who I meant,' he said shaking his head.

'Oh honestly? I think I am going to have to break up with him, but he doesn't seem to realize, he has been getting heavy-handed lately,' I explained.

'I will kill him if he lays a hand on you or my kids!' he snapped.

'Bullshit, you wouldn't say shit really,' I said,

'That mark on your son's head is from Greg being too heavy-handed, and you said fuck all so don't come that crap with me.'

I was so angry that he had even tried to say he would stick up for me, Simon may be a man, but he acts more feminine than me and would never actively get into a fight, he is too much of a soft bastard for that.

'Well, you need to get rid of him, or the kids can come live with me,' he said.

'If you say so, the last thing I need is you on my case too, if you want to help, just have these two at weekends for now, I will split up with him but just might take longer than I want it to,' I snapped back at him.

'I know, I am sorry, I just care about you all, and don't want to see someone hurting my family,' he said defending his last sentence.

'We were your family Si, not anymore, your kids yes, but I belong to no one, and that's how I like it,' I said drinking my milky limy tea.

'You still make shit drinks,' I joked.

We continued talking for an hour, and then I said my goodbyes to the kids and made my way to see Greg. I was dreading seeing him the whole walk to his house seemed to put me more on edge, It was only a twenty-minute walk, and when I got to the front of the house, I saw Greg in the garden having a smoke.

'Oh, she finally comes to see me,' he said sarcastically. 'I did tell you I would be here today,' I said looking down at the time on my phone, 'and I said I would be here now.'

'Come here,' he said. I knew he would be kind to me in front of people, so the worry subsided a bit, but I still flinched as he put his arms around me to hug me.

'I love you, and I am sorry for being a complete and utter knob head lately,' he said holding onto me, he then held onto my shoulders and moved me back, so he could see my eyes, which were starting to well up by this point.

'I do love you, more than you can imagine, and I promise never to treat you like that again,' he said.

I was young and gullible and wanted to believe that this man did love me, but my gut told me something was wrong. I didn't know how to put my finger on it, so I pushed it to the back of my mind and agreed to give him another chance. I wouldn't mind but in the build-up to this point I was convinced I was going to his Nan's to leave him, but already he had a hold on me that I couldn't explain.

That evening with my kids at their Dads, Greg had planned to go out, nowhere special just to the old man's pub we had been to a few times, He loved the bar because his beer was cheap which in his mind meant getting pissed quicker. The pub had a funny smell about it, it was a working man's pub, and I made a joke, saying we shouldn't be drinking in the bar because he didn't work. If looks could kill I would have been dead on the spot, that evening he had no sense of humour at all. I was dreading going home on my own with him but felt like I couldn't say anything, after all, if he were going to start an argument I was going to stand up for myself. We had been in the pub from about lunchtime, it was now almost nine o clock, and all I wanted to do was go home and go to sleep.

'Can we go soon?' I asked.

'Fuck off, I am just starting to relax, we will go when it is closed, or you just go home, and I will see you later,' he snapped.

I already knew better than to go home and leave him. Gregory liked to be the centre of attention and would go ballistic if I didn't put him first, after all, in his eyes I was lucky to have him want to spend time with me, which was a line he had started to use later when we argued.

'No, it's okay, I will stay, but think I will slow down on the drinking,' I said sheepishly to him.

'Do what you want but be a dear and fetch me another pint,' he said winking at me.

I stood for a second and waited and then realized I was to use the money I had on me and made my way to the bar. The whole evening seemed to drag until the last orders bell was chimed, I felt like I was about to be sick, the panic of returning home with him so drunk turned my stomach like I had been winded. I started to put my coat on, and Greg stumbled towards me, he had apparently had far too much to drink, it then dawned on me that we were meant to try and walk home with him in this state.

Once outside, Greg placed his hand on my shoulder and squeezed it harder than needed as he tried to steady himself, I put my arm around his waist to try and steady him, it was no easy task by any means. Gregory was at least a foot taller than me and weighed three stones more, than my tiny, framed body, but we stumbled on towards the bus stop. As soon as we got to the bus stop though, Greg had fallen into a heap by the side of the road, I managed to roll him back near the path, but he was that pissed he didn't even know who I was. I stood up looking down on this stupid drunken mess and wondering what the hell I saw in him; at that point I decided I was going to leave him. The bus stopped for me but only to tell me I was best leaving my drunken boyfriend to sober up as no bus driver or taxi driver would pick him up in that state. In all honesty, the thought did cross my mind just to leave him there, but I knew how badly he would kick off if I had of done that. So, I thanked the driver and tried to pick Greg up and make him walk.

'What, what yaw do-do-doing?' he tried to say.

'Getting you home!' I replied putting my arms under his to try and lever him up.

'I'm fine here,' he said trying to lie back down on the damp concrete.

'Well, I am not, we are not staying here, now get up!' I shouted.

'Do you need any help love?' Came a voice from behind me.

I turned around to see who it was, and a small group of local drinkers had just left the pub behind the bus stop.

'You look like you could do with some help,' he said again.

'I will be okay, I've just got to get him home,' I said, 'but thanks anyway.'

'Look, you are not going to get him home by yourself, let me and my mate help you. You girls can walk behind and talk about nails or hair or summit, my main man and I can carry him back for you, as long as you don't live the other side of Crosby that is?' he said laughing.

'I live on Stoneside if you don't mind helping, I have a few beers in the fridge if you can,' I replied,

'Thank you,' he bent down to the ground.

'No problem,' he said lifting Greg to his feet single handily.

'See how easy that was?' he said looking at one of the girls who he was trying to impress.

It took ages to get back to mine, and Greg had sobered up a bit by the time we got back. I offered the two women a coffee and the two lads a beer out of the fridge, the one girl didn't want a drink, and I guessed she felt put out trying to help me home with the drunk in the corner. Greg piped up that he wanted a beer as well, but one lad told him it wasn't wise, and he seemed to listen, he looked at the floor and nodded off instantly. Once everyone had gone, I got Greg into bed, and I slept in my son's bedroom.

A MILE IN MY OWN SHOES

He's not even two...

Things with Greg hadn't got any easier, but the worst was yet to come. It was the end of August when he finally flipped at me. My kids were at Simon's for the weekend, and I had been out most of the day in the pub with Greg, which had turned into a weekend thing for him, whether I wanted to or not wasn't important to him, as long as he could get wasted at the weekend. So that evening when I got a phone call out of the blue from my Mum, who was very drunk herself, I was shocked and taken back by what she had to say.

'Hey, my love, I am at Billy's Mum's house by yours, and I need to talk to you,' she said.

'What's wrong?' I asked.

Greg was looking at me as if to say, what the fuck is she wanting, I placed my hand over the phone and told him my Mum seemed a little drunk and needed to see me straight away, Greg was on the play station and told me I wasn't allowed to go and see her. I placed the phone back to my ear.

'Sorry Mum, I can't come,' I explained.

'I wouldn't ask if it wasn't important, I need to talk to you now, I need to know what happened to you when you were a kid, it's driving me mad not knowing,' she begged.

Even though I knew if I ignored Greg I would have a huge argument later, I had vodka in my system, and I didn't care what might happen later.

'What's the address?' I asked.

Greg was scowling at me, but I hung up the phone and went to get up off the sofa, he grabbed my arm and squeezed it tightly.

'Where the fuck, do you think you are going?' I tried to pull my arm from his grasp.

'Look I need to go and talk to my Mum; it's a conversation have been waiting for my whole life!' I said defiantly.

'You are not going anywhere,' he said.

I pulled harder to release myself from his grip and stumbled towards the living room door, banging my shoulder on the way out of the room; I continued to bounce off the walls and eventually stumbled outside the front door. Greg followed me and grabbed hold of my waist, lifting me off the ground and into his arms.

'Let me go!' I shouted, and he kicked the front door closed behind him with his foot, I tried to release myself from him, but he just carried me tighter in his arms and started walking up the stairs.

'You are in no fit state to go out, I am putting you to bed whether you like it or not,' he snapped at me.

'I am not a child; you can't put me to bed!' I shouted in his face.

'I can, and I fucking will!' he screamed back in my face, spraying me with his saliva.

He threw me on the bed and was screaming and shouting at me, but I couldn't hear the words. I had switched off and was thinking about how to tell my Mum what had happened to me for all those years; she had convinced herself it hadn't happened so this was finally my time to tell my side of the story. I was suddenly brought back to reality by being shaken; Greg had his arms on my shoulders screaming in my face.

'You are staying in bed; I am going to Martins,' he repeatedly said, until I was nodding in agreement.

Martin lived two doors away, he was an older man who seemed to work hard during the week, but he liked a drink, which suited Greg to the ground, as soon as he knew there was free beer on offer, he would latch on to them. I was told how disappointed he was in me and ordered to stay in bed and that he would check up on me later to make sure I hadn't choked on my tongue. He laughed at me, told me I was pathetic then walked out of the room, slamming the door behind him so hard I thought it had come off the hinges, I got out of bed to check, and I heard the front door slam a few moments later.

I didn't care what might have happened and made my way down the stairs, and I feared Gregory had pretended to go out to catch me sneaking out. I just knew that I had told my Mum I would go and see her, and that is what I had intended on doing. I was still a little unsteady on my feet, but I managed to get out of the front door and round the side of the house. I knew in my sober mind the estate I lived in like the back of my hand and Billy's Mums should have been easy to find, but I was very drunk and struggling to walk in a straight line, never mind get to where I needed to go. After walking around for what seemed like an hour, some random lad stopped me to ask if I was okay, I think the shock of him talking to me had sobered me up a bit, and I looked around me and gathered my surroundings. Billy's Mum lived just behind the cul-de-sac I was stood in; I completely ignored the person trying to talk to me and walked towards the house. I found it easy enough once I had realised how close I was, I had been walking in circles for ages and felt foolish for not knowing the way. Billy answered the door and then ushered me into the kitchen.

'Now then, tell your Mum exactly what happened between you and your Dad,' he said in a deep tone like he was trying to patronize me.

'I don't think I am in any fit state to talk about it, to be honest with you, I have been drinking all afternoon,' I said.

'Well, if you don't tell her what happened, she will believe your Dad's side of the story, and we all know there is more to it than what he has said,' he replied.

'Please just tell me what happened, your Dad said you caught him in the bathroom and refused to leave, and that once he did something he had regretted, but he blamed you and said it was all you're doing,' Mum said, crying while she was talking.

'Once, try more like six years,' I said defending myself.

'You are lying!' she shouted.

'Hey, hold on a minute, why would she lie about it? If she said it to split you two up as your husband stated then why say this now?' Billy's Mum asked looking in my Mum's direction.

'Well?' she said waiting for my Mum to respond.

Billy then led me into the living room and told me to take a seat, I was crying as well by this point, and he asked me if I was telling the truth. I just looked up at him, and I think my look must have said it all to him because he walked out of the room and left me sitting on my own. The television in the room was far too big for the room it was in, it was a big sixty-inch flat screen, you had to have money to own something so grand. The screen showed the outside of the house, so I knew they had seen me stumbling into the garden. About ten minutes later my Mum came into the room with a cup of tea made by Billy's Mum, she placed both drinks on the glass coffee table and sat down beside me, we then spoke about the first night I had walked into the bathroom and how it had all started. She still didn't want to believe me, and after she left me in the room crying to myself, I had overheard her talking in the kitchen and saying that it can't be right. That I must have been lying because she would have known if something was happening under her roof. The truth was I think she knew, but just didn't want to believe it, and part of me could understand why she would think it was easier to brand me a liar again rather than face up to the truth.

I was so intoxicated with vodka that I don't remember leaving their house and found myself walking back towards mine. Martin was stood outside having a smoke and told me to come into his, where Greg was waiting for me. I then shit myself for fear of him kicking off when he saw me, but I hoped he would be fine in front of everyone. When I walked into the front room, Greg didn't notice me straight away; he was sat on a two-seater sofa with a slim blonde girl, they were chatting away and laughing at each other. Greg was apparently flirting but it didn't bother me, I walked out of the living room, down the hall to the kitchen where Martin and a few others were smoking and building joints.

'Do you want a beer, our kid?' Martin asked me.

'I would prefer a smoke if you had any,' I said in a cheeky quiet voice.

'Of course, help yourself,' he replied pointing to the table in the centre of the room.

I sat down and made a smoke for myself, I was talking to Martin about getting a new carpet for my stairs, he was a carpet fitter by trade, and he was telling me how good his discounts were, just as Greg walked into the room with the blonde girl.

'I told you to stay in bed!' he said giving me a cold stare.

'I am an adult, plus I feel fine now,' I said defending myself.

'She seems fine to me,' Martin added.

'Suit yourself then,' he said walking to the fridge to get another beer for himself.

'We will have words when we get home,' he said as he walked back out of the kitchen.

'Don't worry yourself, you need just to ignore him,' Martin said, 'he will be fine, just being a bit moody today by the looks of things.'

'I will be fine, he will probably fall straight to sleep as soon as he gets in anyway, and he has been drinking all day anyway,' I said relighting my joint.

'Are you his girlfriend then, I'm guessing?' said the blonde girl. I just nodded my head, and she walked out of the kitchen too, a few minutes later Greg walked back into the room and said,

'Right were off' he said pointing his finger at me and then towards the front of the house.

I knew better than to argue with him, so I got up and said my goodbyes, we walked two doors away to my house in silence and when we got in Greg locked the door behind him and put the key in his pocket. My heart sank to the pit of my stomach, and I knew he was getting ready to start, he then walked straight past me in the hall with a piercing look in his eyes, which reminded me of my Dad when he used to go mental on me. Greg opened the back door, walked into the rear garden and returned a second later with a can of lager in each hand.

'Where did you get them?' I asked.

'I took them from that old farts house, he is too wasted to miss them, and I have a feeling I will need them later,' he said forcing a fake smile on his face.

I made my way to the sofa and sat down to make myself a joint, and Greg sat beside me. He was cold faced, and as I was putting my two cigarette papers together, he scrunched them up in my hands and squeezed my hands together, hurting me in the process.

'You are going to bed, and I told you that, now fuck off up the stairs!' he shouted in my face.

'I am just having a smoke before I go up.'

'You are fucking getting up the stairs now, you stupid cow!' he said grabbing my arm and pulling me to my feet.

He started hitting me repeatedly across the head with the back of his hand, I raised my arms to cover my face and ran towards the stairs. I was halfway up the stairs when I felt his hand on my ankle, he pulled me hard and I fell, crashing back down the stairs, banging my eye off one of the stairs on the way down, as I collapsed into a heap on the floor, Greg grabbed hold of my hair, ripping some of it from the scalp as he tried to pull me to my feet.

'Where do you think you are going?' he said calmly.

'To bed. Just like you told me,' I screamed back.

'Please let go of me you are hurting me.'

'Good, maybe next time you will have learned your lesson,' he said patronizing me.

'I'm not a child,' I cried out as he pulled me by the hair back up the stairs.

He dragged me into the bedroom, still with a fist full of my hair; he had yanked me so hard, my body felt like a rag doll as I fell onto the bed.

'You can't treat me like this, I won't put up with it,' I snapped.

'I will do what the fuck I want!' he said, releasing my hair and punching me in the leg, making it feel dead in the process.

The next thing I knew I was being thrown around the room, by my clothes. The divan bed had been separated in two, and one half was flung in my direction, missing me by centimetres.

'Get out of my fucking house,' I screamed at him.

'You want me out, then make me you little slag,' he said.

'I am a slag? you are the one who was chatting up a blonde bimbo!' I snapped back.

'Ha-ha, fucking ha,' he replied walking closer to me.

'You are the one who fucked ya Daddy, after all,' he sneered. I just froze and looked at him, I hadn't told Greg about my past, and whatever he had heard was wrong.

'You're a sick bastard; I never fucked my Dad; you twisted sick fuck!' I shouted.

Greg was stood inches away from me, waving his hand in my face; he grabbed my arm and pulled me towards the mirror, knocking all my makeup and perfumes on the floor. He dragged my body across the floor and told me he wouldn't piss on me if I were on fire and that I repulsed him, he then spat on me and walked out of the room. I sat on the floor, shaking until I felt strong enough to get up onto my feet, I made the bed as quietly as I could and climbed under the covers, I just lay in the same position for ages, too scared to move, my eyes fixed on the door. At that moment, I had been taken back to my childhood, with the same horrible feelings I had every evening my Mum was out at work. I wasn't planning on sleeping that night at all; I feared what might happen if I did. Eventually, I had fallen asleep though and didn't wake up till the next morning.

The next morning Greg was full of remorse, he said he had had a stressful day and should never have taken it out on me. He had promised to cut down on his drinking and even offered to make amends with Simon because after all, he was my children's father. So, it was agreed that he would come with me later that day to collect the kids and take them out for lunch together. I texted Simon when we were on our way to warn him that I had Gregory with me, and he just replied with 'ok.' So, after a long talk with Greg, I went upstairs to get dressed, all my makeup and bottles of perfume were still lying all over the bedroom floor, but I decided to clean it all up when we got home later that day. Once we were ready, we booked a taxi and made our way to Simon's flat.

Greg was repeating himself and telling me how sorry he was.

'You know something; I don't believe a man should ever lay a finger on a woman,' he said.

I just looked at him and turned my head away again, looking in the opposite direction to him.

'Look at me,' he said in a calm tone.

'I mean it, Sarah, I have never been like I was last night with anyone, I don't know what had gotten into me,' he said trying to defend his actions.

'Why am I any different to anyone in the past?' I asked.

'Because I love you, and want to make you a better person,' was his reply, I was angry at his comment.

'Who the hell was he to want me to be a better person?' I thought to myself.

'That sounded worse than it was meant to,' he said defending his last comment, he must have seen I was annoyed.

'If you ever lay a finger on me again, I will walk away and never look back,' I snapped. He promised me he wouldn't, and being naïve, I believed him.

We collected the kids and went to McDonald's as planned. Mark had been playing up a little, but that was normal after collecting them from their Dads. So, Greg agreed when we got home, that he would look after him while I popped up to my Dads with Lucy. I was glad of the relief for a few hours because my son had started to become a handful, he was two years old, I guessed that's why it is called the terrible two's after all. I hadn't stayed at my Dad's long as he was all depressed and down in the dumps, and after the weekend I had just had, I wasn't in the mood. I also felt guilty that I had spoken to my Mum about what happened when I was a child, not that she believed me anyway, but the guilt was still eating away at me. I sat opposite him at the kitchen table so after I finished my drink, I made my excuse to go back home. I had been out for less than an hour.

The house was quiet when I got home, I placed Lucy, who was asleep in her moses basket, which was in the kitchen, and I carried her into the living room. I was shocked to see Mark in his sister's car seat, he was far too big for it, I walked over to him, and he was fast asleep. As I stroked his hair, he moved to get more comfortable, and I gasped in horror. He had a sizeable egg shaped lump at the top of his head. I stormed up the stairs to have it out with Greg and find out what had happened within the hour to cause him to get hurt. Greg was very dismissive and told me it was his own fault and that he had to tell my son off for being naughty and clipped him around the head.

'It's more than a fucking, clip round the head; you hit my fucking son!' I screamed.

'He flung himself into the radiator; it wasn't my fault,' Greg replied.

We argued for almost an hour before Mark woke up crying. Unfortunately, with him being only two years old, my son couldn't explain what had happened, just that nasty Greg had hit him, and it hurt. I was livid but knew if I didn't let it go I would get the full force of Greg's anger. I did warn Greg that if it happened again, I would run a mile, and he seemed to understand that I was deadly serious. Greg eventually came down the stairs and apologized to both my son and me and was adamant it was an accident. He seemed sincere, and I hoped he was.

ANOTHER DAY, ANOTHER BATTLE...

For weeks things seemed to improve, Greg did everything he could to keep the peace. He had even brought me flowers, which were new to me. No one had ever brought me flowers, and I appreciated the effort he had made. Mark still seemed a little wary of Greg, but Greg seemed to take it in his stride, explaining to me that it would take my son time to get used to him, but that he was willing to do whatever it took to gain his trust again, because he loved me after all, and he knew when we first met that I had children, and I came as a package. For the past month we hadn't argued either, and I was starting to believe Greg was changing his ways. So, when he had brought me an emerald ring and told me he loved me, I was so made up, but still nervous. We had only been together six months, and I was dreading him asking me to marry him.

'You can get rid of that ring Simon brought you now,' he said.

'I am keeping it for when my daughter is older,' I replied.

'No, you are not,' he snapped.

'Do you still love him?' he asked.

'I never loved Si, and I never pretended to either, but he is my children's Dad.'

Greg just laughed, 'He isn't a dad to the kids, what does he do for them, it is me who is here bringing them up, not him,' he said.

'That is true, but I am still keeping the ring for when Lucy is older,' I replied.

'Get rid of the ring before I snap your fingers off,' he said in an evil, cold tone, so I did as I was told.

I took my ring off my index finger and placed it into my back pocket. 'Are you happy now?' I asked.

'Do not get mouthy at me; I just spent a fucking fortune on that ring for you, you ungrateful bitch.'

'I am grateful, it is lovely,' I said defending myself.

'Well, it beats that silver piece of shit your ex bought you,' he said smiling at me.

Not a pleasant smile either, it was more of a sarcastic grin.

The next morning, I had to take my daughter to the clinic to be weighed. Mark was fast asleep, so Greg told me to leave him at home because I wasn't planning on being out long. Almost as soon as I got to the end of my road, I had a message off Greg telling me my son was awake. I replied saying I would be as quick as I could.

The clinic was packed, and it took over half an hour before I could get my daughter weighed. Lucy was tiny when she was born, so it was no surprise to me when the health visitor told me she was still underweight.

'She is the size of a six month old, and she is almost one,' the health visitor said as if it was my fault.

'She has always been tiny,' I replied.

'I know that, but it isn't the point, the point is she needs to put weight on, and in this past two months she has only gained two pounds, we should try her on the follow-on milk, see if we can build her up,' she said.

I felt like this woman called Val, was looking down on me and I felt shit about myself, even though I knew that my daughter ate all the time, I was going over the conversation in my head the whole way home.

When I did get home, Greg had opened a can of Fosters, it wasn't even ten in the morning and he was drinking, but to keep the peace I didn't say anything. I heard Mark upstairs, so after I told Greg what Val had said about Lucy's weight, I went upstairs to get him. My son wasn't in his bedroom like I expected, he was sat in his sister's cot bed, he was all red-faced and I guessed he had been crying while I was out. I opened the curtains and seen his blotchy face. As I picked him up out of the cot I realized, his blotchy skin was shaped like a hand, a large man's hand and I knew Greg had hit him again. I took him into his bedroom and placed him on the floor to play with his toys; I then closed the stair gate behind me and made my way back down the stairs into the living room where Greg was sprawled out on the sofa, now on his second can of the morning.

'So, what happened this time?' I asked.

'What do you mean?' Greg said sitting up to let me share the sofa.

'My son and the fucking mark on his face again?' I snapped.

'Don't know what you are talking about,' he replied with a big grin on his face.

'Do you think it is funny?' I shouted.

'No, what I think is funny, is that you have the cheek to mouth off at me, I thought you learned your lesson last time?' he shouted back louder than me.

He then got up and pushed me onto the sofa, 'I am going out before I do something I regret,' he said walking out of the room into the kitchen.

'No, I want to know what happened Greg,' I said following him into the other room.

'I suggest you fuck off out of my sight before I smash you in the face,' he shouted.

'Go on then, I am a better match than a child!' I said standing my ground.

'He is only two years old Greg, I don't hit my kids, and I won't let you do it either,' I snapped.

Greg then punched me in the side of the head, and I lost my balance. My face stung, and I felt my nose start to bleed. I got myself up off the floor and ran upstairs to the bathroom, I locked the door and then heard his shouting abuse at me from the bottom of the stairs.

'Get out of my house,' I shouted.

'Don't worry I am going, you stupid slag!' I then heard the front door slam so hard I thought it was going to come off the hinges.

WORKING PARTNERSHIP, OR NOT...

Things had started to get so bad that I feared for not only my safety but also my son's. Mark started to become withdrawn and quiet, and Greg seemed to love the control he had over us. It had all got to a point where I was asking Simon to have our son overnight more often as I was worried Greg would go too far and seriously hurt him. I know that I should have just taken my kids and run a mile, but I wouldn't know where to go, and I know no matter how far I run, Greg will follow us. He has made it very clear that I belong to him and that I will need to be dead to get away. Like who the fuck says that to someone they love? Greg would always tell me that he gets so angry because he loves me but how can he even say those words? I think I have just clicked on to why I am afraid of this vile man. He reminds me so much of my dad when I was growing up. He may not be sexually abusing me like my Father was, but he had the fear factor a hundred percent.

I was on my way to drop my son off; it was a lovely sunny Saturday morning. When I left the house, Greg was still in bed, hung over from the binge drinking the night before. I tried my best not to disturb him as I left the house, which wasn't an easy task with two young children, but it seemed to work, or so I thought.

Simon lived near the town centre; his flat was situated on the other side of the bridge; it was a few minutes' walk down a straight path towards the front of the flat. Something made me turn around as I was approaching the front of the flat and I noticed a tall skinny man stood on the bridge, his build was like Greg's, but I knew he was still in bed so thought nothing of it as I made my way to the front door. Si answered with a big grin on his face.

'Why are you looking so smug?' I asked.

'I want you to meet someone,' he said in his giddy, childish voice, 'Do you remember me talking about Amanda?' he asked.

'No?' I replied shaking my head. 'Mim then?' he said.

I had remembered him talking about a woman who he had been talking to online; he seemed smitten by her, even though they had never met.

'Yes, I know who you mean,' I said smiling back at him.

'Well, she has come to stay for the holidays!' he said rubbing his hands together.

'She is in the living room, come in,' he said beckoning me into the room.

Mim was a small plump lady; she looked as alternative as Simon with her purple hair and a band t-shirt. She smiled at me and introduced herself.

'How did you ever pull her?' she then said looking at Si, who just smiled and shrugged his shoulders.

'I was young and naïve,' I replied.

'Well, it is lovely to meet you finally,' she said shaking my hand again.

I had gone into the kitchen to get Lucy from her pushchair as she had started to stir, just as I got her out of the pram, the door knocked, it was a loud, abrupt knock on the door, and my heart started racing.

'I bet that is Greg,' I said concerned as Si walked to the front door.

'He doesn't even know where I live,' he replied.

I could tell by the increased knocking, that the man on the bridge was, in fact, Greg; he must have got up as soon as I left the house and followed me to Si's. Mim had made her way into the hallway by the time Simon had opened the door.

'I want Sarah now,' I heard Greg saying as the door was opened, so I placed Lucy back into her buggy and kissed my son on the forehead before making my way to the front door.

'Excuse me,' I said wanting to get out of the flat as soon as I could, I could tell by Greg's face that he was ready to kick off and any given moment.

'No, fuck him,' Mim snapped. 'Who the hell do you think you are knocking on this door like that when we have kids in the house?' she said raising her voice at Greg.

'Don't mess with me you fat slag, I want my girlfriend, that's it, the rest is none of your business!' he shouted back.

It soon escalated into a full-blown shouting match between the three of them, as I just stood there, frozen to the spot. Greg then grabbed my arm, forcing me past Simon and Mim, I had run Mim's foot over with the pushchair by accident and apologized as soon as I did.

'Why the fuck did you say you were sorry to that mouthy slag?' Greg shouted as we walked away from the front door.

The whole way home, we argued about almost nothing. Apparently, I shouldn't have stayed more than a few seconds at Simon's when dropping my kids off, I told Greg that I always stayed for a coffee, and I needed to make sure my son was settled, and he replied by telling me I was forbidden from having a coffee with my ex-boyfriend. It was pathetic, but I knew if I had carried on the argument I would not have heard the end of it, so I just agreed with him to keep the peace.

That evening I had been applying for jobs online because Greg had told me I needed to get a job, I already knew that with two children, childcare and rent to pay, I was financially better off not working, but he wasn't having any of it. In his eyes if I were out at work, he would have more money for his beer, seemed like the only thing he cared about. For me, it was a chance to have a breather away from all the stress. I searched online and applied for jobs all that evening, but it was to no avail, a week later I had still not heard anything, and Greg was getting even more frustrated with me always being at home, which caused even more bickering between us.

By the end of the summer, I still hadn't found a job, and Greg was drinking even more. I was expected to buy him eight cans of lager every day, and money was becoming a struggle. Just to add to my stress, my health visitor was still on my case about my daughter's weight and making weekly meetings with me to keep an eye on things. Greg just thought it was funny that this health visitor, Valerie was picking on me and made it clear that he thought I was a poor parent for not being able to control my unruly son. Mark wasn't badly behaved, he just wanted a lot of my time, and if I was showing him time, it meant I was giving Greg less of my attention. My latest meeting with Val was on Friday afternoon, I had already dropped both kids off with their Dad, and she seemed annoyed that I didn't have them both with me, but the conversation soon turned to my relationship. Val said she wasn't stupid and could tell I was in an unhappy relationship; she made a threat about my kid's best interests and said that I needed to put them first before any love interests. As if I didn't already know that, but I was weary of Health visitors at the best of times, especially her, she was opinionated and rude towards me, so I kept my cards close to my chest and told her nothing that could be used against me.

The next day I was due to collect the kids, but with Greg still on at me for going to Simons, it was agreed that that day he would meet me uptown with them instead. I took the kids to McDonald's and did a bit of food shopping; I knew Greg was at his grandparents for the day, so I did not need to rush home. While walking through town, I noticed a sign in the window of HMV asking for temporary staff over the Christmas and New Year, so with kids in tow, I made my way inside and asked the cashier for more details. 'You will need to talk to Matt' she said pointing to the other side of the shop. I made my way towards him and introduced myself, explaining that I was looking for a job, starting as soon as possible. He looked me up and down and then kept his glare on the double buggy with my kids in it.

'I am a hard worker given half a chance' I said feeling like I needed to say something.

'What is your music knowledge like?' he asked.

'I love music,' I replied smiling.

'I didn't ask if you liked music, I asked what your knowledge was like,' he said sharply.

'I would like to think; I have a good knowledge of music; I listen to it every day and have done most of my life. My tastes vary depending on my mood, so my interests span all genres,' I replied.

'In that case, can you come back on Monday, without the children, and I will give you an interview and test you on what you know.'

I agreed and shook his hand, before making my way back out of the shop. I felt stupid for asking for the job while I had the kids with me but working in a music shop was my ideal job, even if the interview was a waste of time, I had at least tried.

Greg was at home when I returned, he seemed in a good mood for a change, and he said he was hoping I got the job, I told him about my interview, and he agreed to have the kids for me while I went. I was worried about leaving my son with him, but he assured me that he would be fine.

'I will just put the little bastard in his room if he starts, but I am sure he will be as good as gold,' he said.

That weekend seemed relaxed, and even with Greg drinking the whole time, we didn't argue once. Greg even seemed to be trying with my son, so when Monday came, I was happy enough to leave him with the kids. My interview went a lot better than I expected and Matt seemed to be pleasantly surprised with how well I had done on my music quiz; I was offered the job and given my start date for the following week. I was made up and rang Greg to tell him my good news.

'That's good, but what will happen with the kids, there is no way I will look after your devil child,' he snapped, talking about Mark.

'I didn't ask you to!' I snapped back.

'Good, his trampy Dad, can have him because I am not,' he said putting the phone down on me.

Every single time he snapped at me or raised his voice, my heart would beat like crazy, I knew I feared him, but I was too much of a coward to do anything about it. Even though my family and friends were all telling me to leave him and couldn't understand why I let him treat me the way he did, it was like he had an invisible hold over me that I couldn't explain or release myself from.

When I got home, Greg was still going on about how he refused to look after my son, so I made my excuses to get out of the house for a few minutes and rang Simon. I had explained the situation and the fact that I was starting work the following week and he had agreed to have Mark, but he stated that if he was having him while I was working, he wanted to have him full time. I was taken aback by this and annoyed at Simon, but after talking for a few minutes, I realised that he was doing it to protect our son. Si had agreed that if I left Greg and wanted my son to return home, he wouldn't stop me, and would help in any way possible. I looked over at the photo of Mark and tears built up in my eyes. Simon can tell I am upset and goes on to explain that it is all for the best and that I know Mark would be happier at his Dad's. Si then repeats that if I don't have Mark living with me that it might push me to leave Greg finally. I knew that was easier said than done but agreed with him anyway.

I didn't tell Greg about the phone call straight away as he was drunk when I got back in, he was a lightweight heavy drinker, which meant after his sixth can he was almost paralytic, and that meant abuse towards me. I had however got to the point that I was used to his erratic behaviour and knew when the best time was to talk to him and the best time to keep my mouth shut, this was one of those moments when I was best not saying a word. Within twenty minutes he was upstairs asleep, which suited me down to the ground. He was still sleeping when I had a knock on the front door. It was my younger brother and one of his friends, he asked where Greg was, and I told him he was asleep. I was then pushed out of the way, and they both came into the hallway and closed the front door behind them.

'I will give the bastard a slap,' My brother Daniel said.

'Why, what has he done to you?' I asked, thinking something had happened between them while I wasn't about.

'Dad told me about him hitting my nephew, and vodka has given me the balls to do something about it.'

I didn't want any trouble, but I was ignored, my brother and his mate made their way up the stairs, I heard the commotion and shouted for them to leave him alone, my heart was racing, and I was scared that Greg would blame me, and later take it out on me. I felt bad but knew I had to ring the police. I ran into the kitchen to ring them and explain what was happening, I then shouted back up the stairs and told Daniel that the police were on their way. His friend came running down the stairs first and shouted abuse at me before leaving through the back door. My brother then followed and warned me he would make me pay for calling the cops on my own family, but I did what I needed to do, to get them both out of my house. Daniel's friend then pushed me to the ground and made his way over my six-foot fence. Once I knew they were gone, I locked both the front and back doors and went upstairs to check on the kids and Greg, I was shocked to see the state of his face when I walked into the bedroom, he was bleeding, and you could tell his face was starting to swell up.

I sat on the bed expecting him to turn on me, my palms were sweating, and my heart was beating rapidly, but he was fine with me, he said it wasn't my fault, and he wasn't going to press charges, as he would do the same if I were his sister. That surprised me as I was expecting him to kick off big time, but the alcohol must have taken a better effect on him.

Once the police had been and gone, Greg had decided that it was best if he looks for somewhere else to stay, I thought he was leaving me, but I should be so lucky. He stated that I was still his girlfriend, but he just couldn't live with me anymore, after what had just happened. I should admit I was glad, and part of me thought it would be easier to leave him if he no longer lived with me.

ANOTHER LIFE RUINED…

It was almost Christmas, and Mark had been living with his Dad for over six weeks and it was horrible. I kept beating myself up mentally about him not being at home with us, but things at home were a lot more settled, and Greg seemed happier living in a shared house rather than with me and Lucy. I would visit Mark once a week at Simon's home, and Si would bring him up to town to meet me on a Friday after work. To start off with it was hard and I cried every time I had to leave my son, but it started to get easier, and seeing how happy Mark was with his dad made me think I had made the best choice in the end. Simon even seemed a lot happier, and I think him taking on a full parent role had brought him out of his shell a little more. Lucy had stays over with her dad too, which meant I had every other weekend to myself and that in turn meant my relationship with Greg had started to improve. His drinking was still as bad, but with me working and only supporting one child, I could pay his rent and keep him supplied with drink, which meant fewer arguments and more time together just the two of us.

Hmv was a fantastic place to work, and I had started to make friends as well as earning cash. I was in work one Saturday when my Dad and one of his druggy mates had come into the store. My Dad had told me a few days previously that he had a load of fake twenty-pound notes, and I knew he was hoping to spend them in the town centre. So, when I saw him, I tried to make my excuses to work at the back of the store hoping I wouldn't get spotted, but I had.

'Hey sweetheart, I could do with you serving me' my Dad said, winking at me.

'I can't Dad, sorry,' I replied, 'I am not on the tills today,' I explained.

'Oh fuck, okay well I will see if I can use my money here anyway,' he said, 'It seems busy enough today.'

I just looked at him and said, 'I had best get back to work.'

I had told Greg about what had happened at work that evening when I had gone to his, and he seemed pissed off at me for it. That annoyed me, and I had snapped back at him because it was nothing to do with me, but he didn't seem to listen. I was meant to be staying the night in his rented room, but with him being in a mood I decided to go home as it wasn't worth the aggro. My house seemed eerily silent as I walked through the front door I quickly turned the hall light on, I knew no one would be in the house, but it still didn't stop me creeping from room to room slowly until I knew no one was in the house with me. Once I felt secure, I locked the front door and sat down on the sofa to watch the soaps. I had fallen asleep on the couch when I heard a loud bang on the front door; my first instinct was to ignore it and pretend I didn't hear it, and then the knocking got louder and heavier.

'Okay I am coming!' I shouted as I got towards the hall.

'Open the fucking, do-door now!' Greg shouted; he had been drinking because his words were slurring.

'One minute,' I replied.

'No, I said now you silly, silly bitch!'

I opened the door, waiting for him to start kicking off but instead, he grabbed hold of me and kissed me passionately, I tried to move from the door, but he just held me close to him and kept repeating the words. I am so sorry; I do love you.

I just smiled even though inside I was screaming for him to release his tight hold of me; I just placed my arms on him and walked him towards the living room. As I walked into the room, I noticed the clock said it was almost midnight, I had been asleep for a few hours even though it seemed like a matter of minutes.

I placed Greg on the sofa, he was intoxicated and could hardly stand up, once I had sat down beside him, he grabbed hold of me again, kissing my neck and telling me how much he loved me.

'I love you too, Greg, but let's just relax, I am tired, it's been a long day,' I said.

He didn't listen, and had his hands all over me, trying to get his hand in my underwear.

'Please stop, I am not in the mood,' I snapped.

He then stopped and looked at me with a confused look, before slapping me across the face, it stung like hell, but I tried not to show it.

'Greg, you should go home,' I said getting to my feet. He pulled me back down on the sofa and started to apologize again, saying that I make him lose his temper because he loves me so much. He then began to grope me again, pinching at my bum as he tried to get his hands inside my trousers. I begged him to stop but he didn't listen, he made it clear that I was to sleep with him

88

whether I wanted to or not. I was his girlfriend, and that was it. Before I knew it his drunken body was on top of me and he was far too rough, I felt sick to the stomach.

The next morning when I woke up and saw him sleeping beside me, I just wanted to hit him in the face as hard as I could, my arms were aching all over, and when I went into the bathroom to get dressed, I noticed why. Where he had pinned me down the night before was red, and you could tell bruising was starting to appear from him pushing on my skin so hard. I couldn't believe he had been so forceful with me, and then to tell me he loved me, how could anyone treat another human being in that way? I will never know. It was safe to say that moment completely mirrored a time in my childhood, where I was forced down, forced to do things I didn't want to do. Even the bruises reminded me of my Father. The difference was my Dad never told me he loved me and back then I had no control. I am an adult now and should have power over my own life, but I don't. From that moment any feelings I did have for Greg had been slowly turning into hatred. I had told myself that I wouldn't let him do that to me again, but the truth of the matter was, I was scared stiff to say no to him.

My real nightmare started a good few weeks later, when I woke up in the middle of the night to him forcing himself on me yet again, he was sober this time which made it even worse. He had woken with morning glory and decided I was a bit of meat for him to relieve himself with. I realized that this would just get worse if I didn't do anything, so while he was on top of me, invading my insides, I continually hit out at him, jabbing him in the face, pulling his hair and trying everything I could to get him away from me. It worked after a few minutes, and after he screamed obscene abuse at me, he stormed out of the house, slamming the door and vowing never to return. I cried my heart out when he left, mainly from the relief that I had finally stood up for myself, but also because he had hurt me so badly. My stomach was cramping up, and I was violently sick all over the bathroom floor. That day I was meant to pick Lucy up from Simon's, but I had rung him to tell him how I was feeling, and he agreed to have her overnight again for me so that I could get some rest. I honestly would have been lost without Simon at that time, and I was a little frustrated that the man seemed to care more about me now than he ever did while we were together.

I had been feeling ill for a week, so Greg had made me take a pregnancy test, which much to my horror came back positive.

'You aren't having a child of mine,' he shouted when I told him the news.

'Looks like I am,' I said back as calmly as I could.

'Nah, this isn't happening, you best get rid of it,' he said coldly.

'I can't kill an unborn child,' I said holding my stomach.

'You think you have a say in this; I do not think so; I will drag you to the fucking clinic and force that pill down your throat,' he said spitting saliva all over me as he did so.

'How can you be so cold? This is your baby,' I said trying to defend myself.

'Like fuck it is it's a small cell at the minute, nothing more,' he shouted,

'Get rid, or I will beat the little bastard out of you!' he snapped.

Later that week an appointment was made for me at the doctors, who confirmed I was in fact pregnant. Greg made it clear to my doctor that we didn't want to keep the baby and that it was a mistake, so my doctor made me an appointment with the local clinic for the following

Monday. I stupidly spent the weekend trying to convince Greg that this baby could be a fresh start for us, but the more I mentioned it, the angrier he got towards me. He said that he wouldn't let me keep the child no matter what, we even spoke about splitting up so I didn't have to have the abortion, but he said even if we weren't together he still wouldn't allow me to keep the child. The threat of beating the child out of me was his favourite saying. So as Monday approached I had realised, this was one of my worst mistakes ever, and the fear of keeping his child inside me outweighed the thought of killing an unborn baby.

The worst was yet to come because after having my scan at the clinic, and it was confirmed that I needed to have an operation as I was over twelve weeks pregnant. Greg just looked smug, he had got his way, and a few days later I was booked into an abortion clinic in Birmingham, which was over fifty miles away from where I lived. Greg came with me to make sure I went through with it, and he seemed happy as we sat on the train on the way there.

'How can you be so cheery at a time like this?' I asked with tears in my eyes.

'I am happy that you listened to me, and that I have my freedom back, well after a few hours anyway,' he said coldly.

'You are sick.' I snapped.

'No, I am the only one thinking straight,' he said turning his head to look out of the window.

'It will be over in a few hours, and then we can go back to the way it used to be,' he said.

'Lucky me,' I replied sarcastically.

Two trains later and then a bus to the middle of the city centre, I had arrived at a big old townhouse.

'Surely this isn't the place,' I said.

'It is, it's the address they gave us,' Greg replied taking hold of my hand.

When we got inside, it was clear we were in the right place after all, the lady at reception asked my name and then checked me in.

'Straight up the stairs and on the right,' she said.

So, we made our way upstairs and came to a waiting room, it was full of women, who were clearly there for the same reason as me, some of which still looked like children themselves, but all of them had the support from loving partners or parents, holding their hands and reassuring them.

'I fucking hate places like this,' Greg muttered as we took a seat.

'I wouldn't know, it's the first time I have been here,' I replied with a forced fake smile trying to lighten the mood.

Greg smiled back at me, and held my hand, like the other couples were doing.

'You okay?' he asked.

I just nodded my head but really, I wanted to scream and shout at him, am I okay? had he really just asked me that. After about ten minutes of waiting, I was called into a side room, Greg got up with me but was told by the nurse that only I was allowed in the room. You could see by his face that he was pissed off, but I just went into the room like I was asked. Inside the room was another nurse sat at a desk, she told me to take a seat and not to worry it was all routine, she needed to ask me questions to determine whether I was being forced into the abortion or not. I had told her that it was a joint decision and that I was happy to carry on with the procedure, that was a lie in some sense, but at the same time I just wanted it all over and done with.

When I returned to the waiting room, Greg looked worried and asked me what that was all about, I told him, and he seemed relieved that the operation was going ahead, he then stood up and said he would see me later.

'Where are you going?' I asked confused at him leaving me on my own.

'I am not waiting around here, while you have a hoover stuck up you! Text me when they have finished, and I will meet you in town.'

I was shocked as he just walked out as if the time to feel alone was here and now, I thought to myself.

Looking around at everyone else, I was envious that they had a loving family around them at what was a very traumatic time, and my boyfriend had just walked out and left me, no doubt to find a pub and drink himself into a mess, while I had to be operated on.

When I came around I was feeling better than I had expected, the painkillers were in full swing, and I felt a little drunk, a little woozy and was falling back to sleep. When I opened my eyes again, a nurse was stood over me checking my blood pressure; she told me to close my eyes again and take my time. All I was thinking was, the longer I stayed in that bed, the more annoyed Greg would be, waiting around for me. I reassured the nurse that I was feeling fine, but my blood pressure told her otherwise.

'Well please make sure you rest when you get home,' she said. I got outside, Greg was nowhere to be seen.

So, I grabbed my phone out of my pocket and rang him. He answered straight away, so I guessed he had been on his phone at the time, because it rang once on my end.

'Where are you?' I asked.

'In town, you can meet me here,' he said.

I explained that I was in pain, and it hurt to walk, so I told him I would get a taxi to him. He didn't sound happy that I was spending money, but there was no way I was walking all the way into town on my own, I didn't know the way if I was honest, and I had expected Greg to be outside when I got out.

'You have the money on you and the card with the number of the taxi on so can you ring them please,' I asked.

'Fucking hell, I have to ring and pay them too, you are unreal,' he said before hanging up on me.

Me unreal, it was my money he was spending anyway, so I didn't see the big deal, I put my phone in my pocket and sat on the wall outside the clinic and waited. A few minutes later I had a message from Greg saying that my taxi was on the way. When I finally caught up with him, he had passed me a plastic bag.

'I bought you something,' he said smiling at me.

In the bag was a pair of trainers, he went on to explain that after going through what I just had, that I deserved some comfortable shoes, I should have been given a frigging medal not some pink trainers, but I smiled and thanked him.

'You can thank me later,' he said grabbing hold of his man parts.

'You have got to be kidding,' I said, 'do you know how much pain I am in?' disgusted at what he had just said.

'You'll be fine,' he replied winking at me.

I ignored his comment, and we sat in silence most of the way home, my stomach was so sore to touch and sitting down on the train seemed to make the pain even worse, but I knew there was no point in saying anything. Greg wasn't a caring boyfriend after all, and he proved that when we got back to his shared room. All I wanted to do was sleep off the pain, but he had other ideas. He told me to dress nicely and put some makeup on because I looked a mess. When I asked why he informed me that we were going to the pub to celebrate his freedom. I was pissed off to say the least, the last thing I wanted to do was go out and celebrate. I had just ended a baby's life, and I felt like shit about it, my stomach pain had eased a bit, but not much and I was bleeding heavily after the abortion. I tried to tell him that I didn't want to go out, but he wouldn't take no for an answer and warned me that I would be in his bad books if I didn't do as I was told. I knew that usually meant I would get abuse and if I were lucky he would just be moody with me. Most of the time, his bad books meant I would get a few slaps till I did as I was told, so I found my dress and went upstairs to the bathroom to have a wash and get changed.

Once I was on my own and out of earshot from him, I broke down. The tears just kept coming, and no matter how much I tried to ignore what I had been through, it was no good, the pain was a reminder of what I had just done. I had killed a child whatever way you looked at it, I was over twelve weeks pregnant only a few hours before, and now I wasn't. That hurt me emotionally, and the physical pain was almost as bad. There was no way I could forgive him for what he had put me through, but I knew if I tried to say anything it would just make my situation worse, so I wiped my eyes and walked back into the room where he was waiting for me.

'You look beautiful as usual,' he said as I walked back into the bedroom.

I just smiled and went to the other side of the bed to put my shoes on, so my back was to him. I clenched my fists as he was talking, god knows what he was saying. I was far too angry to hear him, the only sound I could hear was my rising heartbeat, beating in my chest and my ears. Once my shoes were on I turned and looked at him, forcing a smile on my face.

'Ready when you are,' I said as I got up to walk out of the room. My stomach still reminding me of the pain I was in.

That evening I wasn't in the best of moods, and it didn't go unnoticed with Greg's friends either. I had made out it was the wrong time of the month, and I had my monthly moods. I didn't want anyone to know what I had done earlier that day because I felt ashamed of myself. I tried to convince myself it was for the best because I surely didn't want a child with that monster I called my boyfriend, and at least this way I wasn't tied to him, and I knew one day I would build up the courage to leave him after everything he put me through.

TIME TO MOVE ON WITH MY LIFE...

The arguments continued between Greg and me and had got to the point that I was made to give up my house and move back in with my Mum. I had tried to split up with Greg a few times, but he never seemed to get it through to his thick head, he honestly believed that he owned me and told me on plenty of occasions that no one else would ever love me or ever want to be with me. After all, I was a single Mum from a council estate with not much going for me. Our latest argument was over a stupid guitar. I had decided I wanted to learn to play, and Greg made it his mission to try and put me off. When I had spent his beer money on my first guitar, he hit the roof and told me I would never be as good as him and the money was wasted on me. So, with him out of the way for a while my daughter and I settled into my Mum's house. I had spent hours practicing the guitar in the kitchen, and I was picking it up a lot better on my own, and in my own time, without someone shouting at me and telling me I was shit all the time.

To say living at my Mum's house again was vigorous work was an understatement. My Mum was okay since she left my Dad, but her new boyfriend was an idiot, not violent but just as aggressive and controlling. After an argument with my brother, I was asked to move out, my Mum felt terrible, but she took the side of her new man over her daughter as usual. So, with nowhere to go and my old house now rented out to a new family I was left to contact the homeless department and was told I would be rehoused as soon as they could. The problem was, the only place they could house me was almost a hundred miles away, which was a scary thought. Being so far away from everyone I knew, my son and family. It was a horrible feeling, but every cloud had a silver lining, and at least I was going to get away from Greg.

It was arranged that the homeless needs people would collect my daughter and me from my Mum's house the following Friday. Which gave me a few days to say my goodbyes and pack my stuff. It was quite sad really that all my belongings fit into two black bin bags. I had a whole house full of things before I was made to give my house up, as you can imagine that thought made me angrier with Greg. So, when he asked to see me before I left I was determined to stick to my guns, I had decided to change my number when I got to Stoke and only give it out to a handful of people, which didn't include him. It's funny though because when I did meet up with him, I realised I missed him like crazy, which annoyed me. The man was horrible to me, and in my eyes, I had lost two children because of him, but I still missed him. Greg was so upset that I was leaving, and he begged me to stay, tempted as much as I was after he promised to treat me better, it was out of my hands.

I was homeless and had nowhere to go, as I said my final goodbye, we both cried our hearts out. It was so refreshing to see real emotions coming from Greg, and it reminded me of the man I first met. The caring, sensitive person without alcohol in his system. So, with a heavy heart I kissed him goodbye and started to walk away, he was calling my name, wanting me to go back to him, but I ignored him and carried on walking. I didn't want to turn around because I was a bubbling mess and just the sight of him would have made me weak again. I needed more than ever to be strong and not let him get to me, so I thought of everything he had put me through the past year, and that made me carry on up the road, taking the necessary steps, I needed to get away from him.

Back at my Mums, the atmosphere was tense. My Mum's new fancy man was there and giving off all this spew about how I was an adult, a Mum myself and how I shouldn't be relying on my Mum anymore. The last thing I needed was him nagging me, so I decided to pop up to my mate's house for a smoke, my daughter was asleep, so I was told to leave her with my Mum while I popped out. I didn't like leaving her behind, but I was so stressed that I also didn't think it was a smart idea to wake her, Lucy was unsettled as it was, so waking her from her sleep meant she would probably cry all the time I was out. As I was leaving the house, my other younger brother was on his way to see our Mum, I stopped to chat to him for a few minutes on the doorstep and told him that I was moving away in a few days, he was concerned about where I would end up.

'I will be fine, don't worry about me,' I said.

'It's shit that Mum is kicking you out just because that dickhead has told her to, you sure no one else can help you, Sarah?' He asked.

'Honestly, I will be fine,' I replied with tears in my eyes.

'Look, I've got to go, I will see you later,' I said as I walked away.

It was Thursday afternoon, and I was all set to move away until there was a knock on the door. I was surprised to see my cousin Jody. When I asked what she was doing she explained that she bumped my brother up the town and he had explained my situation to her.

'You aren't going into some hostel in the middle of nowhere with no one,' she said trying to be all dominating.

'I can't see that I have much choice in the matter,' I replied.

'You can come and stay with me,' she said 'after all you helped me when I needed you the most and now it's my turn to repay the favour, and I won't take no for an answer.'

I wasn't going to disagree with her, at least if I went to hers, I would still see my son, so it was agreed that I would get a taxi to her house the next morning.

'It will be nice to have my big cousin back after all this time,' she said as she left my Mums to make her way home.

The next morning, I was filled with excitement rather than the fear I had felt the previous days, the person from homeless needs was due to collect me at ten, so I was waiting for him to arrive and explained my new situation to him. I think he was pleased that he didn't have to take the two-hour drive to Stoke, which meant his workday was a lot easier. As soon as he left I booked my taxi to take me to the other side of town. Greg had been messaging me all night and all that morning, and he seemed pleased I wasn't going to be so far away.

He had begged me to give him another chance to make me happy and stupidly I had agreed; I had hoped that almost losing me was enough to make him change his ways and treat me like any girlfriend expected to be treated. I wasn't high maintenance in any way, I just wanted to be treated normally without all the arguments and fighting, and most of all I didn't want to be hit ever again. Greg agreed to all this and foolishly I believed him.

MY NEW CHAPTER...

It was midday by the time I got to my cousin's house, and she was very welcoming to my daughter and me. She had even given up her bedroom for us, even though I had told her there was no need, she yet again wouldn't take no for an answer. We had dinner that evening, and Jody had brought us something to drink, plus I had some cannabis so as we settled down and got the kids to bed and was looking forward to finally relaxing. Jody had other plans; she had taken my phone while I was in the bath earlier that day and messaged Greg with her address, so that he could come and see me. She had been acting shifty and it all made sense when he knocked on the door just after teatime. I was a little angry that she was trying to play cupid, but I never said anything and just went with the flow. After all, it was her house and who was I to tell her who she could and couldn't invite, so the evening turned into a night of drinking and me playing guitar. Greg was on his best behavior trying to prove to me that he could be a caring boyfriend and even though I had told her about how evil he could be it was evident that she didn't believe me. Not once did he mock me when I got a chord wrong or played a song different to him, and maybe he had changed for the better, but I knew only time would tell.

The evening was going well, and Jody had told us about her new boyfriend, Stuart. She said he didn't like being called her boyfriend and she begged me not to say anything to him because he would go off on one, which I didn't understand at all, but I agreed with her and said I would only speak to him if I were spoken to.

Jody had got changed into something a little more revealing and had done her make up as Stu was due round at any point. She kept going to the windows to check if he was on his way and was getting agitated that he was later than she expected, I had told her not to stress, but she didn't listen. Just as she was starting to think he wouldn't turn up there was a knock on the door, or should I say a loud banging.

'That's him now, remember please don't say anything to him that will cause him to go off on one, and please don't mention the 'b' word,' she said as she walked into the hall to answer the door.

I wouldn't have said anything anyway.

It wasn't just her fancy man who was at the door; he turned up with another girl and a younger lad. Stuart was not what I expected my cousin to fall for, and he was a big built man with a bald head and beer belly, you could tell straight away that they had all been drinking.

Jody introduced me to them, and he just looked at me and laughed. Becky said it was nice to meet me and her boyfriend Jason just nodded at me. When I asked what was so funny, Stuart replied with,

'You aren't that fucking special.'

I ignored the comment and took it as drink talk. We were all sat around the table having a drink for an hour or so, Stuart was all over Jody for the whole time, kissing her and pulling her hair in a kinky manner, at one point he started banging her head off the fridge and said it was because she liked it. She agreed with him, but the situation still made me feel uncomfortable.

It was about midnight when Becky and her boyfriend decided to leave. Stu said he was staying for a bit and as soon as the door closed behind them, I started to understand the situation a little more. He was openly telling me that he had a thing with Becky and that her boyfriend had no idea, he said he had to pretend that he was with my cousin, so Jason wouldn't suspect anything.

I did slightly wonder what either Becky or Jody saw in him, he came across as an arrogant arsehole. Becky was pretty, she had perfect hair and seriously didn't need makeup or fancy clothes to look good, unlike my cousin and I, Becky had a natural beauty and the ideal body. Jody and I were both small, with our flat chests and tiny size six waists. Jody was dark haired but pale and with a few prominent freckles, whereas I have olive skin and blonde hair, but apart from that, we were similar in build.

When Stu had finally gone home, I had asked Jody what she saw in him. She was very defensive about him and said he was showing off because he had met Greg and me, but as far as first impressions went, for me, Stuart didn't seem like the type of man my cousin suited. I didn't like his cocky arrogance or his forcefulness towards her, but who was I to talk, I was with Greg after all.

MAKING FRIENDS, LOSING ENEMIES...

I had managed to get a part-time job at the local fast-food restaurant, and Jody was at home with her kids anyway, so she had agreed to look after my daughter while I worked. We had decided that I would go shopping once a week and buy some electric which was a good deal. One day while I was at work Stuart had come in with Tracey, yet another girl he managed to have at his beck and call. He made an excuse to come in and talk to me, my opinion on him had changed a little over the past few weeks as he had spent a lot of time at my cousins, but I still thought he was an overconfident, arrogant arse. So, when I refused to stand around and chat with him while I was meant to work, he decided to open his milkshake and tip it all over the mirror beside him, so I had a reason to be standing near him if I was seen.

'Gave you something to do now,' he said laughing.

Tracy didn't look impressed, she was a quiet, withdrawn girl, at least sixteen years younger than him, and I wondered why these younger girls all wanted the pleasure of his company. Yes, Stu was funny and good to talk to, but that was about it. While we were talking briefly, the conversation turned to Gregory. Stu blatantly asked what I had seen in him; he told me it was noticed that Greg wasn't nice towards me, and he treated me like some trophy on his arm.

Like you can talk, I thought to myself, but as much as I hated to admit it, he was right, and I liked the fact that it wasn't in my head and that other people could see the same as me.

Once back at my cousins I had hoped to have a relaxing bath and just chill out for the evening, but she had decided to let Greg move into hers with me, without even asking my opinion. I was annoyed at her, and once I was in the kitchen with her, I had told her that she had made a huge mistake, not that she understood what she had done. Luckily for me, he had been drinking most of the day and passed out by nine o'clock that evening. Stu, Jody and I were sat in the kitchen that evening just talking and Jody and I had a smoke while Stu drank his wine. The conversation had turned to my relationship again as Jody asked why Greg living with us was such a big problem, as I explained why I was so annoyed and how it had taken me a year to get my own space, she had started to feel a little bad.

'He won't lay a finger on you while you live under my roof,' she said.

'Chances are he will be fine with me while I am living here, but I don't want to be with him anymore if I am totally honest, I just know he won't let me leave,' I replied.

Stuart joined into the conversation and had offered Greg a room at his, so I could have my own space. I thanked him for the offer, but I knew Greg would disagree, so I just told him I would take him up on his offer if Greg started to be horrible again.

'Offer is always there if you need it, I have space anyway,' he replied.

A few weeks later Greg was an arsehole again; he had invited Martin round to the house while Jody and I were out with the kids. When we returned home, Greg could tell she was annoyed so offered to have her two kids while she went out for the evening. Of course, she took him up on the offer and went to Stu's for the night. My daughter settled straight away, but her kids were a nightmare. Greg just left me too it while he sat in the kitchen getting drunk. I was getting stressed and when I asked him to help it went down like a lead balloon. He started shouting abuse at me, and in the middle of his fit, he kicked Jody's oven, smashing her glass door.

I then raised my voice at him and made the mistake of calling him an idiot, what a mistake. I was dragged around the kitchen and into the hall. Greg had my hair wrapped around his hand, and he pulled me into the hall, Martin told him to let go of me which made him grip hold of my hair tighter. I felt like he was ripping it out from the scalp, and I fell to the floor, next thing I knew I was being kicked in the legs and lower back until Martin dragged him off me. Greg went to turn on him, but Martin who wasn't as drunk overpowered him as I went into the living room. The situation calmed down, but by then I had already text Jody to tell her what had happened. She was fuming and told Stuart she wanted Greg out of her house, so within half an hour, they were both at hers, ordering Greg out.

Stu, being a soft touch offered Greg a room at his. Between him and me, it was agreed that I would pay him fifty per fortnight to have space away from my horrible boyfriend. Greg left with Stu and without a word towards me, not even a sorry for bruising the fuck out of my leg or dragging me about by my hair, not that a sorry would have helped the situation in any way.

Jody and I sat in the living room most of the evening after they had left. Martin had gone home before Stu had taken Greg to his house and the kids had settled while everything was going on. She was telling me I needed to get away from that abusive, vile man and I had to agree with her, but that was easier said than done.

'I have tried to split up with him loads of times, but he keeps coming back like an unpleasant smell,' I said.

'Well, you need to put your foot down and not back down. Otherwise, one day he might seriously hurt you or your kids,' she replied.

I knew she was right as well, and I was lucky I had Martin see it too, if he hadn't been there that evening, it could have been then that I got seriously hurt. My leg was bruised already, and my back hurt. The problem is when you are on the floor like I was, you roll up into a ball, and my back and legs were an easy target for him. The more our conversation carried on though the more I found myself defending Greg's actions. Like it was okay to hurt me. To be fair, in my messed-up head it was normal for the man to overpower the woman, after all, I had grown up watching my Dad always beat my Mum and us kids up. Yes, he had a mental illness apparently, but to me, it was the norm.

I had decided that the next day I would go and see Greg without my daughter and try and clear the air. When I got to Stu's, Greg seemed full of remorse again and told me he loved me and wouldn't do it again. I had heard that line repeatedly, but a big part of me wanted more than anything to believe him, and being the gullible victim that I was, I was taken in by his lies again. It was lovely to have my own space back, but I was feeling a little lonely, so when Greg asked me to stay over that night in his new room, which I paid for, I was tempted but said no initially. Then Jody told me her parents were coming over and I had to stay at Stuart's whether I wanted to or not.

'It will only be for a few days,' she said.

'But you know I am trying to distance myself from him, when are they coming?' I asked her.

They were due the next day, so I was asked to stay with Greg that evening.

'Stu has already agreed and put a small bed in the room for the little one, so just need you to agree.'

'Don't look like I have much choice,' I said pulling a face as I walked out of the room we were in.

Later that afternoon, I packed some of mine and my daughter's things and arranged for Stuart to collect us in his car. When we arrived at his, Greg was in his bedroom playing on my PlayStation. He didn't even acknowledge me walking in his room until I stood right by the television.

'Oh, I forgot you were coming now,' he said sarcastically.

'Charming,' was my only reply.

That evening was okay, Greg as normal had a drink but seemed in a good enough mood, Stu was in the living room arranging to meet a girl we both knew, he asked my advice, but I don't think he liked my response. Carla, the girl in question, was a bit of a player, she liked to sleep about, and I had heard she had contracted shit loads of sexually transmitted diseases. So being a friend I obviously told him what I thought, and after all, he did ask me. The only problem was Greg didn't like me sticking my nose in it, as he said.

He went on to be in a mood with me the whole evening, and by the time it was bedtime, I was told to sleep in the tiny four-foot bed with my daughter. So, I did, but we both woke up at stupid o'clock in the morning which then put him in a mood with me again for the day.

Greg snapped at me to fuck off into the living room with my moaning bitch of a kid.

I was in the living room playing quietly with my little girl from five-ish. She fell back asleep on the sofa within ten minutes of playing, so I just sat in the room in silence, enjoying the peace. At just gone six in the morning, Stuart had woken and walked past the living room to make coffee.

'What are you two doing up so early?' he whispered, trying not to wake my daughter up.

'Greg sent me in here when she woke up,' I replied.

'He's a prick,' was his response before offering me a coffee.

While he was in the kitchen making the drinks I quickly tidied up the toys I had left on the floor, Greg had warned me not to let my daughter make a mess because apparently Stu would be pissed off with me, and I didn't need both the men in the house to be in moods.

'You can leave the toys out, don't bother me,' he said walking back in the room with a cup in each hand, so I got up off the floor to get my drink off him and explained that I was told to keep the place tidy.

'Honestly, I don't know what you see in that man,' he said.

'I do wonder myself some days,' I replied.

'Anyway, I best leave you to drink your coffee, the last thing you need is him getting arsy with you because I am sat in here with you, see you in a bit,' he said before going in the den as he called it, basically his bedroom but with everything a man would need to hide away for the day.

'But between you and me, you deserve to be treated like a princess, and I don't think he realizes how lucky he is to be with you,' Stuart whispered.

'I am not that fucking special,' I said smiling.
'Oh, but you are.' he replied.

MY NEW HOME...

I returned to Jody house a few days later, and I can honestly say I was glad to be back in my own space again. Greg hadn't been the best company but at the same time not as bad as I thought he would be. We had a few little arguments, mainly about my kids, but I left him on good enough terms. Stu's words were ringing in my mind though, and I was starting to resent being with a man who treated me like something he found on the bottom of his shoe. The problem with the type of relationship I was in, you found yourself always wondering if you deserved the way you get treated, you start to believe that you deserve to get a slap for arguing back but no one deserved to go through what I was living with every day. I knew I just needed the strength to leave and leave for good this time.

That evening I had a big conversation with Jody about my situation, and just talking about it made me cry, it was clear that I was unhappy and started to feel depressed. Everything that could go wrong was, and I had never felt this low in my adult life. Greg had to go no matter what.

Jody then decided that I needed something to perk me up, so she had rung someone and asked them to come around, she was being secretive and didn't tell me what she had in mind. Half an hour later Stuart turned up with a female; she was pretty, slim built with dark hair, he introduced her as his bit on the side, and received a slap of the woman and a horrible glare from Jody. It turned out that she was just Stu's friend, her name was Kelly, and she was staying in Stu's spare room off and on while her boyfriend was in prison.

She sheepishly passed Jody something in her hand and then asked if it was okay to make a joint. Of course, she agreed and went into the kitchen to grab some glasses and collect the drink she had put in the fridge earlier that day. She then called me into the hall and asked if I wanted to take any drugs with her, my initial reaction was to say no, but by the end of the night I had taken a small pinch of base, just to keep me awake. That evening and through into the early morning the four of us talked a lot, and I had played the guitar. The night had taken my mind completely off my situation, and I had laughed more that evening than I had done in ages.

Over the next few days, I had seen less of Greg, I had started working part-time at the local fast food place in town, and Jody was looking after my daughter while I was cleaning tables for most of the afternoon. It was Tuesday afternoon, I had been at work a few hours when Stu walked in with Tracey, who was her usual awkward quiet self, and he was in a cheery mood. He asked me how my day had been and tried to get me to stop and talk to him while Tracey ordered his food, I did explain that if my manager saw me she would kick off as I was paid to work, not stand around talking, Stuart then gave me a cheeky grin.

'I will get you to stand and talk to me,' he said giggling to himself.

'Honestly, I wish I could, but I have to clean all the mirrors and doors,' I replied. Tracey returned to the table with their order, and Stu decided it would be funny to take the lid off his milkshake and throw it over the mirror beside him yet again.

'Oops, now you have a reason to stand here,' he said.

'You think you are funny don't ya?' I said as I went to the cupboard to get out the cleaning materials. I am shaking my head at him while making my way back to his table to clean up the mess.

'It wasn't funny the first time Stuart, and it isn't funny now,' I said while trying to stop the milkshake running any further down the mirror.

Just as I was finishing my shift I received a message from Jody, telling me she needed to talk to me, I had guess it was something to do with Stu, but didn't think too much about it. When I got back to her house, she informed me that the council had found her a home and that she needed me to watch her kids while she went to view it.

The viewing was the next morning, and luckily I wasn't due to work again for a few days. Jody was excited and informed me that the house was in Stoneside, I automatically asked what would happen with my daughter and me, as the council knew I was staying with her. She said she would talk to them, but I couldn't help but worry that I would be left homeless again.

Her kids were a nightmare while she was out as well, she had been gone for over three hours and I was starting to pull my hair out, her son was the same age as my daughter. James was so naughty sometimes, and in the space of an hour, he had kicked off four times, resulting in me putting him to bed for the afternoon. Trying to put him in his cot, caused me to get scratched in the face, kicked and bitten.

Jody returned home just after he had finally settled, and informed me that she was moving the following week, I asked what would happen to me, but she said she didn't know.

'I can ask if you can keep this place?' she said.

She had told me all about her new house, how it had a brand-new kitchen with range cooker, new flooring throughout and a brand-new bathroom. I couldn't help but be a bit envious of her.

The next day I received a phone call from the council, they had a temporary house in Dunston Way for me to view. I did worry, as it was out of the way, but Stuart reminded me that he lived close by and that he would help with furniture and stuff and that I had no reason to worry.

So, I agreed to view the house the same day, it wasn't the cleanest of places, but it was a steppingstone in the right direction. Stu did live around the corner from the house, which was good, but it also meant Greg was right around the corner too, and as soon as Greg found out I was getting a house beside him, he was round in a flash.

The few days break had seemed to do us some good, as he was nice for a change, Greg told me that he missed me and asked if he could move in with me. I said I wanted him to stay round Stu's as it was good to have some space, and suddenly his mood changed, he wasn't nasty as such, but I could tell he was pissed off, and yet again I was on eggshells in my own home.

That evening he had been drinking and decided to come to my cousins as I was packing my things and try and talk me round again, but I stuck to my guns. He told me I was stupid paying Stuart for him to stay when he could just move in with me and save myself fifty pounds a fortnight, but I still insisted that I wanted my own space. Greg didn't like being rejected though and soon showed me his true colours when he threatened me; he said I was lucky I wasn't a man as he would have knocked me into next week.

'You wouldn't hit a man, you dick, only pick on females and kids,' I thought to myself, I so wanted to say it out loud, but I couldn't chance him kicking off again.

He then stormed out of Jody's, and I didn't see him again for a few days, by then I had moved into the house around the corner from him, and Stu had taken me out for the day in his car to try and buy some second-hand furniture. I managed to get a microwave, a small hob, a two-seater sofa, cot bed and single bed. It wasn't much, but it was a start. Stuart had also taken the table and chairs from Jody's old place as she was leaving it behind anyway. So, I had enough stuff to cope.

Stu had raided his cupboards for some tins and other food to keep me going until the following week when I was due to have money in my bank. I honestly would have been on my arse if it wasn't for his help.

I was settling into my new home when the door knocked, it was past nine at night, and I didn't want to answer the door, but I did. Greg was standing at the door, with a can of Stella in his hands, he didn't talk, he just stared at me.

'What do you want?' I asked.

He then pushed past me and informed me that he was allowed round whenever he wanted as I was his girlfriend. Last thing I wanted after my long day was to argue with him, so I didn't say anything.

'You haven't even got a TV!' he said.

'I only moved in today Greg,' I said sarcastically.

'I know, you have been getting cosy with my landlord,' he snapped.

'What the fuck you are talking about?' I asked defending myself.

'Stuart, you silly bitch, I know you have been with him all day,' Greg replied.

'He has helped me get furniture and move in, nothing else!' I snapped back.

'Yeah, yeah,' was his response.

'You know what? if you are just going to argue with me you can leave,' I said pointing to the front door.

'Getting brave,' he said as he walked towards me. He pushed me up against the wall, his alcoholic breath in my face, and he stared straight into my eyes.

I am sure he got off on seeing the fear in my eyes. He then placed his hand on my waist and pushed his body towards me.

'Please leave me alone,' I asked.

'No, I came around to fuck you, and that's what I plan to do,' he said in a chilling voice.

'I'm not in the mood,' I snapped trying to push him away.

He then grabbed hold of my hair, and pulled my head to the side, he placed his lips by my ear and whispered.

'I wasn't asking, you belong to me, and I will do what I want with you.'

That evening Greg raped me and left me crying on the living room floor when he finished and walked back out of my house as if nothing had happened.

SINGLE AGAIN...

After the previous night Greg had been around, I had decided that I couldn't cope anymore. I had asked Stuart to call around so that I could talk to someone. I explained that I was splitting up with Greg for good, which also meant I refused to pay his rent anymore. To be fair, he understood and said that if Greg didn't pay him that he would be kicked out of his house as well. He told me to be strong and stick to my guns this time, and I knew I would, I knew no matter what, I deserved a hell of a lot more than he could give me, far too much had happened for me ever to forgive him. The weekly beatings if the vile man drank too much, forcing me to have a termination, and the rape lately was all too much. Stu was supportive towards me but also told me that he wasn't going to fall out with Greg, as he wanted the money that was owed to him for rent.

Greg didn't understand what splitting up with him meant, he still came around to mine, expecting his dinner and inviting his mates to my house for a drink. I didn't want to cause an argument, so just let him do as he pleased, I only lay the law down when he wanted anything more. I would remind him that we were no longer together and that as much as I didn't mind being his friend, that was as far as I would go.

One of the evenings Greg was round with his mate Alan, but we called him Al for short, it was a good evening as we were playing guitars and having a sing-along. I had a bottle of Tia Maria while the boys had a few beers. I had a bit of smoke so wasn't drinking much at all, but Greg and Al were quite tipsy. The night was going well until Greg decided he needed to go back to Stu's to pick up something he had forgotten to bring with him earlier so, he took Al with him. They were gone for about half an hour, and when they returned Greg was kicking off big time, from what I could tell, Greg had been arsey with Stuart, and that resulted in him pinning Greg up against the wall and taking his key off him. He had kicked Greg out, just like he had said he would and had told him not to return to his house ever again. I had tried to ask Al what had happened, and he said he was outside most of the time and that, Greg had gone into Stu's house shouting and kicking off as no one had brought electric. It turned out Stu didn't buy the electric just to piss Greg off, after all, he hadn't paid any rent in over a month. So, he refused to buy the gas and electric. Greg was so pissed off, and upset that he had nowhere to go, and asked if he could sleep on my sofa, and me being a soft touch agreed.

That evening after Al had got his taxi home, I went to bed, Greg tried to follow me, but I put him in his place, telling him that he could have the sofa or nothing. So, he went into the living room and started playing his guitar again. I was getting annoyed as it was almost three in the morning, so I went down the stairs and told him. I was half expecting him to kick off and start a fight, but he didn't, he just lay on the sofa and asked me to turn the light off on my way back out of the room, so I did, closing the door over.

The next morning, I had told Greg that he needed to find somewhere else to stay as it wasn't fair on my daughter, confusing her. I said that I wanted to be his friend still, but I couldn't have him live with me, again I expected an argument and I had spent most of the morning trying to find the nicest way to tell him. Every scenario in my head sounded cold and nasty. Not that he deserved me being nice in any way, but I just didn't have it in me to be horrible even when I needed to be.

Greg left my house in a mood but told me he understood, and that he would go back to his Grandparent's house. He didn't do that though; he had walked to the next square and somehow talked a lady called Carol into letting him stay. Carol was our friend and Martin's ex-wife; she was a lovely lady and as soon as Greg told her his sob story she invited him to move into her spare room. Carol had a son who gave me the creeps a little; he was a ginger, skinny lad who had this habit of staring at me every time Greg brought him to my house. The creepy ginger thought of me as a friend just because I knew his mother and stepdad, but I didn't take to him at all. I am sure Greg had it all planned out, he had visited Carol a few times these past few weeks and at the time I didn't think much of it but again he was only living around the corner from me. I started to get paranoid at night that he might be watching me from his room, which faced the front of my house, so I asked a friend to move in with me for a while to keep my daughter and me company.

Samantha was pleased not to be sat in her flat on her own, and she adored my daughter, it was perfect. I initially met Sam through Stuart as she was one of the many girls he dated for a while. She was incredibly young, and I did have a hand in advising him to call it off with her before she got too close. Sam knows this and has since thanked me as she and Stuart get on brilliantly as friends. I found that I had someone with me all the time which meant Greg stayed away, that was until a few days later when Greg had overheard that I was having my son overnight, and he decided that this was a good enough reason to kick off.

He was drunk as usual, kicking my front door and telling me if I didn't let him in he was going to set fire to my house and burn both my kids inside. I knew Greg hated my son, but this was the first time he had ever threatened my daughter too, not knowing if he was serious or not, I decided to let him in. Lucy and mark were fast asleep upstairs, and I asked Greg to keep the noise down, but he just started shouting at me, telling me that I was stupid splitting up with him and that no one else would want me as I was damaged goods. He hadn't used that line in a while, but it hurt. I knew I was better off single than letting a man in my life again, but I honestly didn't realize how unhinged Greg was, and I didn't want to rock the boat.

'You will never find anyone better than me,' he said.

Then Sam jumped in, she was in the living room and made her way into the hall as soon as she heard me open the front door. Soon she was arguing with Greg telling him how evil and vindictive he was towards me, the next thing I knew, I got punched in the side of my head so hard I fell to the floor. When I looked up he had Sam by the throat.

'Get off her or I will ring the police!' I shouted.

He took his hand from around her throat and looked like he was about to kick me while I was on the floor.

'Think you should ring them before I do something I regret,' he said with a cold grin on his face.

He was shouting in my face for a few minutes, the smell of lager hitting me full force as I was pulled up to my feet. I hadn't realized at first, but Sam ran upstairs to the kids, who were both awake and upset by this point, she was on the phone with the police.

'And you wonder why I left you? you are nothing but a bully Greg,' I snapped getting to my feet myself and pushed him away from me.

I pointed to the door and told him to get out of my house.

'It's okay I am going but this isn't over, you silly little bitch.'

I ran to the front door and locked it as soon as his foot was out of it, he turned around and started banging and kicking the door.

'Go away Greg, or I will ring the Police, little did I know, Sam had already rung them.

Greg got questioned that evening, or at least that's what he told me a few days later when he tried to apologise, the police hadn't been to see me, so I didn't know whether to believe him or not. I explained that he cannot get away with acting up every time he had a drink, and he seemed sorry. I didn't see much of him for the next few weeks, and it was lovely, having no one to answer to.

It was the start of August and I had finally received a loan to furnish my house. Only five weeks late, but as I had almost everything I needed, I decided to arrange a get-together and drink with my mates, out of pity I invited Greg. After all, it was the World Cup and England were playing that evening, Carol had told me that Greg hadn't planned to watch the game as he had no money. So, I texted him and said he could invite Al as well.

It was a good night, Martin and Greg had both passed out on the floor, Sam was asleep on the sofa and myself,

Al and Carla went upstairs and chilled in my room, so as not to wake everyone else up. Al had asked me if I would ever give Greg another chance, he went on to tell me how down Greg had been since we split up and that he was always talking about how much he loved me. I explained to Al that no matter what I would not put myself through a relationship like the one Greg and I had, ever again. Turned out Al was blinded by Greg and didn't realize how nasty and violent he had been towards me; Carla had confirmed that Greg and I were better off as friends.

Over the next few days, I only saw Greg in passing. Which suited me just fine. Sam and I just spent time chilling, watching shit on TV, and chatting shit. It was only just past nine in the evening and the door knocked, I guessed it was Greg, about to bitch or kick-off but it wasn't it was Stuart. He had popped round to ask if I minded him inviting Greg to a club, as it was Stu's birthday the following week, he didn't like Greg but at the same time he was inviting his lodger Nash, and his mate Ade so seemed only fair in his eyes.

So, the next day, Greg had come around and told me he was going out, he wanted to rub it in basically and tell me he was on the pull. It didn't bother me in the slightest. I think that annoyed Gregory even more. So that evening I had invited a few people round to mine for a drink. Stu said him and Ade would come around and meet Greg at mine, which I had agreed to. The evening was going well, but I noticed Greg was drinking the cans quickly, like he was trying his hardest to get pissed. I didn't say anything as it was nothing to do with me anymore, I was just glad he was leaving soon to go to the club with the others.

Stuart had popped home to have a shave and get changed, Greg and Ade stayed at mine, only because I had the free alcohol, they both did love their drink. I was sat at the dining table, on a stool, playing my guitar and having a singsong, when Greg piped up,

'You can only play that because of me,' he snapped, I tried my best to ignore him, so he repeated what he said louder, so I stopped playing and stared at him.

'You taught me a few chords Greg, I taught myself how to play,' I said calmly.

'Oh, shut up, you stupid bitch, you wouldn't have picked a guitar up if it wasn't for me, and you will never be as good as me,' he said standing to his feet.

He started to walk over to the table, to pour himself a drink, I was pissed off with his comment, so my elbow hit of the table, knocking Greg's glass everywhere, I had made it look like an accident of course, but he and I both knew I did it on purpose. In true Greg style, he panicked, and placed his mouth on the table, to suck up the spilled alcohol. I just shook my head at him in disbelief.

Greg stumbled back as he regained his balance and looked me dead in the eyes, 'You think you are so funny, don't you?' he asked.

'Oh, hurry up and go out Greg, you are drunk as normal,' I snapped.

'Silly, silly bitch,' he replied, 'I will stick that fucking guitar down your throat, you silly cow.'

Greg started to walk towards me, but I stood up, still with my guitar in my hand and backed away from him, I grabbed hold of my phone and rang Stu to see if he was almost ready cause I didn't want Greg in my house anymore.

'Is that your new fuck buddy?' Greg shouted while I was still on the phone.

'Ignore him.'

Stu was getting annoyed on the other end of the phone as the abuse continued to flow out of Greg's mouth.

'If it wasn't for me you would still be scum,' Greg shouted.

'Right, that's it, I am coming around now,' Stuart said as he hung up.

Within seconds it seemed he was round at mine. Only half shaven, half his face was smooth, the other half still had his shaving foam covering him. I couldn't help but laugh about it as he walked into the living room, he then ordered Greg to leave the house and he took him for a walk around the corner. Ade was already outside when Stu got to mine, and when he asked his mate what had happened, Ade shrugged, so I explained what had happened. Stu got overly annoyed that Ade had just ignored everything and let Greg threaten me, but we all knew that he didn't treat his partner any nicer.

'Right, they can come around mine, I am sorry Sarah, you won't have to see him again tonight,' I thanked Stuart and he left.

'Enjoy the rest of your night,' he said as he was closing my door.

I wasn't in the mood to party after that, the few people that had come around, left after Greg's outburst, and it was only eleven o clock at night, but I had had enough and was ready for my bed. I left Sam downstairs, as she was on the phone with her Scottish friends and made my way up the stairs. I must have been knackered as I fell asleep quickly. I was woken up at quarter to two in the morning by my phone ringing. It was Stuart, so I thought I'd be best to answer it.

'Hello,' I said all sleepy.

'Sorry to wake you, but have you seen Greg?'

Worried, I sat up in bed.

'No, what's up?' I asked.

'We gave him the taxi fare home, and the bastard is nowhere to be found, we are stuck in town, and your slime ball of an ex-has all our money on him, he was with us one minute, then he was gone.'

'He's a dick,' I said, 'If I see him I will let you know, how are you going to get back?' I asked.

'Not thought that far ahead yet, but can I come and see you in the morning?' Stu asked, and I agreed I would message him when I was awake.

The next morning Stuart popped round for a coffee as planned, he looked knackered and explained that it was almost six in the morning before he got home, and that Greg still hadn't been seen. He went on to say that he had a horrible night, all in all, he had Greg do one, Nash off his face on drugs, and Ade was pissed straight away then to top it all off, my cousin Jody, was doing his head in all evening. If she wasn't texting, she was ringing him, annoyed that he wasn't out without her like I think he had initially planned.

'I wouldn't mind if she were my girlfriend, but I have and do tell her all the time, she is just for fucking,' he said.

'Sorry to be so crude, but I would never want a relationship, with her. I have invited her to Cornwall with me, but I am regretting it now.'

Lucky for some, I wanted to say but instead I just replied with, 'I don't know what you want me to say, but you know she is besotted with you, and you do kind of lead her on.'

Stuart looked at me and then told me he couldn't argue with my statement apart from the fact, that he didn't see it as leading her on.

'Think you and Lucy should come instead,' he said laughing trying to change the subject.

The following day was Stuart's birthday, so I told him, I had no money, but I could always offer him a coffee, and great company, if he fancied popping round the next day. Which he did, he had been at work all day and had told me how Tracey was paying for a meal for him. Stu said he would pop round before they went out. Somehow, he had a way with the ladies, and he wasn't any oil painting by any means, but he was big and bubbly, and it was clear that both Tracey and Jody were besotted with him.

Stuart only really talked about one woman who he loved, and that wasn't even the woman he was with for twelve years; the person who he had three amazing children with. No, Stu talked about Sally, always Sally this and Sally that. I had never met the woman but from what he said about her, she was kinky and had a lovely body, but she was evil and had a mean, nasty streak. Apparently, she would argue with him and throw things at him; he had told me one day, that she had gone at him with a knife. The poor woman had been through a lot before she met Stuart, but with a hateful teenage daughter and emotional wounds, he couldn't help healing her. After years of abuse, he decided to call it a day. He hadn't spoken to Sally in well over a year and didn't even know where she was living or anything, but that didn't stop him talking about her, especially if Jody or Tracey were in the room. It was if he did it just to see their reactions.

Stuart had a game he loved to play, he called it 'Would You Ever', and basic rules were, he would ask you a question and give you the choice of two answers and you would have to answer one or the other. The game had been known to cause a few problems in the past so when he suggested playing it with Sam, Tracey and myself I had to make sure he wasn't in his typical wind-up mood. He promised he would be good and started asking us ladies the questions.

'Sarah, you are on an Island, and you can only take one thing, a man or a guitar?' I giggled and said my guitar as it was more reliable than a man.

The questions stayed like that for a while, until Stu started to get cheeky and started asking more personal question's, like asking Sam if she had to kiss Tracey or me, who she would choose and things like that, trying to make us feel awkward.

Then Sam turned the tables on him, and we started to ask Stu the questions. Sam went first, and Tracey refused to answer anything, so it was just Sam and me asking the questions, they were very personal, but he loved the attention.

Sam asked, 'If you could be with either Tracey or Jody, who would you pick?' he shook his head.

'Neither' he answered.

'You have to stick to the rules Stu, we did,' I said winking at him.

'Okay, I would have to say Jody, as she is crazy in bed, but at the same time too much stress for me.'

I smiled at Stu and looked at Tracey, whose pride was evidently wounded, he didn't, care though and just said whatever would cause a reaction at that time. I giggled slightly but composed myself to ask my question.

'Okay let's stick to the same theme, Tracey or Sally-Ann?' I asked.

'Sally, all day long,' He replied.

Sam then asked her question. 'Sarah or Sally?' she asked looking at me with a massive smile. Stuart blushed for the first time.

'Sarah,' he said looking at the floor.

Sam must have noticed her moment to wind him up, unbeknown to me, he had opened up to Sam and told her he had strong feelings for me, and that he would die to have the chance to make me happy. Samantha loved it, she was forcing him to admit how felt, and poor Stuart hated it. He felt vulnerable and it didn't suit him. Tracey was getting annoyed too, telling Stu he was making a fool of himself, that I was entirely out of his league. That annoyed me for some reason. I wasn't sure why I was annoyed but found myself snapping at her.

'Tracey, who are you to say how I do, or do not feel, you aren't me.'

I then looked at Stuart and said, 'Sorry but it's true, don't get me wrong, I am not saying I feel the same, but I don't like people putting words in my mouth.' Stuart and Tracey then got ready to leave.

'How awkward,' I said to Sam when they left.

CORNWALL...

It was a few days after Stu's birthday when I got a phone call from him, while he was at work. It turned out Jody had been on at him, persistent phone calls and not letting him get on with his job. He was a courier driver and had to drive all day, which meant he couldn't keep answering the phone. Stuart couldn't turn his phone off either, as he needed work to be able to ring him. Stuart honestly sounded upset and begged me to tell her to leave him alone, this thing with her had been going on for a while, and she couldn't take no for an answer, but in her defense, he always played games with her head. He would let her believe one thing, and then it turns out to be something completely different. I am guessing this game had gone too far this time.

Stuart had tried he hardest to break things to her gently; he had even attempted the tough approach, but no matter how much he tried to make it clear he didn't want a relationship with her, the more intense, obsessed and needy she seemed to him. She would spend hours on the phone, crying and begging him to give her another chance, and just could not take no for an answer. At least this is how he made it out to everyone else.

Stuart had asked me to ring her and explain that she was driving him further and further away. I got off the phone feeling sorry for him and sent a text inviting him over that evening when he finished work.

When I rang my cousin, she was an emotional mess already and crying so hard that she could just about get her words out. I talked to her for over an hour, and without slagging anyone off too much I told Jody that she deserved to be happy, and that Stuart couldn't be that person. The stories I knew about them, and how toxic their friendship or relationship, whatever you want to call it, was all going to end in tears. She was into some strange, dangerous sex games and on the odd occasion had got hurt during these messed-up games her and Stuart both played. I worried that one day it would all get out of hand and that she would end up getting seriously hurt. Jody shocked me by agreeing with everything I was saying, she then caught me off guard and said,

'You know he is in love with you.'

'Who?' I asked knowing exactly who she was referring to.

'Stuart, c'mon Sarah you can't be that naive, he is in love with you and has been since he met you,' I didn't know how to reply, so I just told her that, I didn't care how he felt, and I just worried about her.

This drama with them both had been going on for that long, I was sick of hearing about it. I just wanted the two of them to sort their shit out once and for all. Jody agreed to leave him alone and let him get on with work. I sent Stuart a text to tell him I had spoken to her, and he replied with a thank you and an extra 'x'. Stu never sent me kisses; this made me smile a little.

It was almost nine in the evening when he turned up at mine, he had explained in more detail, how much my cousin had messed with his head, he had mentioned Cornwall again and explained that my Mum was planning on having Jody's kids while them two went away for a week. He asked me to tell my Mum it wasn't happening now. Stu then went on to say how he had wished he had never asked her in the first place; he said he made the mistake of firstly saying he would move into her house so that he could rent his bedroom out as well and make more money from subletting. He realized telling her that he wanted to live with her was giving her the impression he wanted more than just 'fuck buddies' as he put it.

He for some reason felt the need to stress to me that my cousin wasn't girlfriend material, then he smiled at me and said, 'You on the other hand....'

I stopped him mid-sentence and reminded him I am not that special. They were the first words he had ever spoken to me, almost a year before.

'You will never let me live that down, will you?' he asked, I just shook my head.

The more we spoke, the more I realized he was going on holiday only a few miles away from my Auntie, she lived in Liskeard and Stuart was traveling to Looe. He then asked if I wanted to join him. I told him I couldn't because of my daughter, and I didn't want to upset my cousin. He then asked why I didn't just travel down with him, with my daughter and go and stay with my Aunt and that I didn't have to worry about money, as it was a free holiday. I agreed to talk to my Auntie and ask if I could come down and stay with her, and within minutes of me sending her a message, she had replied and said that it would be lovely to see me, so it was agreed.

The next day I saw Jody at my Mum's and told her Stu had invited me away, I explained I was going to my

Aunts, so I wasn't going on holiday with Stuart as such, but that he was giving me a lift to Cornwall. She then asked if I could talk to her in private, so we both walked into my Mum's living room.

'What's up?' I asked.

'You need to give him a chance,' she said,

'What do you mean?' She looked at me like I was stupid.

'Sarah, he loves you, and you deserve to be loved more than most of us,' she said.

'No Jody, I don't see Stuart that way, we are friends, and that's all,' I replied.

'I would just be another one of his conquests, I refuse to let myself get treated the way he has treated you,' and I had good reason to argue.

'Are you not listening to me?' she snapped 'He loves you Sarah, and won't treat you horribly, I know deep down that is the truth, he will treat you like a princess.'

I shook my head and said, 'I'm not interested in him in that way, he is a good friend, I care about him, but that is honestly it.'

The next day I start to receive evil messages from Greg, someone had clearly told him I was going away with Stu. Greg was calling me a slag, whore, prostitute and anything else he could think of at the time. Stuart worried that Greg would kick off at me, so invited Sam, Myself and my daughter to stay at his. It was only two days until we were going away, so I agreed.

That evening Sam looked after my daughter and Stu took me out on the back of his motorbike, we went to a small pub called The Hole in the Wall in the next town. I had been asked for my ID but didn't own any so only had a cola. We made our way to a table at the back of the pub. He then told me he would be back in a minute, and left me sitting on my own, when he returned he had another drink in his hand. 'Tia Maria, if I remember right,' he said. I smiled as he poured the alcohol into my glass. He then stirred it with his finger, and placed his finger in his mouth, sucking it more erotically than was needed. We talked about going away, and he managed to talk me into going to the caravan in Looe with him and staying with him and his kids. I adored his kids and eventually agreed.

On the way home, we collected a pizza, I had spicy chicken on mine, his though you couldn't see what was on it, as he had mainly covered the whole thing with anchovies.

'Yuck,' I said as the man behind the counter as he was making the pizza.

When we got back to his, I was shattered and said my goodnights, Stuart wanted me to stay up and talk to him, but I just needed sleep. Sam and I spent the night in the room that once Greg and I shared, it was weird, but I was so sleepy it didn't bother me as much as I thought it was going to.

I woke up the next morning with more abusive messages from Greg, by the sounds of it, he had been to mine the night before and was seriously pissed off that I wasn't at home. I was called a slag and told never to contact him again. Which was fine by me, I thought.

When Stuart woke up I was in the living room, playing with Lego bricks on the floor with Lucy, Sam had gone to her sister's house, so it was just us in the house. I told Stu about the messages, and he informed me that Greg had been messaging him as well, he suggested we leave that day as he had a paranoid thought that Greg would do something to the car to try and stop us going. So, I agreed and spoke to my aunt on the phone; she was happy to put us both up for the night. We started loading the car straight away; my stuff was already packed anyway. I then rang Samantha and told her the plan, and she said she was staying with her sisters while we were away.

She ran around just before we left to get my key off me as most of her belongings were still at my house, and she hugged me just as we loaded the last of our bits in the boot.

'Have fun, you two,' she said as Stu started the engine, he winked at her, and we started driving.

We were on the motorway. My daughter was fast asleep in the back seat, which was surprising, as we had the music up quite loud. Stuart reached into the glove compartment and handed me a little bag. 'What's this?' I asked.

'Open it,' he said looking back at the road.

As I opened the bag, I saw he had got me some cannabis. Stu knew I smoked it; he didn't smoke himself but didn't see any harm in a bit of weed.

'Thank you,' I said placing it in my pocket.

'Are you not going to have a joint?' he asked.

I looked back at my daughter asleep on the back seat, Stu must have known what I was thinking.

'She is fast asleep, just open the window before you light it, you will be fine,' he said, opening the electric window ever so slightly. I rolled myself a joint.

'Plus, you made the mistake of telling me how horny it makes you,' he said smiling to himself.

I looked at him 'Stuart, be good.' I lit up my smoke.

We spent the four-hour drive, talking to each other and realized that we had a hell of a lot in common. I had started to see a side to him I didn't see that often, a vulnerability he had hidden so well from most people, but Stu said he knew he could be a hundred percent himself around me and that must have felt good.

WE'RE JUST FRIENDS…

We finally made it to Liskeard and met up with my Auntie in the pub a few doors away from her house. I hadn't seen Michelle in over four years so was nice to see her. She told us how she had sorted bedrooms out for us, and that I was in with the girl's and Stu had her son's bedroom. I explained that we were just staying the one night, as we had a caravan to go to the next morning. I think Michelle was just grateful for the company. After a drink, we then made our way to her house, via the shop, as she had run out of milk and couldn't offer us a coffee until she bought more.

We walked up a flight of stairs in the courtyard attached to her house, and straight into the kitchen. My Aunt always lived in a messy home, so I did warn Stuart before we got to hers, but I was surprised as we walked through into her living room, at how tidy the house was. Clearly well lived in but a hell of a lot cleaner than any other house of hers I had visited in the past. It was almost bedtime when she told me that Stu cared for me, and she could tell we would be good together. She asked if we wanted a room together, but I informed her we were simply good friends and nothing more. I said goodnight to her and gave Stu a small hug before making my way into the bedroom where my daughter and my younger cousins were all fast asleep. He texted me as soon as I got into bed.

'Wish I was with you,' it said.

'Goodnight Stuart,' I replied,

'Please help me, Sarah, I am sharing a bed with cum tissue,' I smiled and started typing.

'Ha-ha, unlucky, goodnight dude. '

he replied with 'Please,' so I sent him a reply saying that he just needed to ignore where he was and try and sleep.

I had guessed the flirty message next was just because he had had a drink, and decided to put my phone on the floor and try and sleep. My screen flashed as I was turning over, and the text read, 'I love you,' but I decided it was best not to reply.

The next morning Stu woke me up early, I guessed he didn't sleep well in the spunky bed and couldn't help but giggle as soon as I saw him.

'It isn't funny,' he muttered, but I carried on laughing.

'Your nasty to me,' he said.

We had breakfast and then got ready to get in the car and make the small trip to the caravan park in Looe. When we pulled up, Stu pointed out Doug's car. I had met both Debbie and Doug a few weeks before, Debbie was the mother of Stu's children, and Doug was her partner. Stu shook his head when he saw that Doug had left the keys for his car in the boot, so we pulled up, and he took the keys into the caravan. Everyone said a quick hello, then a goodbye just as fast. Within minutes they were gone leaving us with the children and a big caravan.

Stu had explained that they were off for a couple's weeks and it was agreed that he had his kids for the second week of their holiday. Elise and Rachel, both gave me a big hug when they saw me, they spent almost every weekend at their Dads, so I had got to know them well. Carl Stu's son just said he was glad I wasn't Jody; it was clear that the kids were happy to see Lucy and me, and it was nice to feel wanted, but I couldn't help feeling a little guilty that my cousin should have been on this holiday. Our last conversation is still going through my mind.

We all chilled in the caravan for most of the day and about six o clock, the girls and I got dressed up to go out to the club. Stu poured me and his eldest daughter Rachel a drink, it wasn't my normal Tia Maria, but it was okay.

'What's that?' I asked lifting my glass up as to inspect my drink.

'Taboo, it's called, the woman at the shop said you mix it with lemonade,' he replied.

I took a sip of my drink, licking my lips as I moved the glass away from my mouth. 'Well thank you, it is sweet but quite nice,' I said.

'You tease,' he said smiling at me.

'Tease? I don't know what you are talking about Mr.' I said defending myself.

'Licking your lips,' he said.

I just blushed and walked back into the bedroom, to get changed.

Once we were all ready, we made our way to the caravan club. Stu got us all a drink, and we sat at the table watching the entertainment. A band was playing when we first sat down, but after they finished their set; a girl came on the stage, she had a fantastic voice. Elise, Stuart's youngest had said that it was the same girl who ran the kid's clubs during the day and told me her name. I was just watching her minding my own business, trying to ignore Stu's flirty comments about me, and the night was going well. Until Stuart stood up and told the kids, we were going.

'Are we not going to have another drink?' I asked,

'What so you can perv over that girl all night, I don't think so,' he snapped.

'Hey, what's up with you?' I asked standing on my feet.

'Half a bottle of Taboo and suddenly you turn into a lesbian,' he said as he walked away from the table.

'I was admiring her confidence, nothing more Stuart,' I snapped as we made our way out of the club.

'Please don't argue,' Rachel said. So, we walked back to the caravan in silence.

Once inside the caravan I decided to make myself a joint, I was a little stressed and upset that Stu had turned on me for no apparent reason. One minute we were in the club having a laugh and the next thing I know; I was arguing about nothing. He was giving me the silent treatment and refusing to talk, so I decided to go for a walk, it had started to rain and had suddenly gone all overcast and dark, so I stayed near the caravan and club. The rain was getting heavier, and in real Sarah style I had walked out without a coat on, so I stood under a massive tree to shelter from the rain. Just then my phone rang, I thought it might have been Stuart, but it wasn't, it was Jody. He had been on the phone to her though because she told me he was distraught and needed to talk to me and explain why he went moody, but I was still angry and refused to go back to the caravan. About ten minutes later I saw Rachel walking around, she had asked if I had seen her Dad. It turned out Stu stormed off as well. Knowing the four kids were in the caravan on their own I decided to walk back with Rachel and wait for their Dad to return. As soon as I walked through the caravan door, Elise wrapped her arms around me and begged me to stay with them. I calmed the kids down and got them already for bed. I then sat outside the caravan, in the rain and smoked another joint.

By the time he finally turned up, he had blood on his forehead, and he had punched a wall, as his hand was bloodied and swollen.

'What have you done?' I said in a worried tone.

'I am sorry for kicking off, but I think we need to talk,' he said.

I made us both a coffee, and we sat down. Stuart seemed upset, and I tried to find out what was wrong, but he told me to forget it, and that he was okay, he said I should just try and ignore that he kicked off. I bit my tongue while I finished rolling another joint, I was clearly in the mood to get stoned, so I wasn't stressed about the situation. Then I piped up.

'After the stress I have had with Greg; you are the last person I expected to be pissed off at me.'

He looked at me with tears in his eyes.

'You have no idea, do you?' he asked,

'No idea about what?' I said confused by his riddle.

'I am in love with you, I have been since I first met you,' he said.

I couldn't help but smile, I then reminded him that I wasn't that special, and tried to explain I wasn't ready for a relationship.

'How do you know if you don't try?' he asked.

He was getting annoyed again and for some reason couldn't understand why I was being so dismissive of what he was saying to me, he then stood up and looked me in the eyes.

'You don't get it,' he said.

Feeling a little intimidated I stood up and made my way to the doorway to smoke my joint. I felt like I needed it by this point and in all honesty, I just wanted the world to swallow me up and get me out of this awkward situation.

'If you are not willing to give me the chance to show you how happy I can make you, then I will have to cut all ties, I mean it, Sarah. I won't ever talk to you, your Mum, Jody, I will cut ties with the lot of you,' he said passing me a lighter as he could see the lighter in my hands wasn't working.

'Why are you like this Stu, you are my best friend, and I can't stand the thought of losing you,' I said with tears now dripping down my face.

'I have loved you for months, and I have sat around watching Greg be horrible to you, and after that, I sat there watching you and seeing how all these men are fighting for your attention.'

 I looked at his confused 'What men?' I asked.

'All of them, Al, Tabby, Arron. You name it if they have been around your house and especially when you have your guitar out, they are all like; oh my, Sarah you are so good, teach me, Sarah.'

Arron is Carol's son; the weird ginger, and Tabby was the guy Carla was last sleeping with for a while. We had to call her Caz around him as that was the only name he knew her by, so I didn't see why Stuart was bringing them into this.

He paused, looked at me with tears running down his face and said, I can't cope with that anymore, give me a chance or Sarah, or we are done for good.'

I seriously needed my space at this point; I hadn't even romantically looked at Stuart; he was nothing like the men I had been within the past, and he was big built, with a rounded belly. He wasn't ugly just not what I would have classed as my type. As previous partners of mine had been slim built and quite a bit taller than me. I told him I needed time to think and grabbed my coat off the table by the door. I felt so guilty that I had clearly upset him so much, but I had, just weeks before managed to get out of a horrible relationship. I knew deep down that Stu would treat me well. In the back of my mind, I still believed there was a chance that he either wanted to be with me to annoy my cousin or that he would start off lovely and then treat me like he had with most of the women in his past. I honestly didn't think I could cope with another heartache after everything I had already been through, but his words rang in my ear, and I believed that if I didn't give him a chance to at least try, then I would lose him for good.

After half an hour of walking in the rain, I made my way back to the caravan and was greeted with a huge hug.

'Please give me one chance to make you happy,' he said sobbing into my shoulder.

'Okay,' I whispered.

That evening Stuart and I had slept together, I was slightly tipsy still, and very stoned, but I remember every detail of our time together that night. He was very attentive and wanted to make sure I was delighted. He may have been a big man, but god he is good in bed, I thought to myself.

Once we had finished he held me for a while, with the biggest grin ever on his face, he just kept saying thank you to me and kissing my forehead.

'You are amazing,' he whispered.

Stuart then decided that was the perfect moment to make a phone call, it was gone two in the morning, so I was a little concerned who he was calling.

'Hello bitch,' he said as the person on the other end answered.

It was Jody; she was the only person he would get away with calling that too.

'Don't you dare.' I whispered.

'What do I want?' he said.

'I have some news for you,' he giggled at me before continuing.

'I just had sex with your cousin,' he said before abruptly hanging up on her.

'That was nasty,' I said as he got off the phone.

'Yeah, I do bastard well, but it's only your cousin.' he replied.

'By the way, she was at your house, and sounded like they were having a party,' at that point I didn't care.

I was just shocked he had made that call. I'm not sure why as I already knew Stu loved to get a reaction.

'Oh well. I can worry about it when I get home can't I?' I replied.

'If you go home,' he muttered under his breath.

That weekend seemed to go fast, Stuart and I got on well and even though I didn't see him as a boyfriend at first, by the end of the week I was warming to the idea. He was brilliant with my daughter and seeing him being a Dad to his own children had started to change my mind about him. Stu was lovely to me as well; very caring and attentive. My only issue was what other people might think. With that in mind, I struggled to hold his hand in public or I would cringe if he tried to kiss me. Deep down I knew I was being shallow and hoped in time I would fall in love with him the way he said he loved me.

It was the day we were due to leave the caravan site when Stu asked the kids and me if we wanted to go to Devon on the way home, and if all went to plan, we could stay an extra night or two, depending on the money situation. We all agreed and started packing the car up, leaving out a few things each to keep us going for an extra day. On the way to Devon, we drove back into Liskeard and stopped in to see my Aunt again. I think Stu wanted to brag about him and me being together now as my Aunt had tried to talk me into giving him a chance before we had left hers the previous week.

I had to warn the kids that Michelle believed she was a witch, and that she wasn't the cleanest person in the world, but she did have a heart of gold. I was a little worried that my Aunties mind and cleanliness would reflect poorly on me, but the kids seemed to take her in their stride, and after we left her house, they only had good words to say about her. I needed to stop worrying about what everyone else thought and worry about my own thoughts and feelings.

Just as we got back in the car, my phone beeped a few times. I was going to ignore it but decided it was possibly best to see who was messaging me; it was Greg. His message was full of abuse, telling me that I was sick for leaving him for a fat man and that I was worse than the scummy shit he had just removed from his shoe. I knew Greg was a little hurt but to slag both Stuart and myself off so much was just childish and uncalled for. After all I left Greg because he believed it was okay to hit, rape and abuse me. Apparently leaving him for a 'fat man', as he put it was the worst possible thing I could do to him. I obviously told Stu about the abuse, and he told me to ignore it and said he would buy me a new phone when we got home.

'That won't stop him from kicking my door down when we get back,' I said concerned at what the outcome would be.

'He won't do shit to you, I promise,' he said, 'Besides, I think you and Lucy should move in with me, let me look after you,' he smiled and winked.

'I'm not sure; I will need to think about it.'

There was an awkward silence for a few minutes, so I decided to make myself a joint for the drive to Devon. Stu told me if I was stressing to make it strong as he would buy me more when we got home. The problem is, I wasn't sure where my home was. I was stressing about the fallout from not only Greg but also Jody and the rest of my family. I would have happily stayed in Cornwall forever, where no one knew me or my past. I think Stu could tell I was stressed because I had gone so quiet, and my favourite song was playing, he looked at me and made a comment about me not singing, then his daughter lent towards the front of the car and kissed me on the cheek. I had mellowed out by the time I had smoked my joint and was singing along to the music. Stuart was singing too, but in his tone-deaf singing voice, he then looked at me and smiled.

'Were in Devon now,' he said as we passed the signpost. 'I thought we could find somewhere to stay overnight if you're up for it.'

The kids all agreed that we should, and I was glad to have another night away from reality. While driving through town, I had noticed a beautiful white and blue painted building on top of the hill.

'Now that looks like my ideal home, it is beautiful,' I said pointing in front of us.

'Should we take a drive up their dad?' Carl asked.

'Why not,' he replied.

As we got closer, Stu pointed out that it was bed and breakfast and that we should see if they had any vacancies for the evening. The smile on my face was visible. Then he said that he may not be able to buy me the house of my dreams but that we could pretend for just one night if we got the chance to stay over.

'A bit of roleplay,' I said giggling.

We were in luck, there was one room empty for the night, and it was a large family room. They did only have a double bed and two singles; there were six of us, so three beds weren't enough. I then said about all the girls sharing the double, Carl in one bed, and Me and Stu in the other. Carl laughed and commented on his Dad needing a single bed to himself. Stuart then turned and looked at his son, told him he was a cheeky bastard and clipped him round the ear in a joking kind of way of course.

'I just have more to love,' he replied holding his stomach.

That evening was lovely, we laughed and joked, and the kids ran around a tired themselves out, so they were in bed nice and early. Stu and I sat outside under the most precise starry sky I had ever seen. It was still warm, but Stuart had placed a blanket around my shoulders. I was so relaxed cuddling up to him that I had fallen asleep in his arms. I woke in the middle of the night in the single bed on my own, Stuart had fallen asleep on a chair. I woke him and told him to share the bed with me.

'Why were you sleeping on the chair?' I asked.

'You fell asleep outside, and I carried you to bed, you didn't stir, so I didn't want to wake you,' he replied,

'You should have just got into the bed with me,' I said,

'I didn't want to, not without asking you,' I smiled to myself, thinking that was the best possible answer a man could give.

BACK TO REALITY...

We were in the car getting ready to head back home when Stuart realised I had tears in my eyes.

'What's up?' he asked.

I explain to him that as soon as we get home, I am going to have to deal with Greg again.

'No, you don't Sarah. I told you I think you should move in with me.'

I am shocked that he would even consider my daughter and me moving in with him so soon, so I agree to stay a few weeks just while the dust settles around us.

Stu must have told me he loved me at least three times on the drive home and I felt terrible when I would just reply with 'I know.'

You should understand, Stu had months to come to terms with how he felt while I just felt confused, though I couldn't deny that he had been the only man I felt a hundred percent safe with. I know he said that Greg wouldn't have a chance to start any trouble, but I also understand what Greg is like and I can't put anything past him, plus Stu has a full-time job so there will be plenty of times that I will be in the house on my own.

'It's okay, we will get either Jody or Sam to stay there while I am at work,' he said when I voiced my concerns.

Then he repeats it.

'I love you so much, and I will never let anyone hurt you again, I promise.'

I can feel tears well up inside me, but I hold them back for his sake. The last thing I need is him crying while driving. We were illegal as it was with four kids in the back, never mind the smell of cannabis that was lingering in the car even with the windows and sunroof open I could still smell it. Punkrocker comes on the cd player and is turned up full blast, and the girls and I start belting our hearts out, Stu keeps looking at me with that massive grin on his face, and I can't help but smile back.

Stu decides it would be best to drop his kids off home first, even though they have asked if they can come back with us. We explain that I need to go to mine and collect my things and that Lucy needed sleep, so it was agreed. I had never seen his exes house and was surprised when we drove down Hadley Lane. The houses where all massive and awfully expensive. The kid's home was no different as we pulled up outside.

I felt uncomfortable, so I told Stuart I would wait in the car while he said goodbye to the kids. Lucy was wide awake by this point, so he scooped her up into his arms and walked proudly towards the front door. Stu's ex Debbie waved at me, and I guessed she had asked why I waited in the car. She was giving Lucy a fuss while Stu kissed his kid's goodbye. He returned to the car and placed my daughter on my knee. I grabbed the seat belt and wrapped it around the both of us, as Lucy snuggled into my arm.

'She will sleep tonight,' Stu said as he started the engine.

'Where will she sleep actually?' I asked,

'In my bed with you, it is a double, and I will have the spare room until you say I can join you.' I felt at ease straight away and starting to think that staying with him might not be too bad after all.

As we were driving up the road we passed a small chapel when he pointed out of the window and told me that graveyard was the place he wanted to be buried when he died.

'A bit morbid don't you think?' I say shocked with his words.

'Maybe, but I don't expect to be on this earth for too long.' I laughed off his comment.

We pulled up outside my house, and I am surprised when I see the front door is slightly open, I had given Sam the key to look after my house. Now I may not have much in my house, and half the stuff I do own has been smashed up by Greg at some point.

As soon as I walk into the living room it was evident that my house has been used as a doss house while I have been away; beer cans scattered all over the floor and Martin looked like he had passed out on the floor and used a carrier bag as a blanket. I look at Stu.

'I need to grab a few bits from up the stair and then can we go please.'

Lucy has made her way up to her bedroom, and I am in horror as I see Greg's mate Arron stood at the top of stairs holding my daughter. He is steaming drunk and clear he is struggling to keep hold of my daughter who is trying her hardest to release his grip.

'Put the baby down,' Stu shouts while taking a few steps towards him.

'I am not going to hurt her,' Arron says.

Lucy's crying was getting louder as the drunken mess places her on the landing. I run up the stairs pushing past Stuart and straight to my daughter to comfort her. My heart was still in my throat when I look back at Arron who is now pinned to the wall by Stuart's hand.

'Get out of this house and never come back,' Stu growls in his face.

I hate arguments, but I smile as I see him squirm down the stairs and straight out the front door. Stu then picks Lucy up, who stops crying straight away might I add while I start bagging some clothes up.

'Just get what you need for tonight, I will come around tomorrow and get everything else for you.'

I smile at him; he is like my knight in shining armour.

Once we are back at Stu's house, and I have Lucy settled I walk out of the bedroom to find him running a bath.

'Thought you might appreciate this after today,' he says kissing me on the cheek.

'Go and relax. I will call you when it is ready,' tapping my bum as I turn to walk out of the hallway.

I was starting to see a different side to this man, and I was starting to like what I was seeing, he says he wants to look after me, and if it means running me a bath after a long day, I know that is something I could quickly get used to.

Stu tries to stay in the bathroom with me while I have a bath, saying that he will wash my back for me, but I don't feel comfortable enough to let him do that just yet, so I usher him out. The only lock on the bathroom door though is a very top, it's broken, and he has been using a screw as the small handle, I can't reach so I stand on the bath.

'You don't need to lock it you know.' I know I don't but feel better if I do.

That evening I head to bed early, Lucy is fast asleep in the middle of the double bed but being small myself, I don't move her; instead, I just lay on the edge of the bed looking at her, till I fall asleep myself.

It's a few days later when Stuart and I finally share his bed together. He had been out and managed to get Lucy her own bed and had told me I can decorate the spare room for her. With that in mind, how could I even say no when he asks if he can share the bed with me. We had sex the first night, so it wasn't as if I was waiting for a special occasion or anything, I was just not feeling it and couldn't force myself to. I was laying in his arms after talking all night about our plans. Now you would think with him being a bigger framed man, that he would be comfortable to cuddle up to. I was just feeling hot and claustrophobic, so I made an excuse to head for the bathroom, I brush my teeth again to bide me some time, and when I get back into bed, I was slightly relieved that he had already fallen asleep.

The next morning Stu left early for work, and I was left feeling like a spare part, so I decided that I needed some company. Sam turned up about ten and me, her and Lucy headed into town for some much-needed retail therapy.

'I am moving back to Scotland in the next week or so.'

When I asked why my friend was moving away, she said everyone around her was moving on with their lives while she was still stuck, living the same way he had for over two years. I couldn't argue with her but guessed there was more to the story than she was making out. Sam lived with Lucy and me before I went away, so I half expected her to stay at Stuart's with us. Stu had already agreed that she could remain at his before I even had to ask but it seems like she has made her mind up. I text Stuart to tell him her plans, and he replied asking how she was going to get there. It turns out Sam hadn't thought that far ahead yet but just felt like she needed to go home. He replied offering to give her a lift to Fife, which I believed was very generous. Bear in mind it is a four-hour drive each way. Samantha was over the moon and asked me to thank him for her.

'You can thank him yourself later, Stu has asked if you fancy a takeaway with us later?' Her face lit up.

Sam did enjoy her food, and that was the sure way to find her heart. So, it was agreed that Sam would come and stay with us until she left for Scotland, and I was relieved to have some company while Stuart had to work. I wanted a job myself but with Lucy being so young, and her poor life was so unpredictable at that time, that I am unsure if it was the best thing for us.

ROAD TRIP...

It was a lovely sunny evening, but colder than expected when we started to pack the boot of the car. Sam didn't have much stuff to take with her, and I felt sorry for her, having her whole life in two suitcases. I know that feeling well with the number of times I have moved.

'Are you sure this is the right decision?' I ask as we make our way to the car while waiting on Stu.

'I have no choice now,' she says with a deflated look on her face.

'You could always just stay with us?' I say.

Sam smiles at me and explains that as much as she had enjoyed the past week with us, she still felt she needed to get away.

'Plus, all your lovey dovey shit is making me sick,' she joked.

That made me laugh, and I hadn't thought I was being lovey towards Stuart. If anything, he still tells me every day about how much he loves me, and I can't say the words back to him. I know it is hurting him every time I reply with I know, but what else am I meant to do. We have been cuddling and having sex every night, but apart from that, Stu and I had seemed more like good friends. Sam saw something I didn't.

'I see the way you look at him Sarah,' she said as we notice Stuart locking the front door.

She knows I don't have time to reply and just gives me a big grin. I would be lying if I said I hadn't been a lot happier since coming back from Cornwall, and Stu had made me smile more than usual this past two weeks though we still hadn't seen Jody and I was worried how she was going to react around us both. I felt guilty for being with him when I knew how strong my cousin's feelings were for him. She did tell me that I should at least give the man a chance to prove himself before I put my foot down completely. So, I was doing exactly what she said, not that it made me feel any better about the whole situation.

I realise, as we see the signpost for Fife, that I was going to miss Sam and I am wondering if me being with Stu was the real reason she was moving away. She also had feelings for him, or at least she did last summer when they were sleeping together, and even if I am trying to tell myself I don't feel the same way about him, I know I am lying to myself really. That man had been there for me anytime I had needed him. Lately, he had been looking after my daughter and me and said he wanted to worship me. I had never had that in my life, and I think I was just scared.

It was almost ten at night by the time we got to her parents' house. Sam's Dad was upstairs and refusing to come down, so I was guessing there was a family tiff going on which just made me feel even more uncomfortable about being in this house. Stu was thanked for driving all the way up by Samantha's Mum, and we are offered a cup of tea for our effort. Sam had said that her Mum would let us bed down for the night, but after a five-minute conversation, it was obvious that that wasn't the case. We were given the offer to stay with a friend of the family who lives a few doors up, but Sam's Mum had the cheek to say that she wants fifty pounds for the loan of a bed. Stuart had just driven for four hours to bring her daughter home, and we got offered her mates bedroom for fifty pounds. Stu was as offended as me and kindly tells this woman that we would sort ourselves out but thanked her anyway. I gave Sam a big hug, and we said our goodbyes.

'I will just drive through the night,' Stu tells me as I placed Lucy back in her car seat, she is almost asleep in my arms.

'You can't drive all night.'

I was worried because we were all shattered, and I can't chance a crash. Had it been just Stuart and me, then maybe, but not with Lucy in the car. I explained my concerns, and it was agreed that we would sleep in the car. We couldn't even get a room for the night because of how late it was, and between us both, we didn't even have twenty pounds on us. The petrol cost more than we had estimated, and Stu wasn't even offered any money from either Sam or her Mother.

We found a lovely spot to park up, the coast was in touching distance, but the weather had started to take a turn for the worse; it was raining now, and the wind seemed fierce tonight, so we decided to drive a few yards up the road. I placed my now fast asleep daughter and her car seat in the passenger's seat so that Stu and I could attempt to lay in the back. Lucy didn't stir at all. The back of a BMW isn't comfortable at all, and even though I am tiny myself, Stuart on the other hand, isn't, and I could feel his stomach digging into my back every time he breathed out. I didn't want to say anything, and I am sure he was just as uncomfortable as me with his legs bent awkwardly on the seat in front of us. I honestly think I would have been more comfortable and have more space in the footwell, but his arm is firmly around my waist, and I feel him getting heavier as he started to drift off to sleep.

I woke to the sound of seagulls on the roof of the car. Lucy was still silent, and I panicked for a second when I tapped her shoulder to wake her. I sat up and peered my head around and she smiled at me, looking all sleepy and closed her eyes again. I reached for my phone to check the time and it had only just gone six in the morning. My back was aching, but I was grateful that I managed to get a few hours sleep. Stuart, on the other hand, was spark out still. I kissed his cheek to wake him, and I was rewarded with a sleepy smile from him too.

'How are my girls?' he asked as he tried to sit himself up, banging his head on the door somehow in the process. Achy but good I told him.

'Breakfast then we can drive home,' he said.

I needed to freshen up and change Lucy, so it was agreed that we would head to the nearest motorway services.

'I love you,' he said as the car engine starts up.

'I know you do.'

I do believe that he loved me which just increased my guilt for not being able to say it back. Both Simon and Greg told me that they loved me, but never did I believe them. Stuart was sincere, and I know he only said something if he meant it. I can see by his eyes that I had upset him again.

'I am scared to love you; I have seen the way you have been in the past.'

He looked at me shocked as we start to drive down the country road.

'Sarah, please don't ever think for one second I will mistreat you, just the thought of you being treated like shit before used to make me batshit crazy. I love you, and even if you don't feel it back, it's fine. Maybe you will fall in love with me too one day,' he smiles 'A man can only dream anyway.'

The car isn't the place I wanted to be having this conversation, but we had started already.

'I never said I don't feel the same; I said I am scared to admit it.'

'You never need to be scared around me; I promise you that much,' I do think I believed him.

All I had ever wanted was to be loved, and this man had poured his heart out to me lately. I had always liked him a lot but if you had asked me a few months ago if we would be a couple I would have laughed. He was a classic male tart; always had a different lady to chat to online and meet up for sex and being one of his best friends, I had seen every side to him, even parts of him I hoped never to see again. I think that was why I was so reluctant to tell him how I felt, that's even if I knew how I felt myself.

We talked the whole way home, and this man seemed to be saying all the right things at the right times. I felt safe around him, and that is all I could ask for. He commented that everyone before me was just a bit of fun and half of them weren't even girlfriend material, whereas he told me I was ultimate wife material. I almost spat my drink all over myself and looked at him in disbelief.

'You can't say things like that just weeks into a relationship,' I stated.

'In my eyes, you have been mine since we met, so technically we are a year in.'

I shook my head and took a sip of my juice. Lucy was starting to get restless, so I gave her my old set of keys. 'Not as if I need them now.' I said.

MY FIRST FAMILY CHRISTMAS…

I was stressing a little but everything was done, and it was time to relax. We had left out milk and mince pie for Santa and Lucy was fast asleep in bed. Stu and I were sitting in the living room, and he offered me a glass of wine to celebrate our first Christmas together. I didn't know whether to tell him now or wait till tomorrow as planned. I was pregnant, it was crazy I know. Stu and I had only been together for four months, and I was bloody pregnant already. I wouldn't have minded but up until seven weeks ago I was on contraception, but with being small myself and Stu's manhood not so little, he had been starting to feel my coil scratching the end of him every time we were having sex. I had guessed it was uncomfortable for him even if he had tried to deny it; my coil was leaving a lovely inch long scar on the end of his penis, so it was agreed I would have it removed, that happened at the end of October. I had done three tests, and they had all come up positive, and the only person I had mentioned it to was Jody.

Talking about Jody, I was so glad she had started to warm to the idea of Stu and me, she had gone funny with me for a few weeks when we got back from Cornwall, and I couldn't blame her. I found a little note she had written while we were away about how her heart was well and truly broken and I guessed at the time it was old, but it turned out she wrote it while Stuart and I were away after he rang her just to tell her that he had finally slept with me.

I would like to think that he just wasn't thinking straight when he rang her, but I know he did it just to wind her up. As it turned out, it did more than wind her up; the whole situation nearly finished our friendship off. I wasn't about to let that happen so after her avoiding us for weeks I decided just to turn up at her door with coffee and cake. That was the start of our weekly tradition, taking it in turns to provide the cupcakes. With Jody round ours almost every day she was there when I did my first pregnancy test and told me to tell Stuart straight away. That was last weekend, and five days ago.

With that in mind, I kindly turned down Stu's offer on a drink, but I decided to stick to my plan, the Christmas card I picked up for him was signed by me, Lucy and bump, and I had a test hidden in the bathroom to take tomorrow morning. I just told him that I was worn out and not in the mood to drink. He went into the kitchen to fetch himself a cold beer and came back with a tub of silver glitter.

'What's that for?' I asked.

'Santa's footsteps,' Stuart used to put glitter all over the floor when he lived with his own kids even though his ex-partner used to go mad at the mess. He was a big kid at heart, and I think that was why I was starting to fall for him.

Once the glitter had been sprinkled all over the rug towards the tree I stood back and admired how pretty it looked when he informed me that he hadn't finished yet, he then walked in the hall and came back in with his work boots, he placed them on the floor and sprinkled even more glitter. I was starting to see what was meant by all the mess afterwards, but it was Christmas after all. Now it looked perfect; six, big man-sized footprints were leading to the tree. We just needed to grab all the presents from the spare room and arrange them under the tree. We had a lot of stuff too and it had taken up at least twelve hours of my life in just wrapping them, what with five children between Jody's kids and us too. The tree was packed by the time we had finished, and very impressive if I do say so myself.

Stu and I were stood admiring how festive the room now looked when he turned me towards him and kissed me passionately.

'Sarah, I love you so much, thank you for making this year so perfect.' I smiled back at him, gazing into his big hazel eyes.

'I love you too,' his whole face lights up as he leads me to our bedroom.

The alarm goes off at seven, but Lucy is still fast asleep.

'Five more minutes,' I moan pulling the covers over my face.

'But it's time to get up! Santa has been,' my boyfriend is sounding far too chirpy for my liking, but I sit up anyway.

'Merry Christmas beautiful,' he leans down to kiss my forehead.

'Merry Christmas.'

Stu orders me to stay in bed while he makes us a cup of tea, so I pick up my book from beside the bed and start to read while I am waiting for him. A few minutes later he walks back in the bedroom with two cups, he places them on the bedside cabinet while I finish reading the paragraph I am on, that was until the book was snatched out of my hand and flung across the room.

'No time for reading,' he says.

'Great, now I won't know what page I am on,' I pretend to sulk, and he starts tickling my side.

I hate being tickled and he knows it. My outburst of laughter and screaming has Lucy stumbling into the bedroom, 'Stop now,' I say, but he carries on until Lucy is right by the bed.

'Right Sarah, stop now,' he says firmly but with a big grin on his face.

'I swear to god,' that man wound me up something rotten, but I didn't think I could have him any other way.

'Shall we go and see if Santa has been?' he asks Lucy, with his big cheerful voice and Lucy starts getting excited.

She is almost three so finally at the age where she appreciates more than just the wrapping paper and the boxes. I can hear the squeal of delight as she enters the living room. Stuart had already turned on all the fairy lights while making our tea. I put my dressing gown on and picked up the two cups before heading into the living room. Lucy was bouncing with excitement, and it was lovely to see her so happy.

'We should have breakfast first,' I said to Lucy who was now pulling her face at me.

'Don't be tight,' he pipes up, 'It's Christmas, you are meant to fill up with chocolate for breakfast and feel too sick for Christmas dinner.'

Well, that's not happening, I am cooking dinner for nine people today, so no one is filling up on chocolate if I have my way.

'Breakfast before presents had always been the rule.'

I look at Stu who is just shaking his head at me, 'Nasty mummy,' he said pouting his bottom lip out.

'Nasty mummy,' Lucy repeats Stu's words.

I could kill him for ganging up on me, but with the prospect of telling him I was pregnant this morning, I needed to keep him in this good mood. I didn't know why I was stressing about telling him, and he blatantly asked me not to go back on the pill after having the coil removed and said he wanted to leave things up to fate and I had agreed but honestly didn't expect to get pregnant so soon.

I sat on the sofa and sipped my tea while Stuart played Santa and started to hand Lucy her presents, she was beaming and ripped the paper off in record time. Next, he passed me a present. It was a large, squared gift. Bless him, I know I said I like to read, but he had got me six spiritual books about gemstones and Angels. I needed to hear something other than ripping paper, so I placed my book on the floor and turned on the TV to find the music channel. I needed some background noise and I watch on as Stu opens the chunky silver bracelet he had been hinting for last month. He shuffled over to me on his knees to kiss me and say thank you.

That cup of tea had gone straight through me, so I headed to the toilet. I ran my hand behind the spare toilet rolls, grabbing the unopened pregnancy test. I peed on the stick and sat and waited. I had already done three tests, so I was unsure why I was feeling so nervous. I wait a few minutes just staring at the plastic rod in my hand. Once the lines appeared, I flushed the toilet and washed my hands. When I returned to the living room, I asked Stuart and Lucy if they wanted a drink.

Stu's Christmas card was in the third drawer in the kitchen, so that was is my excuse to grab it. Fuck me; my heart was racing like mad as I walked back in with our drinks on a tray with his card in-between them. He got to his feet as soon as he saw my struggle. He then passed Lucy her juice and took his cup of tea.

'That card is yours too,' I said as he smiled at me and took his card from the tray as well.

He opened the card, and I could see his face change as he got to the bottom of the writing.

'And bump?' he asks confused, but surely I don't have to spell it out?

'Yes Stuart, I am pregnant.'

The tears start to stream down his face as I tell him that I had just done a test a few minutes before making the drink, I then made my way to the bathroom to show him. Now he was a sobbing mess, and Lucy was starting to look worried as she toddled over to Stuart.

'You're going to be a big sister,' he said pulling her up onto his knee.

As I passed him the test, he looked at me with the biggest smile I have ever seen on his face.

'Thank you so much,' he says, 'This must be the best Christmas to date.'

He kissed Lucy on the head before putting her down; her interest was back on the presents still under the tree.

'We had best sort these out,' I say pointing to the tree, 'Not sure everyone will appreciate Lucy opening all their presents too.'

Stuart stayed sat on the sofa while I found all the presents for us, leaving everyone else's at the back for later.

Lucy was happily playing in her room with her new baby and buggy while I was in the kitchen preparing dinner. Jody was due any minute with her two, so the house was about to wake up properly. Stu decided this was an appropriate time to ring his Dad which I was pleasantly surprised about because in the whole eighteen months I had known Stu, I had never heard him mention his Father. I had listened to him bitch on and on about how he will never talk to his Mum again. I believed him too, as that man held a grudge. This is the first time he had mentioned his Dad. Stu was stood by the living room window when he dialled the number, but no one answered. He looked deflated now, but I assured him that it was still early and that he could try again later. Just then the phone rang, and he told me it was his Dad's number.

I was busy chopping veg in the other room, but I could hear him proudly tell his Dad that he was going to be a Dad again, they were only on the phone about ten minutes when Stu walked in the room again with tears in his eyes. I asked if everything was okay, worrying that the phone call hadn't gone as planned.

'Everything is perfect, thank you Sarah,' he was a soppy sod, and I put my arms around his big neck while he sobbed on my shoulder.

'Why are you crying then?' I whisper in his ear.

'Because I am so happy.'

I could feel his whole-body jerk and his head get heavy as I console him. I know I don't show my emotions, but this was the first time I had seen a grown man cry so much, and I was unsure how I felt about it.

Stu's kids turned up just before two in the afternoon and dinner was all cooking nicely, so I turned everything down and made my way back into the living room where everyone else was. He then announced to everyone that I was pregnant, and they seemed happy for me. Rachel wrapped her arms around me and thanked me for making her Dad so happy. It felt like a proper family for once in my life and the entire day went more perfect than I could ever have imagined.

By six in the evening, we were all playing Monopoly; well, all but Jody who was entertaining the kids. I was the banker. Stu was fierce at this game usually, but he seemed to be letting the kids take control of the board, yet another trait I admired about the man. Mid game, he asked me if I had a passport yet, but I didn't so it was agreed that we would get one as soon as possible. He then told me that he wanted to take me away on holiday before our baby was born. Apart from UK trips and a weekend trip to France when I was still at school, I had never been abroad, and I couldn't wait, the excitement had me needing a pee again.

That evening we were lay in bed, and Stu starts to tell me how happy I make him, and as much as I had started to fall for him, I couldn't help but feel uncomfortable by his words. I can't really explain it, but my whole life I had wanted to find someone caring, loving, someone to protect me and all I had had was manipulating arseholes my entire life, so this was all freaking me out a little. I tell him that I love him too and he pulls me in for a cuddle. How can I say to him that I hate being cuddled? I had seen a completely different side to him during that past few months and I didn't want to ruin this moment.

The Stuart I had known before us as a couple, was arrogant and abusive and I couldn't help but think that he would soon be like this with me. I had tried to talk to him about my fears, but he just got quite upset and assured me that he will never do anything to hurt me. My ear was now sticking to his arm, and his hand was rubbing my stomach which was just making me feel nauseous.

'I'm sorry,' I said as I got up as gently but as fast as I could.

With my hands covering my mouth I made it to the toilet just in time.

Our holiday...

My pregnancy was going well but with both my other children having a low birth weight I was told that I needed to have a lot more check-ups than normal. This was perfect for our baby's Daddy as Stu was starting to stress that something would go wrong. As much as I know it was out of worry, him going on all the time was starting to get on my nerves, though I daren't have said that to him. Stuart had delivered his youngest daughter when Debbie went into labour earlier than planned. He was in the bath at the time, when her waters broke, and with it being December and heavy snowfall for days the midwife struggled to get to the property. It was apparent that no help was on its way so, Stu had to be an emergency midwife. He successfully delivered his baby girl. With that in mind, I can see why he was worrying, but I have never been so calm about the whole situation, apart from Stu's constant nagging that is.

It was as if he thought, I was going to break or something and had even roped Jody into visiting more often, so I didn't do anything foolish. I don't think it helped that I had moved the bedroom round while he had been at work last week, but this over-protectiveness could become suffocating, I could tell already.

I was getting excited for our holiday to Turkey, and it was less than two weeks away. Luckily, I had my passport now, so all that was left to do was get some summer clothes and a swimsuit. I needed to find something that would cover my belly comfortably enough. I was only fourteen weeks pregnant, but you would think I was further gone, which just added to Stu's constant worrying. You see, you are only allowed to travel while pregnant within the first five months, and he seemed to think I looked like I was further gone than that so maybe be told I was unable to fly. I would pack my pregnancy record so if I was asked I could prove I could travel.

Stuart had been to Turkey a few years ago, so I kept asking him questions about his last holiday. He went with Craig and Sharon and had said that he felt like a bit of a gooseberry and that he was looking forward to it just being the both of us. I know it caused a little awkward moment with Sharon when she found out Stu was taking me on holiday. I am unsure why, but that woman seemed to have taken a big dislike to me even though I had done nothing to her. Unfortunately, Craig was Stuarts' best friend, so I had no choice but to try and get on with her for both their sakes.

'Why did Sharon have a go at you?' I asked.

'She is just a funny one, she hates anyone I have ever been with, but I don't know why,' he said before looking at me and cupping my face.

'Honestly, she will be fine once she can see we are for keeps.'

There was more to this than he was admitting but for now, I took his reasoning and tried and ignore all the hurtful things he had told me that was said.

'It was the heat of the moment, I must have caught her having a difficult day,' he said trying to defend her wicked tongue.

It was clear she wasn't a genuinely nice person, but I must take his word for it, I had known her for a matter of months whereas Stu had known her for over eighteen years. I couldn't compete, and I wouldn't want to try.

Jody was due around any minute to head up to town with me, so I started getting ready. I was dressed, but I hadn't put a brush through my hair all day. Stu said he preferred my hair all messy, but I knew with my hair so dark and me being so pale lately I looked half dead, but he said he loved my witch look as he called it. It was more like I had been dragged through a hedge backwards. I was placing my hair in a high ponytail when Stu startled me by creeping up behind me; I didn't hear him, I just saw his reflection in the mirror.

'You look too beautiful to go up to town,' he says.

I just look at him with a raised eyebrow. I know he must be taking the piss because I looked rough as hell that day.

'And I would prefer you to put on your other skirt that you were wearing yesterday.'

He was looking at my knee-length skater skirt; surely, he didn't think it was short? I wore stuff a lot shorter all the time before I started getting fat, so don't see why it was a problem today. Rather than saying anything, I just bit my tongue and put on my full-length gypsy skirt. It was that long, it slightly brushed off the floor and there was no way he would let me wear heels, so I would have to cope with it dragging all day. I was relieved as Jody walked in through the front door.

'Ready?' I ask as soon as she entered the room, and I was grateful when she turned and walked back out of the front door. I kissed Stu and caught up with Jody who was now waiting at the top of the garden for me.

'Have you guys had an argument or something?' she asked as soon as we walked away from the garden.

'No, I am just feeling a little irritable I think.'

Jody looked at me, and I wondered if she believed my explanation.

'I know what you mean,' is all she said before changing the subject and asked about our upcoming holiday.

'You are a lucky cow, what I wouldn't give to have a man whisk me off to a beautiful hot country.'

I could see the envy all over her face which just adds to my excitement.

'You'd best take loads of photo's,' she said now smiling back at me.

The town was packed, and I wished we had planned this shopping trip for another day, neither of us had much planned during the week, but Jody insisted that we come up on a Saturday morning instead.

'I rarely get my two looked after Sarah, I want to make the most of it and can't remember the last time we were both free at the weekend.'

I agreed with her; it was a welcomed break.

'I just wished it wasn't so busy.' I say looking at the crowds in front of us.

'Stop complaining will you.'

I felt like she had snapped at me a little, but with everything getting to me today it could have just been my hormones again.

'You are meant to be excited; you go on holiday soon.'

I was excited, but it seemed like forever away still, and we still needed to sort out my daughter spending the week with her Dad while we were away sunning ourselves on the beach. I think I was more excited about seeing my son again, apart from speaking on the phone with him I hadn't seen him since Simon moved them both up to Newcastle with his new family. They seemed happy enough, and I would get to see for myself next week.

'I feel guilty leaving Lucy behind,' I looked at Jody who was too busy eyeing up the hunk standing by Starbucks.

'Jody,' I said nudging her with my elbow.

'Don't be silly Sarah, you deserve a breakaway and it's not as if you are leaving her with any old person, Simon is her Dad for fucks sake!' and she had a point.

Simon was looking forward to spending quality time with his little girl too. I supposed I was not the only one who lost out when they moved to the other end of the country.

SUN, SEA, AND MORNING SICKNESS...

We were driving up to Newcastle as the plan was to stop over with Simon and his family the night before we left. Firstly, to make sure Lucy settled and for me to be able to spend some time with my son Mark, who I hadn't seen in almost a year at this point. We talked on the phone every few weeks, but it wasn't the same as seeing my little boy in person. I felt like a giddy teenager all excited for my holiday and Stu had been telling me all morning about his last trip with Craig and Sharon. I didn't realize until now, but he had booked our hotel in the same town he had visited a few years previous.

'I really can't believe you are almost twenty-three and have never had a holiday,' Stuart said as if he almost didn't believe me.

'I have been on the odd UK holiday and used to spend time at my Granny's caravan growing up, but apart from that, I haven't been anywhere really.'

He goes on to tell me that we should have a foreign holiday once a year and I point to my stomach and ask if he was forgetting something?

'Sarah, having a baby will not stop us from doing what we want, I promise you that much,' I just smiled at the thought.

I had the map in my hands as we approached Newcastle, not that I was much help. I was utterly useless at reading the map, so much so, that Stu had to turn the thing the right way up. Lucy was starting to get a little grouchy, but after being in the car for three hours, I was impressed with her behaviour.

'Looks like we are almost there,' I said pointing to where I think we are on the map.

Simon answered the door with the cheesiest grin I had ever seen on him, 'Welcome to my castle,' he said ushering us into the hallway.

This place was far from a castle I can assure you, the hallway itself was crammed with junk from floor to ceiling on both sides of us, and I did have a worrying moment that Lucy could be hurt if she bumps into the precarious mass of what I am guessing must be car boot items. I waited until we were led upstairs and into the living room where Mark was sat on a small plastic chair facing the wall. Simon's newest partner Amanda must have noticed my disgust and went on to tell me that my son had severely misbehaved all morning.

'It might just be excitement?' Stu said defending him, but we didn't know the ins, and outs of the situation, so I just looked at both Simon and Amanda and told them that as much as they do know best, I hadn't seen my little boy for months on end. Simon could see where I was coming from and told Mark he could move off the chair and go and say hello to his Mummy. He didn't though; Mark didn't even look at me but instead ran straight to Lucy and hugged her and asked if she wanted to play. I smiled as they embraced for a few moments.

'No mess this time,' Simon said, as both the kids make their way to the bedroom.

'I am a little worried about the stuff in the hallway,' I said as I sit on the small sofa beside Amanda's son Tom. Tom had a few social problems, and it was apparent when he kept staring at me.

'I have met you before.' he says.

I wasn't sure if this freakishly small twelve-year-old was telling me this or asking me, but I nodded at him and explained I had met him a few times when they stayed with Simon.

'Oh yeah, that's right, I thought you might have forgotten.'

He was winking at me now and it was weirding me out. Amanda's daughter was in the kitchen doing the dishes, and Simon had just shouted into her to make us all a hot drink.

Steff emerged a few minutes later with two extra-large cups; I am hoping one of them is not for me as the cups look larger than my entire face. I let out a small sigh of relief as she passed them both to her Mother, she then returned to the kitchen. I was glad when I saw Stu's, and my own mugs were of a normal size. I took my coffee and thanked Steff. She smiled and soon scurried back into the kitchen to finish cleaning up. Steff was a polite young girl, and I had got on well with her anytime we had met in the past, but she seemed a little deflated today. I placed my cup down on the dirty floor. I noticed the old ringed tea stains covering the cup. I really didn't want to drink it, but I knew it was rude if I didn't at least try. Stuart picked up his cup from the floor, and it had hairs and tobacco dangling from the bottom. He had picked up half the floor with the base of the cup. I heaved as I felt the bile start to form in my mouth, this being pregnant business had my poor stomach as tender as ever, but I composed myself and lifted my own cup, I just avoided looking at the base or even the cup altogether. I was hoping the tea tasted better than the sick that had just invaded my mouth.

Again, I mentioned all the stuff stacked unstably in the hallway and Simon told me that Lucy won't get into the hall and that I had nothing to worry about. Of course, I would still worry. I was leaving my daughter in his care for a week and seeing the state of the kids and the house I was starting to wonder if going to Turkey was such a bright idea.

I voice my concerns to Stuart that evening, but he was quick to settle my nerves telling me that if he trusted her staying, then I should too. He was usually a good judge of character, so I agreed, and we fell asleep almost straight away.

The next morning, I was woken to the sound of Tom shouting at the top of his voice, it didn't help that our bedroom for the night is in, what I am guessing was meant to be a dining room. The kids were awake in the living room next door, and the walls seemed paper thin. Tom starts shouting again, but this time I heard Mark crying, so I got up out of bed, trying not to disturb Stu who was still snoring away. Lucy was awake and following me out of the room. As I walked into the living room, I saw Tom had hold of my son and was very angrily shaking him. I pulled Tom off Mark and demanded to know what the hell was going on.

'He kicked over my drink on purpose,' Tom snapped.

I looked at Mark who seemed sheepish and then back at Tom. 'Even so, there is no need to hurt him!'

Stu had woken up by now and was standing in the doorway and from what I could tell he had heard the conversation.

'He is four years old, and you are twelve, go to your room till your Mum gets up,' Stu said pointing to the living room door. Tom didn't argue and went straight out of the room.

It was an hour and a half later before Simon emerged from his pit looking somewhat worse for wear. I offered to make a coffee knowing that if I made it, the drink would be in a clean mug. Simon sat on the sofa and started rolling himself a joint. Once Amanda had come downstairs Stu told them both about the argument between the boys. It transpired that Mark had this new naughty habit where he would spill over drinks or trample his food into the floor.

I wouldn't have believed it if I hadn't of seen him do it later that lunchtime myself. He wanted ham sandwiches and when he was told there was no ham left he had a major meltdown, kicking and screaming, and after he had seemed to calm down and the dust seemed to have settled, he walked over to everyone's freshly made drink and kicked each one over. I couldn't believe how naughty he had been and in all honesty I was relieved when Stu said we had to leave shortly for our flight.

I now had nervous butterflies in my stomach. I was going on holiday! And to a hot country at that but I did wonder if the baby would like flying. I was only about four months gone, but I could already feel movements. The last time I was on a plane was over fifteen years ago when I went stewardess accompanied as a child. Stuart on the other hand always had family holidays growing up and said he tried to go abroad at least once a year. Family holidays wasn't something I was ever used to, but we moved so much that every year kind of felt like a holiday.

177

Once we were at the airport, Stuart informed me that we had the VIP area because he had sweet talked a deal when he booked our flights. He had told them that this was my first ever holiday and apparently that was enough to give us special treatment. The VIP area was quiet, and drink and nibbles were free of charge. Not that I could drink anyway, but Stu decided he needed a drink or two before we boarded the plane, it transpired that he was nervous as hell at the thought of flying. I must say it was nice to see this side of him as he always seemed to have it all together. After Stuart necked the third bottle I did inform him that he needed to slow down, I was sure they wouldn't let us on the plane if he was pissed.

'Just because you can't drink doesn't mean I can't take advantage of all this free beer.'

It was another two bottles before we were called to the gates, the VIP area was right by the gate we needed, and I was grateful when I saw Stu wobble to his feet, he seemed to compose himself by the time we were boarding.

'I hate flying,' he said as we take our seat.

'Do you mind sitting by the window?'

I didn't mind at all but seeing how unsettled he was, was starting to rub off on me. I fastened my seat belt, placing the strap under my baby bump. The take-off is always the worse bit, but I was fine as soon as we were in the air. Stu was still squeezing my hand.

The flight was almost four hours, so I really needed to try and get some sleep, this morning had taken it out of me, and all I wanted was my big warm bed. Stuart was watching whatever movie was showing and had his earphones in so didn't hear me when I told him I was closing my eyes. I must have drifted off to sleep straight away, and I was woken by the captain informing us we had almost reached our destination. Stu looked at me and told me he was glad I was awake because he needed my hand again. I just smiled at him and placed my hand in his. I felt him squeeze straight away.

As soon as we left the plane I felt the heat straight away, the tarmac felt warm under my feet, and I wouldn't have minded, but this was in the early hours of the morning. We made our way to the baggage counter to collect our cases, and then a Turkish man ushered us down a small dark corridor saying the word 'coach'. I was a little weary because this passage went on for a while and we seemed to be the only ones walking in the same direction, but as soon as we got to the end I noticed a few people who were on our flight so, I guessed it must be the coach we needed. Stuart said our hotel was an hour away and if I was honest all I could think about was sleep. The heat didn't seem as bad now that my body temperature had adjusted but it was still stupidly warm. I was so exhausted by the traveling that I was hoping I would just pass out. Stu had other ideas though and had already told me he was heading straight to the bar.

'Are you sure it will still be open?' I ask knowing that it will be almost three in the morning by the time we arrive at the hotel.

'Of course, it's a holiday, and we are paying guests,'

I was hoping he was wrong, but I let him think he was having a cold Turkish beer after sharing a bus with other people. You see, he was a little funny about getting in a taxi, never mind getting in a coach. Stu had driven since he was seventeen so had never needed to rely on public transport. Even when he came here a few years ago, they all rented 100cc mopeds just because Stuart pulled a face about trusting anyone in this foreign country. I was surprised when we sat in our seats, and he happily sat down by the window.

'This was going to be amazing,' he said.

I tried to smile but ended up yawning instead.

'I think someone will be asleep any minute,' I heard him say, just as I close my eyes.

I was woken by Stu telling me that we were almost there. As far as I knew I had only drifted off for a few minutes, but I had slept for just under an hour.

'I needed the sleep,' I said rubbing my eyes.

'Another reason I wish you would stop wearing makeup,' Stu said.

Another little dig, for some reason every time he saw me with a little bit of makeup on he was throwing a little dig. Yes, I may have had panda eyes as I had just rubbed my eyes, but this must have been the tenth time he had mentioned my make up this week. I wouldn't mind, but I have only been wearing it now and again after his dig a few weeks before that it made me look like a pregnant teen when I had my face done up. I know I look young, but I did think he was being a little dramatic. Now he was bitching at me because I had smeared it. Well luckily, I didn't plan to wear any on this holiday, I wanted to get my face to tan as well as my body, but it had annoyed me. I decide not to say anything because I didn't want to start this holiday with bickering, plus I was pregnant so no doubt my hormones were contributing to my irritant state of mind. I would have to say something when we get home though if the sniping didn't stop.

We were called to the front of the coach as it came to a stop, I was guessing this was our hotel, but I couldn't see anything apart from a small bar a few hundred yards away and a muddy track.

'Are you sure this is the right place?' I asked Stu worried we were just being dropped in the middle of nowhere.

'Yes, yes,' the Turkish driver said passing Stuart our case and pointing down the muddy track.

'Only one way to find out,' Stu said walking away from the coach, so I naturally followed him. We were only walking for a minute when we saw a small man stood by a fence in the wall.

'My English friends?' he asks.

Stu responded with a nod of his head, so we followed the little man down this garden path, as the garden opened, the hotel was in full view and looked just as lovely as it did in the brochure, the pool flickered as the mood reflected in the water. The gardens were very well looked after too, and I was looking forward to seeing it all properly during the day. The man lead us to a sizeable hut-shaped building opposite the hotel, and as we walk inside the man said he will get us our room keys, but first, we needed a drink.

'Told you so,' Stu said pulling his tongue out to me.

'Okay, sorry must be hard always being right,' I stick my tongue out in response.

'I am a mighty Leo, I am always right,' he said holding a proud stance and pushing his chest out, well his belly really but I let him think it was his chest he was pushing out.

'Can I just have an orange juice please?' all I want is a Tia Maria, but I can't drink and even if I could drink, I wouldn't expect them to stock it here. I think I am going to stick with tea as well while on this holiday because I didn't think I wanted to trust Turkish coffee. Stu warned me that I needed to use the bottled water while on this trip, even when I was brushing my teeth.

That wasn't the weirdest thing about this country; he also informed me that, if I needed to use the bathroom I had best take nappy bags with me. The pipework was so small that you were not allowed to put the toilet paper down the toilet like we are used to at home. Instead, a small bin was provided. He said he didn't know this the first time he stayed out here, and the heat mixed with a bin full of used toilet paper wasn't a pleasant experience.

It was almost four in the morning Turkish time by the time we headed to bed. The window was wide open with a netting over it to keep all the bugs out, but I was still too warm. I end up falling asleep in just a pair of knickers and a small vest top which was now riding up my belly. I may have only been a few months pregnant, but my stomach was already starting to show a perfectly formed bowling ball shape. And I could only sleep on my back, which wasn't comfortable at all.

The next morning, we woke just after ten and decided to have a lazy beach day. Stuart wanted to show me the blue lagoon on Joseph's beach and a small bar right on the seafront. We walked for a few hundred yards before Stu informed me that he wanted to rent a bike for us. I look at my growing stomach and back at him. He said he would never put our baby or me in danger and that he would be safe with me on the back. I asked if I could think about it during the morning and he agreed. The beach is a good hour and a half walk away from us, and even though it was all downhill, he was worried about me walking that far in the heat. We decided to get on the local bus instead. The coach looked like an old run-down school bus, and I did wonder how it was even on the road. No way would it pass a mot in the UK. We climbed on, and even though it was busy, a Turkish lady offered me her seat, she pointed at my stomach and beckons me to sit. Stu smiled at the lady, and I offered my thanks to the lady as I took my seat. I am surprised when the bus started to fill up quickly, we had only got a few hundred yards down the street. I call it a street; the footpath was a stoned thin strip, and the road itself was dry loose mud, a far cry from our roads back home. There was no room on the bus, we were like sardines, and I was grateful to the woman who gave up her seat for me. I can guarantee that

I would have been knocked about had I not been sitting. I looked at Stu who was now squashed up against the window; the sweat was pouring off him. It wasn't even midday but already must have been over twenty-five degrees. The bus stopped again, but surely, we couldn't fit anyone else on here. I didn't think the driver cared if he was making money, and by the looks of things the locals were happy enough to get hot and sweaty and pushed and pulled about every time the bus stopped.

I was so relieved when we finally made it down to the beach. I needed air in my lungs more than anything, and the breeze from the sea was welcoming. The water looked crystal blue; I had never seen the water look so clear. We started walking down a sandy path rather than heading straight to the beach; I just followed Stuart as he has been here before and apparently knew where he was taking me. The pathway headed behind a few small shacks; one of which was a little café by the looks of things, but it was closed which I honestly thought was crazy when this place was so busy.

'Just a few more yards,' he said looking back at me to make sure I kept up with him.

We ended up walking through a small woodland area before I was stunned with a small, isolated beach with a bar right on the sea. The seating area hung over the edge of the sea and was held up on big wooden stilts. It looked safe enough, but you can't tell the place had taken a battering from the elements.

'This looks magical,' I said smiling.

'This, my dear is Joseph's beach.'

I took in the amazing sight in front of me and pulled out of my daze when a man started to walk towards us. Then I noticed we were the only people here.

'Are you sure it is open to the public?' I asked Stu who has just put his hand up to the approaching man.

'I have been here before; this is the blue lagoon it's a public place.'

I had heard of the blue lagoon before but guessed that was the more substantial part of the beach we walked past earlier.

'Good day,' the Turkish man said taking Stu's hand to greet us.

The man doesn't look at me; he just talks to my boyfriend. Instead, he talks in Turkish, and Stu said he welcomed us and offered us both a drink.

'I would love a nice cold beer,' Stu said, 'and my wife will have an orange juice.'

Wife? He was getting ahead of himself. I joked with him as the barman walked back into Joseph's bar.

'I am not your wife yet?' I reminded my arrogant boyfriend.

'In my eyes, you already are my wife.'

I am unsure if that was sweet or a bit creepy. Was he trying to propose to me, because if he was, then he would need to work harder than just to assume that I am already his? I was happy, and even though this baby had happened far too quickly for my liking, I had no real complaints. Saying that I was nowhere near ready to marry this man, I love him, but I was not ready to commit my whole life to him.

'Maybe I am not ready to get married Stuart, you think of that?'

I sounded snappy, but I didn't mean to, his comment about already being his had annoyed me more than I first thought.

'Calm down Mrs. Hormonal,' he laughed, and I find myself laughing along with him.

'Were getting married before my child is born,' he informed me.

'Don't I get a say in this?'.

Oh, I wish I hadn't said anything, I was not liking the way this was heading.

'No offense Sarah, but my child isn't going to have the same surname as your Dad, I know you are both friends now, but I still don't want my child to have any name but my own.'

I could see where he was coming from but why did we need to get married just so our child had his name, we can do that when registering our baby, I reminded Stuart of this fact, but he still insisted that we need to be married first. This beach was so relaxing that I honestly did not want this to turn into an argument. So, I let Stu have his way and think that we were getting married.

'Our baby is due in six months, not enough time to plan a wedding' I reminded him.

'Plenty of time,' he said before leaving me on the sun lounger and making his way into the sea.

'Come in,' he shouted, but I just shook my head.

I can't swim and couldn't remember if I had told him this fact about me, but I felt silly that I was an adult and couldn't swim.

You see, I had an accident when I was a child and almost drowned, and since then I haven't tried to swim again. I refused to take any chances while pregnant too, so I just stood my ground and informed him that there was no way he would get me into that sea.

'You are missing out, the sea has so much salt in it, that you just float,' he said as he lay on his back.

He must have weighed eighteen stone, so I was surprised, but he still wasn't getting me in that sea.

The waiter returned with orange juice for me and a beer for Stu, I did tell him that he could leave his drink with me, but he said it was okay and walked out to the sea where he was still bathing on top of the water. I shouted over to tell him his drink was here, but the waiter kept walking straight into the sea and handed him his glass in person.

'Now, that is customer service,' I joked, but I was surprised.

I couldn't imagine anyone in the UK delivering a drink into the sea. I got my phone out to take a photo of Stuart looking immensely proud of his pint in hand.

That evening as we head out for dinner, I was a little apprehensive about eating out because I am a fussy eater at the best of times, but here the fear of trying new foods is heightened. After looking at a few menu's which were in English as well as Turkish, I still couldn't decide what to eat, so Stu asked if I wanted steak. I must have looked shocked or something because he sarcastically informed me that it was pork they don't eat in Turkey, not steak.

'I know it is pork; I am not that uneducated.'

He just laughed and told me he knows a restaurant around the corner who cook a lovely steak. My mouth is watering at the thought, and I am now looking forward to dining out for a change.

The restaurant was small but very well laid out and even though it was busy, the place still somehow seemed quiet. The music was soft Bollywood style, and the restaurant was decorated in browns and golds. Very relaxing after a sweltering day, and I was pleased when we were given a window seat. It must have still been at least twenty degrees outside, but there was a gentle breeze coming through the blinds. I ordered my steak well done and ask for a glass of water. Stuart had a beer.

The food was delivered very quickly but as the waiter placed my plate down, I could see that was far from well done. Stu asked them to send it back, and I sat waiting as he started to devour his food.

'I guess you were hungry,' I said as he took a massive mouthful.

Possibly the least attractive thing I had seen lately, and I was almost sick as a little as a drop of blood from his practically rare steak dripped down his face. He could see he was turning my stomach and acted on it even more so.

'If I am sick, I will blame you,' I warned.

My food arrived, and even though it looked a little more cooked, it was still pink on the inside. The thought of eating rare meat turns me at the best of times.

'It is better for you when it is still red, more iron which a lot is better for the baby too.'

Still, even if it was good for me, I was unsure. After a few moments of trying to persuade me I finally cut a corner of my meat and placed it in my mouth without even looking at it I started to chew, thinking that it was going to make me sick, but it was the tastiest steak I have ever tasted, juicy and so much flavour.

'This is good,' I said cutting myself another end. I already knew I won't eat the middle, it's almost raw but the end bits were fine, and I was happy with myself for trying new foods. It was so out of my comfort zone that I couldn't help but smile to myself the whole time we were out.

The next morning, we woke up early, and Stu was renting a motorbike, so we could head to the nearest city. I was still unsure if I even wanted to take the chance and get on the back. I had been on the back of the bike with him a few times, and he was a careful rider, but I was four months pregnant, and I had more to think about than just myself. Stu had tried to reassure me, but I had told him I wouldn't know till I saw the bike he had in mind if it looked safe enough and I felt safe then fair enough but considering the state of the buses and cars here, it didn't fill me with much confidence.

Stu had me giggling most of the way into town, he started off with acting silly and pretending he couldn't walk up a curb. we were stood at the side of the road for a good few minutes with him swiping his foot across the floor but not lifting his foot high enough to place it on the step.

'I was about to wet myself.' I warned as I was holding my stomach watching my fully-grown man acting like a toddler.

'Lift your foot up,' I said, but he just looked at me confused.

Not as funny now, so I lifted his foot for him.

'I didn't know how to walk,' he said in the best baby voice I had heard.

'Stuart, we are about to have a baby, I could do without having a big baby too.'

He laughed and informed me he is just giving me a practice run. Like I need that, I already have two children. That had me thinking about Mark, I did miss him, and I could tell Lucy did too, so I was happy that they were getting to spend a week together.

'When we get home, I might invite Si and Mim down to stay if you don't mind?' I ask.

He was slightly offended that I had even asked him that question. 'Why would I ever mind? it's not as if you would ever begrudge my kids for staying over, is it?'.

He was right; I would never say who couldn't and couldn't stay over, apart from anything else it was Stuart's home, not mine.

'You know I love your kids Stu, that comment didn't even need to be said,' I reply.

'Same goes for you, anytime you want your son to stay over he is welcome, you don't ever need to ask.'

Once we got to the bike rental place, I was a little less apprehensive about going on the back with him. The bikes themselves looked very well looked after and Stu had assured me the whole way here that he would never put either of us in danger, and that we would be safer than ever. He had the choice of bikes as his licenses showed he could drive any vehicle. He stayed with a small moped, a 100cc engine and after ten minutes of looking at the bike, he was happy enough to pay the man his deposit and handed over his passport.

'What happens if they lose it?' I asked concerned that this young Turkish man just throws the stuff handed to him straight into the small portacabin office. I don't even think he had looked where he had thrown my boyfriend's passport.

'Then we are stuck here,' he laughs, 'Well no, I should say I am stuck here, you still have your passport so could go home and leave me here.'

'Like I would do that,' I replied.

'If I lost my passport you would have no choice; you have a daughter to collect in a week.'

He had a point, but I was just hoping it didn't come to that.

'I will be worrying all week now,' I warned Stuart as he passed me a helmet and helped me fasten it under my chin.

'It will be fine, people hand in their passports all the time, and it's a clever way to guarantee that they bring the bikes back.'

I was still unsure about all this but did see what he was saying, 'What happens if the bike gets damaged or breaks down?'

I was full of questions. 'Then we have to pay for the repairs before they return our documents.'

'So, in other words, if we don't break the bike, we can go home.'

'Exactly.'

Stu got onto the bike and tilted it down to make it easier for me to get on the back.

'Fancy renting a speedboat too.'

That would be amazing, but I couldn't swim. I try and put that big lead balloon of a thought to the back of my mind and agreed. I had never seen a speedboat in real life, never mind been on one. This holiday was turning out to be perfect so far. Stuart started up the engine, and we were off down the sandy roads towards the beach. The wind against my skin felt fantastic and was cooling me down perfectly. Thank god, we didn't have to get on a cramped bus again.

The sea looked even clearer today, and Stu said it would be because the tide was in, and that there was more salt in the water because of it.

'That means if you fall in you will float?' I ask.

'Well not as much as you would on Joseph's beach but yes, you would float a bit.'

He smiled, 'This beer belly will keep me afloat anyway,' he joked.

I sat on the sand just down from where we had parked the bike, Stu went and talked to the man who rented out the boats, looked like we were in luck as I was beckoned over to them both.

'We need your passport,' Stu said, and he was lucky I checked it was in my bag before we left because I almost left it in the bedside cabinet. I fished it out of my small shoulder bag and passed it to the man. He then walked us towards the boats.

'This one,' he says pointing at the bigger of the three available.

'Perfect.' I started to take my sandals off and place them in my bag.

I expected the water to be freezing but should have known what with this sun beating down all morning that it would be warm enough. Stuart helped me into the boat first before getting in himself. The Turkish man who now had my passport got on too and I wondered if he was our driver for the next few hours, but instead, he showed my boyfriend the controls and jumped off. He shouted a few warnings at us about not going out too far that we get lost and to stay safe. There were four life jackets under my seat should we have needed them, but I didn't plan to get out of this boat. I sat back and looked out to the sea as Stuart proudly started the engine up.

'Get in there,' he said excitedly.

'Did you have a boat last time you were here?' I asked.

'No, Sharon was too much of a pussy and wouldn't let us rent one.'

'What, and you listened to her?' I was surprised because he never listened to anyone, he could be very stubborn and fixated on his plans that a woman telling him he isn't allowed to do something would have usually made him more determined to do the opposite.

'I was on holiday with her and Craig, so I didn't have much choice.' Even so, I was surprised.

It was halfway through the day when I realised I hadn't put sun cream on. I was regretting it now as I saw my legs are starting to go pink and I am feeling hot. Stu had tried to tell me to have a dip in the sea, but I just gave him a knowing look.

'I won't let you drown,' he assured me, but I was still not getting into that ocean.

'It will be called the dead sea for all the wrong reasons; I think I could die just from the panic never mind drowning,' I thought.

'You go for a swim, and I will keep an eye on the boat' I said.

He threw his already wet t-shirt at me and called me over to control the speedboat, it was only at crawling speed, so I made it to the other side without even much of a wobble.

'You use this handle to increase speed,' he said, showing how gently I needed to move the throttle. 'And obviously, this is how you steer,' his other hand was on the steering wheel.

Looked easy enough. I took over as Stuart made his way to where I was sat moments before. 'Show me then,' he said egging me to speed up.

'Stuart, I was waiting for you to sit down.'

With that, I pulled the throttle closer to me, the front of the boat lifted almost causing him to crash to the floor.

'Not that fast, you crazy cow.' I laughed at him, and even though I have never driven a speedboat before I do wonder what this fuss was about, this was a piece of piss. 'Aww, did I scare you,' I say sarcastically.

'No, just I wasn't expecting it.'

I can tell I did freak him a little as I slowed down, and he got comfortable in the seat again.

'That wasn't even fast, but this is,' I say pulling the throttle towards myself, a little faster this time and I held the handle in place a little longer.

I was in fits of giggles as Stu slid straight off his seat and rolled towards the back of the boat. I released the handle because I couldn't see because of the tears streaming down my face.

'That was just too funny,' I roar at him, trying to catch my breath.

He was still laying on the floor on his back looking deflatingly at the clouds above us.

'You are lucky you are carrying my child, or you would have been overboard by now.'

'Yeah, yeah,' I say as he sat up.

I could tell he was trying his hardest to keep a straight face, but it didn't last long. 'Do you think you can drive us gently over between them two small islands?' he asked, so I nodded my head and crept slowly in that direction.

'You piss taking cow. Sure, you can go faster than that.' I started giggling again.

'I can but don't want my mighty lion to cry now do I?' Stuart smiled the biggest grin as I gained a little more speed.

'Your mighty lion?' he said, 'I like it.'

That evening after I had taken a shower I realised just how severe my sunburn was, my legs mainly were red raw, and since my shower, they were stinging like fuck. I tried to put after sun spray on my legs, but as soon as the mist hit my skin, I wanted to recoil in pain. Stu looked at me helplessly knowing there was nothing he could do.

'It is my own fault for forgetting sun cream this morning,' I said.

'No Sarah, had I not rushed you, then I doubt you would have forgotten it.'

I shook my head at him; the man was silly if he wanted to take the blame for this. I was a twenty-five-year-old woman who could put cream on!

I couldn't sleep at all that evening and spent most of the night in the living room reading my book and trying to take my mind off my stinging legs, by this point my arms were starting to go just as red but for some reason didn't seem as painful as my shins and feet. I eventually fell asleep about four in the morning. Stu was in bed when I drifted off, but I had woken with him asleep on the hard-tiled floor below me. I woke him and asked if he wanted a coffee. Once he has woken properly, I asked him why he felt the need to sleep on the solid floor when we had a bed in the other room.

'You didn't come to bed, and I woke up, and you weren't there, I panicked,' he said.

'Why would you panic?' I asked.

'We are in a Muslim country, and you are a beautiful woman, why wouldn't I panic?'

I think he was over paranoid, but I tell him I understood where he was coming from. I didn't really but could see that this clearly upset him.

'Sorry for not coming to bed, but I eventually passed out after reading.'

He then looked at me as if he was annoyed.

'What now?' I ask.

'So, your book got all your attention, and I didn't?' he replied. I hoped he was winding me up, but sometimes it was hard to know with Stuart.

He was drinking the previous night when we returned to the hotel, so I was guessing he was a little hungover and sensitive, so I said no more. I let him have a five-minute bitch about how rude it is to read while in another person's company and even worse if you forget to come to bed because of it. I could not believe he had got so uptight about this, so I tried to break the conversation by showing him how bright red my legs were.

'The book didn't stop me coming to bed, this did.'

His face said it all as he remembered how much pain I was in the night before.

'We will go to a chemist as soon as they open.'

Silly really but I didn't expect them to have a chemist in Turkey, I don't know why I just hadn't noticed one at all while we had been out in the town.

'The markets on today if you fancy it?' he said in a cheery voice.

What the fuck? he was just snapping at me a few seconds ago, but at least he was in better form now I supposed.

'That sounds good, as long as my legs feel better.'

They were loads better and looked more painful than they were, but I played on it a little.

We headed into town on foot, even thou we had the bike. Stu agreed that I should wear a long skirt to cover my burning legs. The chemist was a few minutes down the road from our hotel, and we had passed it every day, but I had never noticed it before. A middle-aged Turkish man was stood behind the counter, and as my concerned boyfriend tried to explain to the man why we were there, it was evident that the man spoke little English. I lifted my skirt to reveal my sunburnt legs and the man behind the counter went off into a small side room.

'That was hard work,' Stuart said just as the man reappeared.

'This,' the man said pointing to the bottle, he then makes a spraying sound and said the words, 'cool down.'

He handed me the brown glass bottle and Stu told me to try it. So, I took a seat and lifted my skirt to just above my knees. The mist cooled me down instantly and the Turkish man nodded at me. I stood back up as Stu paid him.

'That spray okay for you?' Stu asks.

I could still tell that I had sunburn, but the stinging had definitely eased off a bit. We headed into town to the market. I was amazed as soon as we started getting closer to city, you could hear the hustle and bustle of the market. The place was full of smells, colours and textures and this had the be the most cultured market I had ever seen. The spice man tried to call us over, but Stu told me to keep walking. We stopped at a small stall that sold handmade spoons, and other small items all with Hisaronu painted on them. We purchased a clock which he said will look lovely in the kitchen and a black decorated mixing spoon. The man wrapped the items up and told us to be careful with the bag. The next stall we stopped at was a spice stall; I looked at Stu a little confused because he had only just told me five minutes beforehand to walk straight past the spices.

'Thought we didn't want spices?' I asked.

'No, I just didn't want to buy off someone who was trying to force me to buy. This lady hasn't tried to force anything on me'.

I smiled at him and looked back at the Turkish woman.

'Boy or girl?' she asked pointing to my stomach.

'We don't know yet.'

She looked back at me and smiled. 'Well, I think a boy.'

Stuart and the woman had a small conversation about how he was hoping for a boy. I, on the other hand, had been drawn to the stall next to us. There was a small old lady behind the counter, and you could have easily missed her in the vast array of wooden carved items. I was especially drawn to the boxes at the front. They had Buddhist symbols on them. I picked a medium shaped box up, by now Stu was stood beside me wondering what I was looking at, so I passed him the box.

'It is a magic box,' the lady said seeing us looking.

'What's magic about it?' he asked the woman.

'Try to open.'

So, he did but like the woman had just said it seemed magic and had no way of opening, no visible clasps and no obvious places where it would separate.

'Show me,' the woman said placing her hand between her merchandise.

So, Stuart passed it to her, we couldn't see her hands because like I said she was so short you could hardly see her above the counter, but her hand appeared again with a now opened box.

'See?' she said, and I heard a giggle leave her lips as she clambered behind the counter.

'How much is it?' he asked. She replied but I didn't hear what she said.

'Can we afford it?' I asked but I am gutted when Stu said we can't, and we placed the box down and walk away from the stall.

'I am sorry, but if you want I will order you one online when we get home.' I was not that bothered to be honest, but he seemed annoyed that he couldn't get me the box, so I thanked him and told him that even if it is one similar, I would be happy. Thus, it was agreed.

Today was our last full day in Turkey, we were to travel home the next evening, and I was glad because this heat had worn me out, but most of all I had missed my daughter like mad. There had been a few moments this week where I had got a little teary seeing her photo as my phone's screensaver. Now don't get me wrong, this has been a well-earned break, and I had loved every second of it, but I just wanted to hug Lucy.

PRIOR ENGAGEMENTS...

Turkey was a fantastic holiday but being back home was as much of a treat as a holiday at the minute. I am six months pregnant now and feeling it. I was so glad Lucy was in a nursery for three hours a day. She was starting to test the boundaries with me at the minute. She was good as gold for Stu but a right pain in the bum for me. She can be lovely all day long and then as soon as I get home the temper tantrums start. Stuart had joked that she mustn't like me being pregnant, and as much as it was a joke, I was starting to think he had a point. I was also thinking she was annoyed with me for leaving her with her dad for a week, even though Simon had said she was good for him and if anything, it was Mim's kids who had played up the most while we were away. I still think she didn't enjoy it as much as he said she did. I asked Lucy if she had fun while I was away, but she just went in a huff; she had apparently told Stu that she didn't like staying with her dad and had asked if she could call him Dad instead. The second part I could believe because I heard her calling him Daddy Stu before we even went on holiday. I did think he would love her to see him as her dad and I couldn't ask for a better person to help bring her up. He is amazing with her and treats her like she is his little princess.

Jody had offered to pick my daughter up for me today and was taking her to town for dinner, so I didn't need to worry about collecting her, which was just as well because my sickness seemed worse today. It might be something I had eaten because I did pig out on munchies the previous night while catching up on Saturday's X Factor. I had been lucky enough to not suffer from morning sickness really, but it would be just my luck to have it now.

It was my birthday in a few weeks, and I already knew what I was getting, Stu took me shopping with him last weekend to pick out an engagement ring. I had tried to pick one of the cheaper options and went for an emerald and diamond cluster ring priced at just under three hundred pounds. He took offense and told me his wife wasn't going to be wearing anything cheap on her hand; he said I would be wearing it most of my life, so I had to pick something I wanted. My second choice was the ring I had been eyeing up since we entered the shop, but it was priced at four grand, so I never thought for one second he would spend so much money on me. Now, he hadn't proposed to me yet, so I was guessing he would do it on my birthday when he collected the ring. I know Jody had got me my favourite perfume because she got me it every year, even if we hadn't been on talking terms she would still try.

Oh, I still felt sick by the time Stuart got home from work, he looked pissed off as he made his way up the garden, I sat upright waiting for him to come into the living room but instead, he heads straight to the kitchen.

So, I made my way into him. He had just opened a can of beer and drank it in one.

'Thirsty?' I asked.

'Long arse day,' he sounded snappy, so I didn't say anything back I just squeezed past him to make myself a cup of tea.

'You look like you have just sat on your fat arse all day,' he sounded sarcastic and arrogant.

'I have felt like shit all day,' I explained.

'Yeah, I can tell, what, did you forget to pick up your daughter?' he was still snapping at me, and the hormones were really at their peak at the minute, I didn't know what had got him in this bitch fit mood, but I didn't deserve it.

'Jody has Lucy.'

He opened the fridge and grabbed out another can, this time he poured it into a glass.

'I can't believe you couldn't even be bothered to do the dishes.' What the hell was he bitching about now?

'There are two bowls a plate and a cup Stu, what is your problem?'

He grabbed his glass and walked out of the room, leaving me left wondering what the hell I had done to be told off like that. Tears were creeping down my face as I poured the hot water into my cup. Just then the front door opened, and it was Jody with her daughter and Lucy. I heard Lucy running straight up to Stu and hugging him, while I sipped on my tea, hoping Jody couldn't tell I had been crying, but she did.

'What's wrong with you?' she whispered.

'Nothing, he is just in a funny mood,' I explained.

'I tell you something Sarah, that man might have bullied me, but I won't let him do it to you,' she was still whispering, but her voice was a little louder and I worried he would overhear us.

'Shhh, talk about it another time,' I whispered back, and she nodded in agreement.

'Coffee?' I asked in my usual tone.

'Yes, please I am wrecked today.'

Jody said slumping into the only chair in the tiny kitchen.

Stu walked back into the kitchen, 'No coffee for me thanks, I have beer' he sounded normal again, a lot calmer tone to his voice.

'Hey Jody, how's, you? I hear my future wife had you collect Lucy today?' he looked at me and pulled a face.

'No, I offered because she needed a rest, look at her, she is pale as fuck.'

He walked back out of the room and Jody started to tell me about her day. She was having a tough time of it lately, and her son really was testing her limits. I know Lucy can be challenging work, but James really does push the boundaries more than any child I had ever met.

'Where is James today?' I asked.

'Oh, your Mum offered to have him for a few hours to give me a break,' she said, I looked at my cousin a little confused and asked why on earth would she offer to take my daughter if she needed a break from her own child?

'This is James we are talking about; your daughter is a delight for me, you know she always is, plus she and Stacey have been playing lovely all day.' I looked over at Jody's daughter fast asleep in her pram.

'Worn out bless her.'

My stomach started to twinge, so I sat on the side. Stu walked in a few minutes later and asked Jody to leave the kitchen so he could have a word with me. She took her cigarettes and reached behind me for the ashtray before heading out of the kitchen, Stu closed the door as she goes. He just stands there and stares at me for a while.

'What is up with you?' I asked.

'Like you need to ask?' he replied.

I honestly had no idea why he had returned home in such a stinking mood, so I told him if he doesn't talk to me then I couldn't help the situation.

'First, you have sat on your fat arse all day, and might I add you have been here on your own, how do I know you haven't had anyone around while I am at work?'

'Stuart, do you honestly think I would have someone around, and like who? I snap.

'I don't know, maybe Greg,'

Now he must have been pissed or something because he knew how much I hated that man; this was all over me bumping into Greg last week when I was in town with Lucy. Greg had tried to talk to me and had taken offense when Lucy acted like she didn't remember him. To be fair, my daughter hadn't seen that vile man in almost a year, and I will be glad if she really doesn't remember him. I only mentioned it to Stu as I thought he would be happy knowing Lucy ignored him. Had I known it would turn into an argument a few days later, I'd have kept my mouth shut.

'Why would you even bring his name into this?' I asked.

'Well why else do you have makeup on?' he snapped walking towards me.

I had forgotten I had even put makeup on that morning when I got up and looked in the mirror, my reflection had me looking ten years older, I looked worn out, so I had decided that a little bit of makeup might make me feel better, and it did. I felt more comfortable dropping Lucy off that morning. Was he really starting all this over a bit of makeup?

'I wore it to make me feel better,' I explained.

'So, you do not give a shit about how I feel?' he was shaking his head at me, 'I told you I do not want what you to wear that crap on your face, I don't like it,' he stated.

He had mentioned it a few times, but not once had he told me I was not allowed to wear it, 'I think you are being totally unreasonable,' I said as tears started to form in my eyes.

'Oh, don't start your tears with me, it didn't work for your cousin, and it won't work for you either,' he said.

I jumped down from the kitchen counter and squeezed past my unreasonable boyfriend. 'I will go and wash it off,' I said as I walk into the hallway.

'Make sure you wash it all off and throw the rest of the shit in the bin!' he shouts.

Jody was in the living room looking a little sheepish, she gave me a look of concern, but I just walked straight into the bathroom, standing on the edge of the bath to lock the door. As I was washing my face I could hear him in the living room talking to Jody, she sounded like she agreed with him over something, and I guessed it was me being told off for wearing this stupid crap on my face. I was scrubbing a little hard, but I had no makeup remover, and most of what I owned was waterproof. That was a habit from being with Greg, that man made me cry most days, and no one looks as rough and ugly as they do with tears, snot and mascara running down their face.

I spent a good ten minutes washing my face, and then another five minutes just sitting on the edge of the bath, that was until Jody knocked on the bathroom door.

'You okay?' she asked.

I shouted through that I was fine, and I would be out in a moment, she then offered me a fresh cup of coffee.

'That sounds lovely,' I said getting back on my feet and making my way over to the mirror again.

It was obvious that I had been crying and the last thing I wanted to do was go out there with a red blotchy face. I washed my face gently this time and used cooler water to help settle my face. Jody knocked the door again.

'Coffee is in the kitchen, Stu said he had to pop to the shop.'

He had had two cans since he got home, so I was hoping he wasn't driving, the last thing we needed was him in an accident because he was wound up with me, I would never forgive myself. I climbed into the bath again to unlock the door but as I leant over the screw, which is acting as a handle, frustratingly fell on the floor. As I clambered back down, I realised this belly of mine was starting to get in the way. I bent down to reach the screw and attempted to open the door again. Jody was standing in the doorway with my coffee in her one hand and a joint in the other.

'I know you don't smoke it as much now, but you look like you could do with a few drags,'

She handed me the smoke and a lighter and I walk towards the kitchen; I looked out the window as I passed through the living room, and I was relieved when I saw Stu's car still parked on the grass.

'I guess he walked to the shop then?' I asked my cousin who was now in the kitchen with me. Lucy was playing in the sandpit at the back of the garden while Jody's daughter was still fast asleep.

'Your guess is as good as mine,' she said a few minutes later.

For a second, I didn't click on to what she was talking about but realised she must have meant when she stated that the car was still on the grass.

'That's why I said that' I explained.

Jody was already rather stoned which explained why she took ages to reply to any of my questions.

'So, I can't believe you are not allowed to wear makeup, Stu used to love your makeup and would often comment on how even I should do mine more like yours.'

'That was before I was his girlfriend,' I said lighting the badly rolled joint.

I choked straight away and passed it back to Jody. I was guessing that it was my body's way of telling me off. I did smoke this stuff every day until I found out I was pregnant, and even though Stu had told me that I was still allowed to smoke with his child I never had done, but I wished I could have a smoke now.

'I can't believe he has bitched at me for wearing makeup, yet he told me I could carry on smoking weed,' I was more annoyed now I had realised how petty his argument seemed.

'Yes, but Sarah, that is only because both Emma and I smoked it all the way through our pregnancies, so he said he doesn't see the harm in it,' she seemed like she was trying to defend him.

'Sarah, you are beautiful without makeup on, you don't even need it, but I do see where he is coming from, you look incredibly young at the best of times. When you wear makeup, you look like a teenager.'

I knew they were both right, but I was a little annoyed that my own cousin was defending my unreasonable boyfriend. Talking about him, he had been at the shop for over half an hour, and it was only a two-minute walk up the road.

'I wonder what is taking him so long?' Jody asked as if she had just read my mind.

'I was thinking the same.'

Jody tried to pass me the joint again, but I didn't have any. Instead, I made my way over to Lucy who seemed to be in her own little world as she didn't even notice me walking towards her until I was right beside her.

'Mummy play,' she said as I sat in the sandpit with her.

I heard the front door open and guessed it was Stuart back from the shop, Jody went into the kitchen and then popped her head out of the door and called me in. I really was not in the mood for another argument, but I got up anyway, Lucy followed me.

'Daddy Stu,' she shouted as she saw him standing in the kitchen.

He picked her up in his arms and then told me he was sorry for being a dick towards me. It turned out that my dickhead ex had been messaging him throughout the day saying things like he would get me back no matter what. I am surprised that Stu had even let this man get to him, we were engaged and about to have a baby, why the hell would I want to go back to a man who used to beat my son and me up on a weekly basis. I explained this to Stuart when we were all sat in the living room. Jody had gone into the kitchen to make a coffee, and I could hear her daughter starting to stir in her buggy. After a long talk, Stu tells me he is sorry again and that he was scared of losing me. That wasn't going to happen, I assured him.

Lucy was all ready for bed, and Stu had run me a bath. Jody was staying over tonight, so had gone to pick up her son from my Mums before it got too late. The sun was still high in the sky, and it was almost seven in the evening, I didn't think Lucy was going to settle too well tonight, she never did in the summer months. When Stu got back, I mentioned us needing some thicker curtains for Lucy's room, and he agreed that we would go shopping the next day. I had never been to Ikea, and I know it sounds a little sad, but I was really looking forward to having a gander. I had been told the place was massive and has almost everything you could need moving into a house. I may get some innovative ideas for Lucy's bedroom, and I really did not mind flat packed furniture, if anything I thought I would be good at putting the stuff together.

We lay in bed, and I was almost drifting off to sleep when Stu mentioned that he had nearly paid off all my ring. I still can't believe he spent so much on me, but I get why he had. He then told me that I won't be getting it on my birthday because that would seem so obvious. I turned to look at him and raised my eyebrows.

'Who said I was expecting it on my birthday?' I asked.

'No one, I just didn't want you thinking you were' he replied.

'So, in that case, what are you getting me for my birthday?' my birthday was in just over a week, and I wouldn't have expected him to get me anything really, I was just pushing my luck.

'I was thinking maybe a pram or a car seat,' even though the light is off I could still see that he was smiling.

'Don't even wind me,' I say. 'The baby will have its own birthday. I am not letting it steal mine,' I explain.

'Oops' he said as he turned over to go to sleep. Just because I was pregnant doesn't mean I don't get my own birthday. Surely?

It was finally the day before my birthday, and just because Stuart said I wasn't getting my ring the next day, I was starting to think I was because Jody had just offered to pay for me to get my nails done. I felt like a bitch, but I kindly turned down her offer. I had never been a girly-girl, and I just think fake nails would look stupid on my tiny hands. I didn't think she had taken offense though because she said it was just a thought. Why else ask if I wanted my nails done, unless I needed to have pretty hands for maybe a lovely ring? Stu still swore that he had got me stuff for the baby as it was more practical than buying all the stuff in the next few months. He had a point, but I knew I would be gutted if he hadn't got anything at all for me.

My Mum was heading round later that day, she had moved away for a while there but always came back. My brothers and I had started having a bet on how long she would last this time and to be fair to her; it had been a good six months since I had last seen her. I am not sure why, but she seemed a little upset or something on the phone that morning, that's why I invited her round for dinner. I was thinking a beef madras for lunch. Stu's kids were due around about six that night, so we would have a house full. With that in mind, I got dressed and started cleaning this house. Not that it was messy at all; I just needed to give it a quick once over before heading to town to meet Jody.

I walked into the kitchen to make myself my first cup of tea of the day. I was feeling slightly nauseous, so I grabbed two ginger nut biscuits from the cupboard while fetching a cup. Stu laughs at me for being so fussy with my cups, but I only like drinking out of a thin mug, whereas he has these massive thick mugs. I don't know how he can drink out of them. I like the rim of my cup to warm up with the drink otherwise it is cold against your lips, while the drink is scolding hot. There was a note beside the kettle from Stu wishing me a good day and asking if I would put some money in his bank while I was in town. He hadn't said how much though, so I sent him a text to confirm.

I washed, got dressed and ready to take dander into town but he still hadn't text me back. I didn't want to ring him because I knew he was driving the big truck to London, and I was guessing he should be almost at his drop as he left over five hours ago. It was going to take me half an hour to walk to town, so I would text him again when I met up with Jody. I had called her to tell her

I was on my way, and she informed me that she was running a little later than planned. That was cool with me because it meant I didn't have to walk as fast now, and the sun was beating down on us that day. Now don't get me wrong, it was nowhere near as hot as it was that last month in Turkey, but this heat was having the same effect on me as it was then, I was lightheaded and a little uneasy on my feet. I was grateful when I turned the corner of my street and saw the long path ahead of me was shaded.

This was the one thing I hated about living at Stu's house, no matter which way I went, I still needed to walk past my old house to get to the town. Knowing that Greg had mates still in the area didn't help either, and with bumping into him the other week near the town, I could do with not seeing him again. The door to my old house was open, and a small girl was toddling about in the garden, so I was guessing new tenants had moved in. That gives me a form of relief because I had been told that Greg had been squatting in the house after I moved out. I was going to ask him when I saw him if it was true but, in all honesty, I couldn't wait to get away from him. The man still scares me and that few minutes seemed to last ages, and the sweat that had poured out of me was unreal. The last thing I cared about was where he was living or how he was doing.

I had told Jody I would meet her in the café. She should be here any minute, so I headed to the counter to order our drinks. I was fully drained after walking in the sun, so I ordered myself a coffee instead of my regular sweet tea. As predicted Jody walks into the café just as I place both our drinks down.

'Coffee?' she asks noticing two bowl-shaped cups.

'I feel like I need it today, I am worn out,' I explained taking a sip of my drink.

'You do look it, to be honest,' she smiled, 'only joking but seriously you should have said if you weren't up to a meeting, I could have popped to yours instead.'

'I am fine, I needed to get out of the house for a bit anyway and seems weird, but I have to buy a birthday cake,' I said giggling.

'Sarah, you are not buying your own birthday cake, I will buy one instead,' Jody explains, 'I have got my something already but wanted to get you more bits today anyway so let me get the cake.'

I asked if she was honestly okay with the idea, and she assured me that she was but that she needed to pop to the bank beforehand to withdraw money. That reminded me, Stuart still hadn't responded to my message, so I explained to Jody what was going on and dialled his number. It was just ringing out, so I guessed he was driving again. I just put off spending any money that day and transferred what we had over to his account, that way he could use what he needed, and I could spend whatever was left over on our shopping the next day if need be.

'I am hoping he sees the missed call and rings me before I need to head back and collect Lucy from nursery because I have seen a lovely gypsy skirt on sale and was hoping I could get it today,' I said to Jody as we walked past his bank.

'I can always get it for you, and you can give me the money back,' she said but she had already offered to get my cake, I couldn't expect her buying my dress too.

I knew Jody struggled just as much as the rest of us, so the fact that she still offered to help is such a lovely gesture. I know she struggled too because at least once a week we invited her down for dinner and she always talked to us about how she had had to go days on end without any milk or bread etc. That annoyed me a little because she knew that all she needed to do was ask and I would give it to her. Jody was brilliant at helping others, but not so good at looking after herself.

'So, do you think you are getting your ring tomorrow?' she asked.

'I am hoping so, by the way, I am sorry for turning down your offer of getting my nails done,' I felt bad.

'Don't be silly, I know it isn't really a Sarah thing to do, it's like me offering you a fake tan!' she laughed.

'Stu might have loved me having non-bitten nails though.'

Jody stopped and looked at me 'What's up?' I asked.

'I am glad you said no now, thinking about it,' she continued, 'the fact that you argue over what you can wear and not being allowed makeup. He may have flipped out at you having your nails done actually.'

She had a point there. I was asked to throw all my makeup out because he was insecure and said I looked too young wearing it. Stuart said that he couldn't understand why I would want to try and improve my looks if I am in a happy relationship. Even when other people had told him that it was normal to want to make yourself look and feel better, Stuart couldn't get the concept; he could be very narrow-minded at times. I wouldn't want to imagine how he would react to me making myself look even more girly with long fake nails.

BIRTHDAY BUMPS...

It was the morning of my birthday, and my Mum had just rung me to wish me a happy day, she wasn't able to pop around like planned last night and told me on the phone that she wanted to talk to me face to face.

'Your Dad has moved back to Belfast, the bastard said he was just going on holiday,' she said.

My Mum and Dad had split up two years ago. Dad was left with my two brothers while Mum moved out with Daniel and they both moved in with her new boyfriend.

I didn't like him as he seemed to bully my Mum a little but who am I to say anything? I stayed with Greg long enough. On top of that, Mum had just found out she was having a baby with this new man as well. Maybe that was what had made my Dad finally move back home.

'Has he taken the boys?' I asked.

'Yes, he left Daniel with me,' she sounded like she was about to cry.

'Why didn't he tell me, so I could say goodbye?' I asked.

'He left last Saturday Sarah, I was told not to tell you, and I should have known then that he wasn't planning on coming back.'

I was shocked 'Why?' I asked.

'Because your Dad blames you,' she paused and took a deep breath. 'Greg has been shooting his mouth off, and now your Dad's crack dealer has heard wind of the shit you were saying,'

'Mum, I haven't said anything in over a year, since that day I came to see you when I was drunk,' I said trying to defend myself.

'Sarah, I know, and you know what your Dad is like.'

As you can imagine, I was not feeling the birthday buzz after that phone call, and I made my way into the living room to see where my boyfriend was. I could hear him in the kitchen, so I popped my head around the door.

'Morning you,' I said, making him jump a little as he apparently hadn't heard my footsteps.

'You made me jump!' he said placing his phone on the counter, 'I was making you breakfast in bed, my birthday girl. You are not allowed to see.'

Stu kissed me on the forehead and ushered me out of the kitchen.

'Either go back to bed or sit in the living room, but you are not allowed in the kitchen until I say,' he tapped my bum lightly. 'is that okay?' he asked.

'That is perfect.'

I was liking this special treatment today and could have got used to him waiting on me, hand and foot. Though I knew, that would never happen, if anything it was me who did most things in the house, like the cooking, cleaning, and general up-keep but I couldn't complain because he could work anything up to sixty hours a week. Even more so at that time as he had offered to do all the London runs knowing there was more money in those jobs. He said he will work every hour; the kids and I never should go without. He is a good man, and I was smiling to myself when he came into the room with a freshly made cup of tea for me and a ginger nut biscuit. I swear to you these little cookies had been a godsend for me in that pregnancy. I wish I had known about them when I was pregnant with Lucy.

'Thank you love,' I said, as he places my tea on the table beside me.

'Who was on the phone?' he asked.

I had almost forgotten to tell him about my Mum's conversation and had he not asked me; I may well have forgotten entirely. I had total pregnancy head, and my mind was like mush most of the time.

I explained to him my Dad had moved away and how it might be somehow all my fault, but Stuart just looked at me confused. My boyfriend knew the basic outline about my whole ordeal with my Dad growing up, but he knew enough to wonder why I even cared where the man lived.

'He has taken my brothers away with him too,' I explained, 'Plus, you know me, and he were friends lately, or at least I thought we were.'

He shook his head at me and told me not to worry about it and that I shouldn't be getting stressed because I am carrying his child. He then rushed back into the kitchen saying the word fuck a few times. I was guessing he was burning the breakfast. The man wasn't the best of cooks, but at least he tried. Greg would have never attempted to cook for me, and Simon could be just as bad. Apart from when I first moved in with Simon, he showed me how to prepare a few dishes, but once I knew how to make them, the cooking was left for me to do.

'I have lost half of my family,' I said, but my voice is low and more of a mutter.

'That is his loss, Sarah, besides, it is our family that I care about.'

Stu was looking directly at my bump now, being almost seven months pregnant had me looking like a beached whale, even if Stuart kept telling me I was beautiful I felt he only said that because he was my boyfriend.

I know I should have been relieved that my Father was moving away but being told it was because I had opened my big mouth was the last thing I needed to hear. Last time that man thought I had told anyone, my life was in danger. I worried what stress he would cause for me this time, and now it wasn't just me I had to think about it, this whole situation. I decided I needed to talk to Mum as soon as I saw her and find out the whole story. Stu had already told me off as such for stressing over things I couldn't control. Where half my family lived was one of the things I had no control over.

Stu returned to the kitchen to finish off my breakfast while I headed into the bedroom to retrieve my phone. I had a text, so I opened it. Jody was wishing me a happy birthday and informed me she was on her way around with her kids. I looked up at the clock and it wasn't even nine in the morning, so I made my way back into the kitchen to tell Stu. He was on the phone in the back garden, and the toast was starting to smell burnt, so I popped it up.

'Hey out of my kitchen,' he said from behind me.

'Sorry, you were on the phone, Jody is on her way around already,' I explained.

'I know she is I invited her.'

That surprised me a little because he had been going on and on lately about how much arduous work Jody is to be around. It wasn't so much Jody but more her son

James. Stuart didn't help by winding the child up at any given chance.

'Can you please not wind them up today?' I asked putting on my sweetest smile.

'I would never,' he smiled.

'Honestly Stuart, please be nice to the kids, I already have a sore head.'

Stuart informed me that Jody was staying at ours for the weekend but that he would be on his best behaviour, I knew what he was like and wondered how long it would last.

Sure, enough as soon as James walked through the door Stu started his winding up tactics, telling James that his Mummy had a big bag of sweets in her bag, knowing full well that she didn't. James went into the living room while Jody was unstrapping her daughter from the buggy and started emptying the contents of his Mother's bag all over the place. Jody had missed my boyfriend's comment and ran straight into the room shouting at James. That is until she saw Stuart pissing himself laughing. Jody was annoyed within a few minutes of getting to our house.

'Stu, please not today, I have been up all night with them,' she begged.

Stuart informed us that he needed to pop into town and collect a few bits for my party spread later. Jody had said she would help me prepare the food, so I was not worried when he told us he may be an hour or two.

'Take your time,' I said as he kissed me on the cheek goodbye.

Jody and I were in the kitchen when she asked to see my hand.

'No ring yet?' she seemed surprised.

'I told you I wasn't getting it today.'

'I know but Sarah, he told me he was collecting it last fortnight, I am surprised he hasn't given it to you by now,' she said.

'Two weeks ago?' I thought he hadn't even finished paying for it yet.

'I am almost sure he told me the other evening that he only had a few more payments to make before I could finally have it, maybe that's where he has gone now, it doesn't take two hours to collect a few party bits!'

'Do you think he will propose tonight?' she asks me in her high pitched excited tone.

'Maybe?'

We had been talking about being engaged for months now, and Stu had been working all hours just to be able to pay for the ring, so I was starting to lose a little interest in the whole conversation.

'He will do it when he is ready; I just have to wait and see.'

The food was all prepared, and Stu had now been gone for over three hours, I wondered if I should give him a call and see where he was. I text instead just in case he was driving. He replied straight away saying that he took a detour to collect his kids from Debbie's on the way.

'Kids are on their way.' I informed Jody, who was sorting out the balloons in the living room. She started stressing when we heard James messing about in the bathroom. He was only four years old and trying to fill a balloon with water. He had seen Elise and Carl with water balloons. I laughed but Jody started going mad saying that Uncle Stu is going to flip when he sees the mess on the bathroom floor.

'It is just a bit of water,' I said.

'You know what Stuart is like though Sarah, he will flip his lid.'

'He won't because I will not let him, besides I have a mop and bucket.'

The door opened, and for a second it sounded like a mini stampede as Stuart's kids all walk in through the front door talking to one another, I could hear Stuarts bellowing laughter just outside the door, he must have been talking to our neighbour John.

'Happy Birthday Sarah!' they shout making their way into the hall where Jody and I were still mopping up the water. James had managed to soak the floor that much it had seeped into the carpet on the landing as well. Stu popped his head over all the kids to see what I was up to and when I told him what had happened, he just laughed and went to find James to give him a high five.

'See? told you he would be fine,' I assured Jody who looked stunned that my boyfriend didn't just kick off.

'Wow, the old Stu would have sent us all home,' she laughed feeling more relieved now.

'What can I say? I have tamed the lion,' I smiled knowing that everyone had seen a substantial change in him lately. He seemed to have mellowed out a lot compared to the arrogant and moody Stuart we all remembered. Stuart passed his arms around me and pulled me closer, so he could kiss my forehead. Just then the door went again, this time it was my Mum. She was alone which seemed weird and when I asked where the kids were she informed me that they were with my Aunt Eliza.

'Thought it would be too stressful with mine here too,' she said handing me my birthday card.

'Sorry it is not much, but I have struggled this week,' she explained.

'Mum I don't care what you have or haven't got for me, all that matters is that you are here,' I hugged her lightly and gave her a small peck on the cheek.

My Mum was the same as me, we both felt uncomfortable when being hugged or touched in any way and I think it showed as Stuart tried to squeeze my Mum and me into a tighter embrace.

'Stuart John Irvin, I am warning you,' she said waving her finger at him.

'Come on Laura, you are as tiny as your daughter, so I can't see you kicking my arse anytime soon.'

Stuart had a point, but just because my Mother was small, didn't mean she couldn't hold her own. I think years of abuse from my Dad had finally given her a backbone as she and Stuart started play fighting. Lucy was standing in the doorway, and I could see that she was starting to get upset so I moved past them as soon as I saw the chance. I picked her up in my arms, which wasn't easy when your stomach was as big as mine. As soon as she was in my arms, I explained that Daddy Stu and Nanny are just pretending. That seemed to be enough when she wriggled to get down and made her way back into the bedroom where James was playing.

'Someone will get hurt in a minute,' I warned, just as Carl and Elise jump onto the sofa where their Dad and my Mum were still wrestling each other.

They started to calm down, but Stuart never knew when to stop and slapped my Mum quite hard across her bum. She cursed at him and then jumped back to get a sharp dig in. Within seconds Stuart had my mum pinned against him, and as she wriggled and tried everything she could to release his hold, I hear Elise yelp.

'Shit, I am so sorry,' my Mum said jumping up to see if Stu's eight-year-old daughter is okay.

'I'm fine, it's okay,' Elise sounded so grown up.

'Accidents happen,' Stu said trying to reassure my Mum who was feeling guilty.

She started to panic as Stuart began to squeeze a little too tightly and when digging her nails into his hands didn't help loosen his grip, she decided to bite him instead. Elise was trying to help my Mum by pulling on her Dad's arms and unfortunately got bitten in the process. She seemed to have taken it well though, and I think she squealed just in time because the teeth marks were barely visible. I took mum into the kitchen to get her a drink and, I was hoping to find out more information about my Dad's sudden move.

In the kitchen, mum explained that he had rung her at stupid o'clock in the morning to ramble on about how he was threatened and that it was my fault for saying shit about him. Dad did this a lot when I was growing up and sometimes it would be over something as little as someone giving him a dirty look in the street. That actual incident resulted in my Mum and me being threatened with a knife. Mum must have suffered the most back then as he was convinced that she was trying to kill him off so slept every night for almost a week with the knife in his hands. I only had it placed against my throat for a few minutes and had spent the next month or so feeling scared to fall asleep. I can only imagine how she must have felt.

Jody walked into the kitchen to see what was taking us so long, the conversation stopped, and I gave my Mum a knowing look to say that we would talk about it later. I didn't even mind Jody knowing what was going on as I told her most things anyway, but I think Mum must have felt uncomfortable. I didn't see why she did; maybe it was because he hadn't fought to keep my two brothers here, but we all knew you could not get through to my Dad when he was like this, and any arguments now would just escalate the matter even further. I am sure even with that in mind; she must have felt shitty about the whole situation.

I went to bed that evening feeling a little deflated and kind of upset that yet again I had been blamed for one of my Dad's episodes. Stu was trying his best to get me to sleep with him, and with him being a little drunk he wasn't taking no for an answer, it was as if he couldn't even tell that my mind was elsewhere.

'Not tonight,' I said, gently pushing his hand off my leg. 'I just want to go to sleep.'

Stuart took offense and thought he had done something wrong but seemed to listen to me and rolled onto his back. I was on my side facing the outside of the bed, and all I could feel was the bed shaking. With my Dad already on my mind, I started to remember when that monster I called my Dad was masturbating at the bottom of my bed while I pretended to be asleep. I turned over, half expecting Stuart to be doing the same, but he was laying on his back with his hands forming a steeple shape on his stomach, the bed shaking was him annoyingly waving his feet.

'Please stop that,' I asked, but I just got a dirty look instead.

He wasn't listening to me because I finally fell asleep to the motions of his feet.

The next morning, I woke up, and Stuart was already awake, and I heard movements in the kitchen, he then returned with a cup of coffee for me and a smiled at his face, he apparently couldn't remember being a moody sod just before we had gone to sleep.

It was a week after my birthday when Stu told me that he was collecting my ring, I can't say I had forgotten about it, but when I didn't receive it on my birthday I kind of lost a little interest. Now he had said he was collecting it I was full of excitement again. The ring was beautiful and dainty, and at four thousand pounds you can imagine the cut of the diamonds was something else.

I had never really had much money and felt like we were living hand to mouth that past month or so and I knew that was all because Stuart wanted to get me the best ring possible, even if we couldn't afford it. He had also been working long hours to be able to afford the three hundred pounds a week that was agreed when he purchased it. He was sent to London to do another delivery that Sunday and had left at three in the afternoon; I didn't see him again until the early hours of the following Tuesday night. The joy of being a truck driver I suppose.

Stuart needed to go to work again today but said he would drop into town on the way to collect my ring first; he then commented hoping that he didn't lose it on the building site, and I warned him that I wouldn't make dinner if he kept winding me up about it. Stuart loved his food and even more so my cooking, one of the reasons he said I was wife material. That thought made me smile as he kissed me passionately before leaving for work. I said my goodbyes at the front door and then made my way into the kitchen to put the kettle on. Shit, he had forgotten his lunch so, I ran outside to try and catch him before he left. Luckily for me, he hadn't started the car up as he was on his phone.

'Aww you are a lifesaver, what would I do without you?' he said taking his bag of sandwiches off me.

'Starve by the looks of things,'

I could hear my mobile ring just as I got to the front door, by the time I was inside it has rung off. Whoever it was can wait a minute I was thinking to myself as I carried on making my cup of tea. I felt a little sick, but that was more down to the baby moving around inside me, the child had some strength already, and I felt bruised from the inside out. I finished making my cuppa and returned to the living room where Lucy is still fast asleep on the sofa, doesn't surprise me as she was up half the previous night restless and ended up coming into Stu and I until gone three that morning. Not that Stu noticed as he had passed out after I did, and a bomb could go off in the house, and he still wouldn't see. I, on the other hand, wake up at any little noise or movement and I have done since I was a child.

I switched over the TV because there is only so much Peppa pig I could stomach; Jeremy Kyle was on now, and some rough looking woman was shouting at a man who was said to have slept with her Mother. I could not wait to see what her Mother looked like. My phone rang again, it was Jody.

'Hey cuz, do you fancy some company in a bit?' she sounded very quirky which was nice to hear.

Jody was at mine within half an hour, and Lucy soon woke up as Jody crashed through the door with her buggy, shouting at James who was apparently being naughty again.

'Oh, Sarah,' she sighed as I appeared in the doorway.

It turned out Jody woke up to James in a pile of mess, while she was asleep, he decided it was a smart idea to trash the house completely. Cereal all up to the stairs, half opened packets of crisps down the toilet. She was hoping that them all being at my house he would be better behaved because he usually was better behaved around me. I think it was because I was very laid back and it took a lot for me to shout at him, whereas Jody spent all day with him so by the time she had calmed down over one of his outburst, James was starting another one. In this house, though he knew to sit and be good otherwise Stuart would shout and being a bigger man with a big bellowing voice, James knew to do as he was told.

'So that's the only reason you come to see me then?' I joked.

We were chatting for a few hours when my phone started to ring; It was Stuart just warning me that he would be home a lot later than planned. His boss has sent him on another job knowing that he could do it in the hours and would need a night out in the truck. Stuart had messed up his tachographs a few times, so he could drive through the night but last time he almost got caught out, he had been driving over thirteen hours instead of the ten hours allowed. The hours Stu would be driving meant he needed to take the nine-hour rest period in-between. I offered to go to the bank and transfer some of our money, so he could at least find a hotel, but he assured me he would be fine. The bed at the back of the cabin was spacious enough, and before I became so heavily pregnant, I would go with Stu on his nights out while Jody stayed with Lucy.

'If I had known earlier, you could have come with me,' he said.

'I am not sure it would have been so comfortable with this belly of mine expanding,' I explained.

'Or mine.'

I laughed probably louder than was needed, Jody must have heard as she appeared in the hallway where I was standing.

'It's okay love,' I said, 'I will just get Jody to stay over and keep me company tonight.'

'No rude business in my bed,' he laughed as we say our goodbyes.

'Your boyfriend has a sick mind,' Jody said as I hang up the call.

'Don't I just know it.'

Jody agrees to stay the night but has asked if we can pop over to her house later to collect some things that she was going to need for the evening. We headed to hers just after five in the evening.

Once we are back at mine, I cook us all a quick dinner while Jody baths her two. Lucy was sat at her little table in the kitchen waiting patiently for her food. She was well behaved that day which was nice to see. Usually, when Stuart worked, and she had the other kids to bounce off she could get somewhat moody, but she was full of smiles asking me different questions about when I was a child. I am clearly going to sugar coat everything as I talk to her about holidays with my Granny and all the various places I had lived. Lucy told me that she wanted to go on holiday as I did as a child. Funny enough Stuart and I had been considering going away after the baby was born on our first Butlins holiday together. He had been a few times but was thinking about the park in Surrey as it was near to his Dad, and they could travel to meet the new addition of the Irwin clan.

Once the kids were all settled in bed, Jody and I sat in the living room while I was strumming my guitar.

'I miss you playing.'

'This belly gets in the way,' I reminded her.

My baby either loved me playing or hated it because as soon as I started to play, it was doing summersaults inside me, sometimes kicking so hard that you could hear it on the guitar.

We went to bed just after eleven, but I text Stu to say goodnight. When he didn't reply I assumed he was asleep.

WILL YOU BE MINE?

It was July the tenth when Stuart finally proposed to me, and it wasn't all romantic as you would think. He had spent most of the day winding me up and telling me that he had collected the ring but somehow misplaced it. Stu then tried to say that it was my fault because the only place it could have been was in his work trousers and that I was the one who did the washing. Did the laundry? I am sure he meant to say that I do everything. I understood that he went out to work and I stayed at home, but I was almost eight months pregnant and with it being the middle of the summer I was knackered ninety percent of the time. We were in the transit van as Stuart needed to return it to the yard, he was meant to take it back the previous night but as he didn't get back till after teatime and the yard was closed at the weekend, he knew it wasn't in use. Lucy was at my mum's house for the afternoon, so I agreed to keep him company, I wish I had stayed at home now.

'I know you are just winding me up,' I said.

'Do you think I would lie about losing four grands worth of jewellery Sarah?'

I did think he would, but the more I said I didn't believe him the worse he was getting.

'Maybe it is a sign that we shouldn't get married then,' he said with a big smirk on his face.

Now I was in tears as the hormones, and my childish wind-up boyfriend all gets too much.

'Stop your crying you silly woman,' he said, 'I was winding you up.'

'I knew you were, but as usual, you never know when to stop!' I snapped.

I was pissed off that it had taken for me to cry before he realised enough was enough. He had been at it for over three hours by then, not giving in and honestly trying his hardest to convince me that the ring had been lost in the washing machine or tumble dryer. If it had been in his pocket then surely it would have been in a box, you don't carry around a four-grand ring in with your pocket change, do you?

After admitting to that whole morning being all part of his childish game, he threw the box with my ring in it, onto the passenger seat between us. It bounced and fell into the footwell.

'Here, you moody bitch, have it!'

I picked up the ring box and placed it on the seat.

'Well, you better put it on after all this fucking drama,' he snapped.

'Stuart, you have been winding me up all morning, what did you expect?'

'Not to be marrying a moody bitch for a wife.'

Oh, he was in a mood for Christ sake. I am never moody but those past few weeks hadn't been the easiest. I reminded Stuart that I was carrying his baby who was due in seven weeks' time. Winding me up seemed crazy considering how petrified he was that something would go wrong at the start of my pregnancy, just because I had a little bit of stress.

'I don't want to talk to you, put the ring on,' he sulked.

We pulled up to the yard as I placed the ring on my engagement finger, it fit perfectly. I found myself staring at the shiny new ring as I clambered out of the van almost losing my footing on the step. Stuart was already halfway across the yard and heading straight towards his car.

'I can't move as fast as you!' I shouted, but he kept walking on.

We travelled home in the car in silence, and I noticed Stuart has taken a wrong turning.

'Where are we going?' I asked.

'To pick Jody up, she can keep you company while I am out. I will collect Lucy later,' I was confused where he was going, we had planned to go out for lunch later.

'What about food?' I asked.

'You can feed yourself I am sure.'

I wanted to know why he was suddenly off out, but I knew by now that I was best just waiting till he got out of his mood. Jody was ready by the time we got to hers, so I was guessing Stu already had this planned. Would have been nice to know.

'Hey Cuz,' she said as she placed her daughter in Lucy's car seat and told James to get in the other side of the car.

We had a Landrover by now, so there was plenty of room. Stuart still had his BMW, but it needed a new fuel pump, and he was waiting for Daniel, not my brother, but the local mechanic to get back off his holidays. The Landover was run down and smelled like the farmer who used to own it, but at least it was a car.

Stuart dropped us off outside the house but didn't say anything or move; he just kept looking forward, waiting for us to all get out of his car.

'See you later,' I said, but he just started up the engine and wound the windows up.

'What has got into him?' Jody asked as we make our way to the door.

'He has been in a funny mood since he woke up. I think I ruined his proposal.' I explained.

Jody put the kettle on as I went on to explain how I managed to get my ring off him and send him off in a mood all in the space of a few hours.

'Sounds like he is just on one, don't let it get to you Sarah,' she said handing me my cup. 'Let me finally see this ring he keeps banging on about.'

I turned my hand to show her my beautiful emerald engagement ring, and she looked stunned. 'As beautiful as its owner,' she said.

Stuart returned home a few hours later; I had already prepared dinner and was just waiting for it to be put on. Jody had helped me tidy the house too, knowing that Stu would pick on any detail he could if he was still in a mood. Surprisingly, he seemed fine and apologized to me for acting like a dick earlier on. He said that he didn't mean for it to go that far and then asked if he could have my ring back.

'Stuart, it took long enough for me to get it, surely you are not going to take it from me just yet?' I smile as he kissed me.

'Let me at least be the one to put it on your finger.'

So, I agreed and took my ring off, placing it in the centre of his palm. He told me that he wasn't willing to get on one knee, but only because he was worried he wouldn't get back off the floor. So instead, he picked me up and placed me on the kitchen worktop.

'Wow, you are getting heavy,' he said.

And I felt it; I must weigh two stone more than I did at the start of the year and with the baby due soon I was starting to feel heavy. Stuart then took my hand and placed the ring on my fingertip.

'Sarah Louise Rosmond, will you please make me the luckiest man on this planet and marry me?' a tear drips down his face.

'Of course, I will.'

'I am still marrying you before that baby is born,' he said, kissing my bump just as the baby started kicking.

'See even she agrees.'

'We don't know if it is a boy or a girl yet,' I reminded him.

'Well, I know it isn't an 'it'.' he smiled helping me down from the worktop.

That night Jody was staying over and had gone with Stuart to pick up Lucy from my Mums. I was left with her two kids, but they were playing nicely with the Lego in the living room. That was until James started throwing the bricks around the room. I managed to calm down his shouting temper tantrum just as his mum walked through the door. I told Jody about the sudden outburst, and she informed me that he was going to bed as soon as we had all eaten. I will be honest I was slightly relieved as I was hoping to watch X factor in peace later. I don't watch much TV usually but being stuck most of the time indoors is starting to take its toll on me, and I find myself looking forward to relaxing with my feet up in front of the TV munching on rubbish, it was bad that this was the highlight of my weekend most weeks. I told Stuart I wanted to get a job and it turned into a little bit of an argument at first. He said he worried that if I got a job, I wouldn't have time for him. Ridiculous I know.

A few day later Stu informed me that we were going to book the registry office and that I needed to start looking for my dress. I was getting married, and it was finally starting to sink in. I honestly never believed I would ever trust anyone enough to agree to the marriage. Stu and I hadn't even been together a year yet, and I was due to give birth to his baby and walk down the aisle with him. I was starting to think I may be a little crazy, but I did love the man, and even if he was a moody sod at times, he made me feel safe and loved and that is all I have ever wanted since I can remember. When we got to the registry office, Stu tells me that he wants to get married as soon as possible and the registrar explained that you needed a three-week notice, as we must put our bands up. I didn't understand exactly what she meant but by the time we finished filling out forms and planning for the day; we left knowing that we are getting married on the twenty-sixth of August. That was only two weeks before my due date. I thought it was going to be fun trying to fit into a dress with this humungous belly of mine, but we would give it a go.

Once home we sat and worked out our finances, and it turned out that this was going to be a wedding on a very tight budget. So much so, that I had a whole fifty pounds to spend on my dress and shoes. Well, that was a proper dress out of the window, but I couldn't complain. Stuart had worked so hard since I got pregnant to make sure we had everything I needed for the baby, getting married in a few weeks didn't make any financial sense, but in Stuart's mind, he seemed to believe a hundred percent that I need to be his wife before I gave birth. All evening we were talking about our special day, and it turned out that I didn't have much say. Stu was sat at the computer designing our home-made invitations. He had put a comment on there about how I am a Pagan and that he would appreciate it if everyone could attend wearing black.

'That's ridiculous Stu!' I say shocked that he would even suggest it.

'We can't ask everyone to wear black; it will look more like a funeral,' I explained.

'But it will be different, and different will be remembered.'

Again, he had a point, but I thought he was crazy. Next, he will want me to wear a black wedding dress and be wearing dark gothic makeup. Well maybe not the makeup, I would be surprised if he even lets me wear makeup on the day.

Well as guessed, I was asked to wear a black dress. I was stressed because it was a week before our wedding now and we had done nothing but send out invites. We were around Michael's house. Stuarts friend of twenty years and I was sat in the kitchen with his wife, Sal. I explained that we had done nothing, and the money was just being absorbed into life.

'Well, we have Shelly's tiara here, and I can make you a cake,' she kindly offers, and at this point, I was grateful.

'What about your dress? that's the most important part,' she said.

'The budget is down to twenty pounds now, but this stomach needs to fit into it, and Stu has asked me to buy a black dress,' I explain.

'Black dress?'

'Yes, I guess you saw the invite?'

'I did and laughed when I saw the message from Stuart in it, is he expecting everyone to wear black?' she asked.

'Apparently so,' we giggled as she made us both a cup of tea.

Our next stop was to go and see Ade and his ex-girlfriend Gemma to invite them. Gemma wasn't in; she was now living in the flat directly above Ade with her new Scottish boyfriend. Ade seemed okay with it though as he still got to see their girls whenever he wanted to as they were so close. Ade and Gemma were together for years, and we were anything but surprised when Gemma finally had enough and walked out on him. Ade drinks a lot, and while I was with Greg he just stood there and let the man run abuse at me, so he was still in my bad books, but I get on with him for Stuart's sake and his only.

While we were at Ade's we are introduced to a young lad called Charles, he was clearly into his rock with his studded belts and great black trench coat. He reminded me of a better-looking version of Simon. Stuart decided to invite Charles to our wedding too as he was Ade's friend, but it was just because Stuart admired the man's dress sense.

Turned out on the day of our wedding Charles took a shine to Jody and I could see them all chatty while we are waiting outside the registry office. Stuart was already inside, and I was told he was shitting himself. I managed to fit into a Black gypsy-style dress that seemed to accentuate my baby belly. I was due in two weeks, but I heard the guests had a bet on as whether I would go into labour that day. I hoped not even if I couldn't wait for this wiggling child to be born. I felt sore most of the time now, and I was sure it had bruised my insides beyond repair.

Even though I was feeling somewhat fat today, I did look pretty. I borrowed my Mum's makeup that morning, and I had done it in the way that it still looked like I hadn't got much on, but it had accentuated my green eyes. My hair was placed in an up do with big curls and thanks to Sal, I had a lovely golden tiara with matching earrings. I couldn't wait for my husband to be to see me.

A few moments later I was called into the building by the registrar I had met a few weeks previous. She lead me into a small room and handed me my flowers; she then told me that we would begin in ten minutes and that I should take a seat and relax while she got all our guest seated. Now, I was getting nervous. Stu and I had been together just over a year now, and we were getting married already. I may be a little crazy, but I do love the man, not entirely in love with him and I confessed this to my Mum when we were talking about how quickly everything seemed to be moving. I told my Mum that I would learn to love him the way that he loved me and that at the end of the day he treats me the way I want to be treated, and we were about to have a baby, so I guessed marriage was inevitable.

I was called into the hallway, and I hadn't got anyone giving me away or anything, in fact, I was just asked to walk through the back of the room and head straight to the front where Stuart was waiting for me. I was a little nervous and know that everyone was going to be looking at me, but I couldn't help but look down at the floor. I only lifted my head up when I saw Stuart's shoes. I couldn't believe he had worn jeans on his wedding day; not that can say much, this dress I am wearing only cost me eight pounds. Simon was at least wearing his blazer jacket. I knew our wedding was on a budget, but I was secretly disappointed that this was it. When I looked around me, the only members of my family were Jody and my Mother. The rest of the room was all Stuart's side, his friends, and his Father. I had met Stu's Dad Malcolm and his wife Judy earlier that day, and they seemed kind enough. It would be nice to talk to them properly at our reception do. Well, gathering was the best way to describe it. We ended up at the local carvery restaurant where we had told our guests that they were to provide their own food and drink. Stuart did put this on the invitations which at the time I thought was a little cheeky and made us sound like right cheapskates. With only forty pounds in my purse, I was grateful that everyone kept getting my new husband his drinks. The cola was making me feel all bloated, so I opted for water which the staff served to me free of charge. Our meals were on a two for one offer too, so it was ideal as none of our guests were flush with money. Well, apart from Malcolm, Stuart had always talked about how both his Mother, who we don't mention and his Father both had a few quid lying about. Stuart's half-siblings on both sides all wanted for nothing whereas Stuart has always needed to fend for himself. I could see why there was a bit of resentment on his side. Malcolm was talking to Debbie, who seemed to be stuck to their sides all day so far. I didn't mean to sound jealous, but she was their son's ex, and I am his new wife. They hadn't tried to speak two words to me.

It was just after we had all eaten when Judy finally came over to make conversation with me. Malcolm was outside with my husband who was starting to get a little drunk with all the free drinks being handed to him. He hadn't even eaten his dinner, so I knew that the alcohol was taking its toll. Judy told me how happy she was that her stepson had finally settled down, she said that he has been onto the phone with his dad most of the week making sure that they could attend our wedding.

'We wouldn't have missed it for the world' she said.

'Though we do need to head soon, Malc doesn't like driving back when it is dark.'

I was a little gutted that we hadn't been able to spend much time together, but I understood that they had a five-hour drive ahead of them. I walked with Judy outside to find our husbands.

'We will be up again in a few weeks when this little one has arrived,' Malcolm says hugging me before getting in the car.

We waved them off as Stuart started to stumble a little, we agreed to sit down inside and go easy on the drink for a while. It had only just gone seven in the evening, and we had plenty of time to celebrate.

I was sat down at the table removing my shoes, pregnancy had them swelling at night-time on me these past few days, and if I could avoid it by walking barefooted now then I would give it a go, I put my feet on the table to let the blood regulate correctly. Carrying an extra two stone almost was a hard job I can tell you.

Stuart headed to the toilet making a funny remark about my feet smell, they may well have done, but I could not get close enough to them to smell them. Just then I saw Jody and Charles walking towards me.

'You will never guess who has just turned up at your wedding?' she says all flustered and stressed.

I honestly had no idea who she might be on about, so I give her my best-dumbfounded face.

'Greg! yes you heard me right, Gregory has just turned up, and it is sitting at the back of the pub with some lad I don't know.'

'How fucking dare, he!'

I chucked my shoes on the floor and stormed over into the direction where Jody said he was sitting. I could hear Jody shout after me but before I knew it I was stood at a table with Greg's smug face looking at me.

'You look nice, special occasion?' he asked.

Oh, I could have just punched his face in, the man made my blood boil and how dare he turn up here. There were plenty of other pubs that he could have visited that I didn't see why he would be here in the first place. Besides the fact that the Gregory I knew, never had the money to drink out in a pub unless I was paying for it and secondly, he didn't drive as he was banned for drink driving a few years back and this bar wasn't on any bus routes that I knew of.

'How did you know I was here?' I asked gritting my teeth as I did so.

'I didn't,' he said, but I could tell he was lying to me.

I was honestly going to lose the plot if I stayed here so I told him to stay the fuck away from my family and me and we would be fine. I was about to walk away from the table when I saw Stuart marching over to us.

'Sarah leave this to me please?' he asked, so I made my way back over to where Jody and Charles were last seen all flirty and very friendly earlier.

Jody was staying over at our house that night with Lucy and her two, and she had been brilliant so far at keeping the little ones entertained. When I returned to the table, Lucy was sat with Charles, who I didn't know and with Greg being there as well I just wanted to get my daughter away from all this. It didn't feel much like a wedding day at all. Feeling on edge, I asked Charles if he knew where my cousin was, and he pointed outside and said she was trying to calm her son down. Most of our guests are outside, so I made my way towards the door, with Lucy holding my hand. After being inside for the past half an hour, it took me a moment for my eyes to adjust to the blazing sunshine.

It was twenty-three degrees, and I was in this big black dress. If this heat had its way, I could have possibly go into labour that day. I caught a glimpse of Jody running through the parked cars, she had her daughter in one arm and trying her hardest to catch up with James who thought it funny that his Mum couldn't catch him. I took my daughter over to my Mum and asked if she minded watching her for me while I help Jody out. I then walked over towards them hoping James wouldn't see me. Jody had clocked me straight away and nodded her head at me in acknowledgment. James didn't see me and almost ran straight into me, banging his head on one of the wing mirrors on the car, which slowed him down. James fell into my arms as I crouched down to him. He wasn't crying, but I could tell that he had just hurt his head. Now that I was sat on the floor with James giggling that his Mum couldn't catch him, I didn't want to move. I couldn't see any of the guests and could pretend I was not even there. James asked when my baby would be out of my belly and I told him, at this rate very soon.

'James! Aunty Sarah shouldn't be chasing you; she is about to have a baby,' Jody scolds him with her words.

'Very soon,' he said getting up off my knee, all I could do was laugh.

Jody helped me to my feet, and I told her about my encounter with Greg, she asked me where Stuart was, and I told her that I left him at Greg's table.

'Shit Sarah, everyone has been feeding your husband whiskey, I will be astonished if Greg doesn't get knocked out.'

Seemed weird her saying he was my husband out loud. I know she was right as well. Stu was a little unsteady on his feet earlier, so we made our way back to the front of the restaurant where everyone was and just as we got to the bottom of the steps, Stuart was stood in the doorway with my guitar.

'I have been looking for you,' he said.

'He even went into the girl's toilets,' Craig said.

I explained about James running off and winding his mother up._ Stuart looked at me and told me that I shouldn't be getting involved in anything but enjoying my special day. I smiled at him, but if I was sincere, I was not enjoying this day as much as I had hoped. I knew it was a wedding on a budget but with Stuart's family hardly talking to me, kids being bored and restless and then my abusive ex showing up to cause trouble, you can imagine why I was doing anything but enjoying myself that day.

'What did you say to Greg?' Jody asked.

'I just told him that if he keeps his distance, then we will all get on fine,' Stuart said very proudly.

I was passed my guitar, and Stuart told me that he had ushered everyone outside, so he could read his speech. I didn't think he was going to go ahead with it as he had mentioned earlier that it could get him in a lot of trouble. I hoped he wasn't expecting me to stand up and say anything because I did not think any words would come out.

Stuart's speech was priceless; he was the only man who I knew could get away with slagging people off to their faces and they still smiled at him. Stuart had a line for almost everyone, but his chapter about Debbie was the one I worried about the most.

'And would everyone please raise a glass for my ex Debbie, the lovely mother of my children, who without her taking me for every penny I have ever had, I wouldn't be standing here today as a poor humble man, marrying a beautiful woman who, might I add is almost half my age,' everyone erupts in laughter, I just wanted to bury my head.

'Yes, our wedding may have been on a budget, but I couldn't see my Dad putting his hand in his pocket, and as for my Mum, well we won't go there today.'

Stuart was pushing it, but everyone took what he was saying as light-hearted banter. I, on the other hand, knew that everything that man said holds a half-truth.

After the speech was done Stuart asked me if I would play my guitar. My wedding, and I am my own entertainment. It was weird because Stuart doesn't like me playing the guitar in front of people. He has gone as far to say that I am not allowed to play it in front of people that don't know us in case they fall in love with me as he did. Stuart said he knew he loved me the day I moved into Jody's house and played Tracey Chapman song, Fast car. He says that as soon as he heard me sing that song, he knew he was enchanted by me. Pretty sweet I know but banning me from playing in front of others I thought was a little over the top.

Knowing that he felt uncomfortable with me playing today had my hands clammy and my throat dry. My Mum went to get me a drink while I made sure the guitar was in tune. When my Mum returns I sipped the water and asked Stuart what I should play, of course, he asked for Fast car.

Everyone was singing along as I started to play another song followed by another. I was just about to put the guitar down when Jody asked me to sing Linger by the Cranberries. It was one of those songs that you either love or hate, but I do think it was the one song that suited my voice the most. I started to play, and just as I was about to sing, Greg walked out of the pub and stood on the steps watching me, I was still strumming the tune, but I couldn't sing now. Stuart then saw Greg as well and told me to ignore him and play. Apart from anything else, it was nice to feel a little smug and show Greg that I was a better guitarist than him nowadays.

Stuart started singing along in his most prominent, bellowing voice. His words were crude as Greg began to walk across the car park. He must have got here by foot because he was heading towards the car park entrance. He had only turned up to make a scene, and I was glad he was going away quietly for once. I finished playing the guitar, and some of our guests had already started leaving. Stuart was talking with Charles, and he had asked if he would accompany Jody and the kids back to our house. Jody looked as shocked as me, but they both had seemed to get on well that day, and with the rumours circulating about dodgy taxi drivers in the area lately, Stuart believed he had a valid point. Jody agreed that she will text me as soon as they all arrived safe, but she told me that she would be sending Charles off on his way as soon as the kids were indoors.

'You have to offer him at least a drink,' I said knowing Stu always had a few beers in the fridge.

'Maybe, if he is lucky,' she said hugging me.

She rounded the kids up, and I gave Lucy a big hug and asked her to be good for Aunty Jody, she looked shattered bless her, and I was guessing she would go to bed with no fuss.

Once all the guests had started to leave, Craig and Sharon invited the rest of us back to their house, which was ideal as it was only a few minutes' walk from where we were. I put my shoes back on, which in all honesty even though they are wedged sandals, my feet were still screaming out to me. Craig, Stuart and his brothers were all walking ahead. Sharon, I guessed, had gone on ahead because I couldn't see her, and I am left trailing behind all Sharon's kids. Ade must have spotted me struggling to get up the grass embankment and gave me a hand. He seemed slightly worried about me and started to tell me about how Gemma went into labour on a day out with her eldest child and that he shit his pants. I was telling Ade about how Stuart delivered Elise on the landing, and he said he remembered it being in the local newspaper at the time but didn't know Stuart back then.

Stuart was still in front of us and looks annoyed when he turned around to see Ade steadying his new wife. We were seconds away from Sharon's house when Stuart waited for me to catch up.

'You go on ahead I want to talk to my wife,' he said to Ade, he just looked at me and looked away. I waited for Ade to turn the corner and asked what was up with him.

'Did you invite Greg today?' he asks.

'Why would I do something like that Stu, he is the last person I wanted to see today,' I was so annoyed that he had even the cheek to ask me that.

Stuart then just turned in the opposite direction and started waving the Vs. at me, miming the words fuck you to me. I tried to get him to calm down and come to Sharon's, but he wouldn't listen and just kept walking further away, keeping his eye on me. He shouted and told me to go to Sharon's, and he would meet me there later. I didn't know if I should keep following him or turn back but with my feet killing me now I decided to let my husband have his little mood, and I agreed to meet up with him later. We both had phones so if I hadn't heard anything from him by ten, I would call him.

Back at Craig and Sharon's, it transpired that she didn't want us all heading back to hers and had gone upstairs in a huff. Sal then invited us to have a drink outside hers, which was ideal because it means Stuart's kids could come and join us as they only lived a five-minute walk from Sal's. By the time we all got to Sal's house, it was gone ten, and I tried to ring Stu's phone. It just rang out which set everyone off on a hundred questions on where he could be. Stuarts brother Owen then asked if Stuart could have gone back to our house and told me to ring Jody.

'Why would he have gone back there?' I asked while dialling Jody's number.

'He did use to sleep with her, so who knows?' Owen joked, but I didn't think this was a joking matter.

Stuart had been gone for over three hours now, and no one seemed to have heard a peep from him. If he hadn't been so drunk when I last saw him then I wouldn't be so paranoid now. I just hoped that he hadn't gone off to try and find Greg, that was my primary concern.

Jody hadn't heard from Stuart either and told me that she would ring me if she did. It sounded like Charles was still with her, so I told her to enjoy her evening and ignore the fact that I had only been married a few hours, and my husband had walked out on me already.

It was almost one in the evening when Stuarts brothers told me that they needed to head back to their hotel before two to check in. They asked if I wanted to join them as Stu and I have a room booked in the same hotel, so I agreed and started gathering my belongings. We were about to say our goodbyes when Stuart walked in through Sal's front door.

'Where the hell have you been?' I heard Craig ask.

Stuart had gone off for a walk and decided he wanted Chinese so walked the nine-mile round trip just for some crispy lemon chicken. He said he went to Sharon's house thinking we were all still there, but instead just got a load of abuse from her for waking half her house up.

'I sobered up after that,' Stuart joked.

I was still annoyed with him, so I didn't say anything as his brothers explained that we needed to go back to the hotel soon. We headed out the door, and Stuart tried to put his arm around me and told me he had missed me. I was glad he was where I could see him, so that I didn't need to worry anymore.

The hotel was a bit of a distance away, so we decided to book taxi's, it would be double time by now, but Stuart's brother had offered to pay for both the cabs. Once inside we were invited into Owen's room for a little drink before we headed to bed. Owen said that he hadn't had much chance to talk to his sister in law and that Stuart didn't have a say in the matter. Stuart's younger brother Lloyd was annoyed and said that he was planning to go to sleep.

'We can always have a drink in our room,' I said.

'No, Lloyd is just a pussy, ignore him,' Owen opened the cupboard and passed us both a glass.

'I can't drink,' I remind him.

'I am sure you can have one little glass,' Stuart assured me.

Once Stuart and I were in our own room, I realised that I hadn't even a change of clothes with me. Stu told me that I could sleep in his t-shirt, which, might I add he had been wearing all day in this heat, or sleep naked. I opted for the second option. He then told me that he would go back to ours early in the morning and pick me out a set of clothes. I was shattered and wanted to go straight to sleep but it was our wedding night, so I couldn't just roll over and say goodnight. Stuart was very gentle with me as we are lay on our sides. He told me that he was sorry for his outburst earlier and that he was so happy to be my husband. I thought it's going to take a while for it to sink in that I have a husband.

LABOUR DAY…

Stuart and I had been talking a lot lately about starting up our own business. He knew it had always been my dream to own my own little witchy shop and this plan had been in my mind since before Lucy was born when I helped Si with his business plan. Stuart agreed that I had enough knowledge about the products and where to source them from, that we shouldn't let it all go to waste. I reminded him that we didn't have the money to set up a shop and as usual, he told me he would think of something.

So, I did it. I drew up a business plan and headed to my local job centre to ask for their advice. I was put in touch with a man called Martin Green. He was the regional chairman for the Prince's Trust, and he was assigned to mentor me. It turned out that my business plan was fine and that I didn't need the six weeks training, which I was extremely glad of, as I was about to give birth in the next few weeks. I could already feel the baby getting heavier as my stomach started to drop.

Within a week I had a thousand pounds transferred to my bank as a business loan. Stuart had also put another two hundred into the kitty.

'You can order stock now,' he said with a massive grin on his face.

'Don't you want to help me?' I asked.

'No, maybe next time. I want it to be a surprise and be like Christmas when it all gets here,' he was bouncing on the spot like an excited child.

I was sat in the computer chair, but Carl had been spinning on the chair and somehow managed to twist it through the top of the seat. To be honest, though, the chair was a hell of a lot more comfortable with the big cushion on it anyway. Carl had done us a favour, but I wouldn't tell him that. You can tell he is Stuart's son as they both seem the have the same natural banter, Carl can get very cheeky and not know when to stop, but his Father is just as bad.

I cannot explain the feeling of seeing my order completed on the screen in front of me. I was now feeling like a big kid and could not wait for Stuart to see what I had ordered so far. Now to purchase from my other wholesaler. I used three all together as it was apparent that some were better priced than others and it made more financial sense. Just as I was typing in the web address, I started to get a sharp twinge in my stomach. This happened the previous night, but I took no notice of it and fell back to sleep. Now I couldn't ignore it.

'Fuck!' I shouted out loud. Stu came in from the kitchen.

This pain seemed to be lasting a while, and I hoped it was just the baby turning.

'Shit! are you okay?' Stu asked, silly question really when he could see I was in pain, but I still said I was fine.

Then I felt it, it was like a balloon popping inside me, not painful as such but uncomfortable and then I felt it, a long sharp pain as my waters broke.

'Think we need to go to the hospital,' I said once I had caught my breath. 'Glad there is a cushion on the seat now.'

Stuart laughed at me and told me I was not allowed to move just yet.

'But my waters have gone, this baby could arrive any minute.'

'You are not going anywhere till you place that order.'

What the fuck had he just said, he may have said it in a jokey manner, but I could tell he was serious.

'Our baby is coming.'

'I know, but you are doing the order first,' he stood with his arms folded across his chest. He sounded patronizing now.

'Are you serious?' but I already knew he was.

Right, it was clear that I needed to go to the hospital, but I knew my stubborn arse of a husband thought he is being funny right now and wouldn't budge. The sooner I spent all this money on stock the quicker we could be on our way. I asked him to go and fetch me some clean clothes while I stayed sat on this drenched cushion and carried on placing the stupid order. I must be honest, I did think about ordering significant value items just to spend this money quicker, but I would only be doing it to spite him. I already had a rough idea of what I was ordering anyway so, I was hoping this wouldn't take long.

With me washed and changed and Stuart happy that he got his own way we were ready to walk out the door when my phone rang. It is my Mum, and for a second, I had completely forgotten about my daughter. I was so glad that Lucy stayed over at her Nan's last night in hindsight. As I answered, my stomach started to hurt again as I had another contraction. Stuart took the phone out of my hand and told my Mum that I was now in labour and that she will have to keep hold of Lucy for now. Of course, she was okay with that, and he hung up.

'Let's get you to the hospital,' Stuart said trying to help me stand back up straight. This was what they meant when they said crippling pain.

I didn't remember it being this bad with either Mark or Lucy, and I was guessing it was because I had gone full term with this baby, whereas my first two were both over three weeks early. Did that mean my labour was going to be harder? I would soon see.

I had tried to count how long the gaps were between each contraction, but it was just a guess when I said eight to ten minutes. I was lying in a hospital bed, and the midwife had her hand inside me feeling for my cervix. I felt sick as I felt her hand moving back out of me.

'You are only two centimetres dilated,' she said, 'You have a while to go yet,' another contraction, but this one seemed to last a little longer.

'I know it is uncomfortable, but you need just to go and have some rest and maybe grab something to eat, your bed won't be ready until eight.'

I looked at Stuart who just looked at his watch, and he informed me that we now had a five-hour wait. I was booked in to give birth in the main city hospital, which was a good half an hour away, but Stuart brought me here first just in case the baby was already on its way.

'Food?' he asked helping me to my feet.

The midwife returned with my pregnancy record and told me to relax and take some paracetamol if the pain got too much. I wished I could swallow tablets I thought to myself as she passed me a blister of painkillers.

We headed towards the city and pulled into the pub car park. Stuart picked The White Horse because it was a stone's throw away from the maternity ward. The last thing I wanted to do was eat, but I knew I was going to need the energy in a couple of hours. These contractions were starting to get closer now, and I was grateful we were close to where I needed to be. I think Stuart could tell I was not eating because he has just reached over and grabbed a handful of my chips.

'Aww, is my husband hungry?' I wished I was, but I couldn't stomach anything but the baby.

It was almost seven in the evening, and we had been sat at this pub for just over an hour. All I wanted to do was lay down and go to sleep, so I asked Stuart to take us to the hospital early. He agreed and told me he was just popping outside to ring my Mum first because he forgot to ring her back earlier.

I tried to stand up thinking that I was best to grab some fresh air, it was the end of the summer, but you wouldn't think so in this heat today, Stuart said it was because I was fat that I was so warm. Like he could talk. Just as I went to stand up, I felt my leg go from underneath me. A woman was over to me in a shot, helping me to my feet.

'Oh, dear are you okay?' she asked.

'No, I am in labour,' I felt like crying, but I didn't.

'I can tell but don't you think you should be at the hospital, and not in a pub?'

I couldn't agree with her more and tell her that believe it or not it was the midwives idea to grab a bite to eat before heading to the hospital. I can tell the woman doesn't believe me, but I was in too much pain to care what anyone thought right now. Stuart saw me wobbling slowly towards him and opened the main door between us.

'After you my lady,' he said holding the door open.

'Let's have this baby wifey.'

I put my seatbelt on as Stuart started the car. I could smell cannabis so badly in the car beside us, that I could almost taste it. I did miss having a smoke with Jody, but I had told myself I would keep off it even when this one was born.

'At least they can give you proper pain relief when we get there,' Stuart said seeing me clench the sides of my seat while a contraction kicked in again.

As soon as we got to the reception, I was given a wheelchair and taken straight into the delivery suite. The midwife came into the room with us and asked me to undress and put the cotton gown on that was folded at the bottom of my bed. Getting my clothes off was a bit of a struggle as Stuart helped me. As soon as my t-shirt was off, he reached around to undo my bra.

'No!' I snapped. I didn't mean to snap, but I was uncomfortable at that moment.

'That can stay on,' I said, 'Sorry for snapping.'

'I think you will be a lot more comfortable with it off,' he says concerned.

'Please just leave it on me and help me get this gown on,' I had no energy to argue.

The midwife returned just as I screamed out with the worse contraction that day. It was sharper and lasted longer and only seemed like a few minutes between them.

'Can you lie down on the bed while I check baby?'

She assured me that everything was fine and that now it was just a waiting game, she then attached me to a big monitor. I had had this on me before; the one strap has a circle dish to monitor my heart rate, the other one monitors the babies. Stuart looked petrified, but I explained to him that I had had to wear this contraption in my previous labours. I was born with a hole in my heart which did close on its own over the years, but I was left with a slight murmur as an adult. Now don't get me wrong it wasn't half as serious as it might sound and in everyday life, it doesn't affect me, I get out of breath quickly, but that is about it. The doctors just keep an extra eye on me during pregnancy as they say the baby puts pressure on my heart. It felt like the pressure was on my backside right now. I was glad when the midwife turned the gas and air on for me, she then made sure all the monitors were working before heading back out of the labour room.

'You okay?' Stuart asked.

Silly question but I told him I was okay, he did look worried, but he had no reason to be, women give birth every minute of the day, and we were reminded of that fact just as a woman started bellowing out in pain in the room next door. You would have thought she was right beside me with her set of lungs.

'I hope I don't scream that loud?'

The monitors started to make a buzzing noise as my contraction began again, Stuart was far too fixated on the numbers increasing on them to notice me waving in the air for the gas and air.

'Please?' I said with a whimper.

I placed it straight in my mouth, hurting the corners as I put the nozzle in my mouth. Long deep breaths. This stuff made you dizzy after a while, and I didn't want to be dizzy and in pain. The midwife returned just as my stomach started to settle down again. The baby was moving lower, and I could feel it kicking my ribs. My insides had felt bruised for weeks now, but right now every little movement was having me wince in pain.

'Can she have anything for the pain?' Stuart asked the midwife, but I had already told him the answer.

'Sorry, she is far too gone, and I don't think she is able with her heart condition, I know it is hard, but it will all be over soon,' she said trying to reassure us.

'I just have to check on another mummy, will you be okay?' I nodded my head as she exited the room again.

Stuart took the gas and air out of my hand, and I think it was because he wanted to hold my hand, but instead it was because he wanted to try the gas and air out for himself.

'This is better than my super strength beer,' he said proudly.

'Can I remind you, that it is for me.'

Here it went again as the numbers started to increase on the screen, it measured the strength of my contraction. Full blown labour is up between eighty and ninety. I was already hitting fifty and counting. Stuart was counting out loud as if to egg me on and again he still had the gas and air in his hand. I snapped at him to pass it to me because I was clearly in pain, and you should have seen the look he gave me. You would think I had asked him to chop his manhood off with that stare.

'I am in pain here!' I said as I put the nozzle back in my mouth.

Stuart then thought it was a brilliant idea to get his phone out and take photos of me in this state. I understood that he wanted memories, but not of this part surely?. I asked him to put the camera away, but he wouldn't listen. When he returned to the head of the bed to show me the photos I was horrified at the state of me.

'You still look beautiful to me,' he kissed my forehead. I still had the gas and air in my mouth, but I had stopped breathing in so deeply. I was sleepy now.

I soon woke up as I start to feel the pressure intensify again, the midwife walks in and asked if I was in pain and my thoughts slipped out of my mouth.

'What do you fucking think?' Shit, had I just said that out loud? From the look on Stuart's face, I clearly had.

'It isn't her fault you are in this state,' he said sounding a little patronising.

'No, it is yours.'

'Sarah, don't bother.'

I looked over at the medical posters on the wall while the midwife took a blood sample, I hate needles, but I hardly noticed her sticking it in me. She then pottered about in some drawers at the other end of the room and told me she would be back in a second to check how dilated I was now.

'When she comes back in the room you best apologise for being so rude,' Stu scolded me with his words and cold look in his eyes.

'I am in pain, what do you expect?' I had tears running down my face.

'You will say sorry, or I will walk out and leave you to do this on your own.'

'You wouldn't?' I asked.

'Try me.'

I didn't want to argue with him; this was meant to be a happy time, well for the one not giving birth anyway, we shouldn't have been arguing with me swearing. He had never said shit in the past about me swearing, so I couldn't see what his problem was now. The midwife returned, and I apologised to her and explained that it was the pain.

'Honestly, it's okay, I have had a hell of a lot worse than the Mum's saying fuck!' she smiled. 'Shall we see if this baby is ready yet?' she asked placing surgical gloves on.

She told me I was almost fully dilated and said to me to get some rest between contractions which were now just over a minute apart. I only knew that because the midwife had just told Stuart, my eyes were closed, and I really couldn't stay awake.

'One last push!' the midwife was at the foot of the bed.

'One last big push, come on Sarah, you can do it!'

This was too much; I couldn't push anymore; my body wouldn't even keep my eyes open.

'Push!' I could hear Stuart beside me.

'Open your eyes Sarah look!' with all my power I pushed as hard as I could until I felt a ripping sensation and I heard our baby start to cry. The relief you feel in that second when you hear your child's first breath is something I can't explain, but any parent feels the same. All that pain was worth every second and I would do it again to feel like this.

'Boy or girl?' I asked, my voice was weak, and I needed a drink.

'Beautiful baby boy!' the midwife said proudly. 'I will just clean him up a little, and then we can place him on your chest.' I sat forward as Stuart tried to undo my bra. Another midwife walked in and examined me to make sure I hadn't ripped myself in two. I hadn't, and I was fine, though I was expecting to need a few stitches after that ordeal.

'You have a few grazes, but no stitches needed,' she said, placing a clean bed pad underneath me. My legs didn't want to work, and I could have slept for days, but my midwife brought our son over to us. He was perfect.

'Sorry for being moody, wifey,' Stuart said sheepishly to me.

'You know I turn horrible when I can't handle a situation,' he explained.

'Stuart, I know, let's just forget about it and enjoy this moment,' I kissed his sweaty forehead.

'I love you, Sarah, thank you so much,' he said as our baby was placed in my arms.

'I love you too, both of you.'

CONTROLLED BEHAVIOR...

Family life seemed perfect for a while, and I honestly didn't have anything to complain about. Our son Harry was a dream child, he never cried unless he was hungry, and then it was just a moan more than a cry, and he slept all night through, almost from day one. I did worry at first when he wasn't waking up for his nightly feeds, but the midwife assured me that I was best leaving him to sleep if he was quite content. Harry was always content and a very smiley baby.

Stuart was out a lot working while I ran our market stall business. My only issue with that was that Sharon was looking after Lucy and Harry. Sharon apparently still had a problem with me, and I still didn't know why, but I am guessing half of it was down to jealousy. Stuart told me to ignore her, but she wasn't an easy person to ignore. Not only had Sharon talked Stuart into letting her buy my kids clothes, which I can provide for my own children but now she had Lucy calling Sharon's Mum Nanny! It was creeping me out a little because I swore she was telling other people that Harry was her son.

Being at the market four days a week was starting to take its toll on me a little. I had noticed black bags under my eyes, and it wasn't from being a mother of a month-old baby, because like I said he slept most of the night through. I did love my business though, and this was Stuart's compromise about me having a job. He had joked a few times about quitting his job, so that he could be at the market to keep an eye on me. He said it is a joke, but I know deep down he would drive himself crazy with weird scenarios in his head. Every evening he asked me what I had sold and to whom. He even went as far as to ask me how many male customers I had had in the shop. It was starting to grate on me, and he tried to say that he trusted me. How could he say that when I got interrogated almost every day? I think if he had his way he would have spent every second of the day with me.

Jody had had an exciting few weeks as well, she moved in with Charles which I did think was far too soon, they had only known each other a matter of weeks, but she insisted that they were both madly in love. It was nice to see her happy, but I did worry she was rushing this all a little bit too much. Who was I to talk though? I moved in with Stuart straight away, but firstly I knew Stuart for a good year before we got together and secondly, I had Greg always threatening my daughter and me. Moving in with Stuart was my protection in some sense.

Stuart and Jody seemed to be clashing a lot lately too which had me feeling like I was stuck in the middle. Half the time I didn't even know what they were arguing about. Jody is my best friend and my cousin, and I don't have any other adults I can call my friend. The latest argument between them both was apparently because Jody told him to fuck off after he told her she wasn't allowed to go home until she had rubbed his feet. Stuart had been winding her up all evening, and if I am honest I did join in a little, but that was only because she did let us manipulate her a little. The whole thing started over Stuart winding her up and saying that she was still obsessed with him if she was willing to do anything he was demanding. I did think it was a little weird that my cousin sat at the bottom of our marital bed and rubbed my husband's feet but in the same breath, I was glad that he wasn't trying to treat me the same. When Jody was about, Stuart treated me like I was his queen and would often say Jody was our little maid. He even had a bell he would ring when he wanted anything.

Mum was visiting last week when Stuart was bragging about how he had Jody as his little slave girl and told my Mum about the bell. At the time, Jody and I were in the kitchen having a smoke, when we heard the bell ring. Joking I told her that she best see what he wanted, and she went bolting into the living room. Stuart then started taking the piss out of her for running in; I think she only went because I told her to, so when she started crying I felt guilty, but if I didn't stick up for my husband no matter what, he would see it as an act of unfaithfulness. He believed that I had to have his back no matter what because he said that if the shoe were on the other foot, he would always be on my side. I know that in an ideal world I would never disagree with him, but this game with Jody was getting too much, and unfortunately, she just kept coming back for more. If it were me, I would have told him to fuck off long before now.

She did text me that morning and asked if she could call up that weekend as she had news for me. Stuart said it was up to me, but I could tell that he wasn't too amused. I know I keep talking about his moods, but when he was in good form, he was the life and soul of the house and must be the most immature man I had ever met.

It was a few days later when Jody comes and announces that she and Charles are getting married in a few months. Stuart was in the bathroom shaving his head and had called me in to check him; he had missed loads of hairs at the back and around his mole on the back of his ear, when I said that I didn't want to shave his head as I was worried I will cut him. Stu called Jody into the bathroom; she agreed to shave his head straight away, happy to have been asked. From what I could tell Stu asked her because she used to do it for him before I had met him. I went into the bedroom as I heard Harry wake up and when I returned Stuart was horrible to her, I took Harry into the living room and placed him on his play mat, when I turned around Jody was leaving the bathroom in tears because he made her feel so bad. Stuart was convinced that she was only marrying this man because she was jealous of me being married to him. He then went on to tell her that she would never make him suspicious of her either and that she needed to stop trying to be like me. All I could do was watch on and apologise to her when he wasn't in earshot.

'He isn't the man you think he is,' she warned me as she left.

Jody ended up getting married, and we were not invited. I have heard that she has been talking about moving away, but anytime I have mentioned messaging her to find out more, Stu has told me not to.

'She has made her bed, she can lie in it,' he would say.

Stu's kids had started staying every weekend now, and we had been asked if we could have Carl on more of a full-time basis as he was playing up with his Mum and stepdad. Stuart agreed and straight away started to move the room around to create more space for his son. With the flat slowly filling up with toys and baby stuff we realised that it might be time to move to a new house. We decided to look for a home closer to his kids. It only took two weeks to find a house, and it just happened to be opposite Stuart and Sally's old house. Not that it bothered me, but Stu did like trying to wind me up about it, he ended up getting himself more frustrated because I refused to bite back.

Carl moved in just before Christmas and to start off with everything was fine and Carl seemed to enjoy living at ours. I did, at one-point wonder if Debbie was making up lies about her son just to make us have him, but one evening when Stuart and I were sat in the living room, Carl walked in after arguing with his Mum and started shouting at me. Stuart was a soft touch and let Carl get away with most things, but one thing that boy never got away with was shouting at me. Carl would be challenging work almost every morning and trying to get him up for school would result in a major argument, which meant nearly every evening we would end up sitting in the living room with Stuart going on at his son for the way he spoke to me. I couldn't lie, and if Stu asked me what his son was like getting up, then I would tell him the truth; that would end up with having to sit quietly for over an hour while Stuart repeated himself and told his son about how my previous relationship was very abusive. Why he needed to tell his son that, I don't know, but he repeated himself.

'Don't you think Sarah has been through enough without you shouting at her?' Stu asks Carl.

'Well, she shouldn't piss me off,' he replied.

'She pisses me off too son, but I don't shout at her.'

I looked over at him and raised my eyebrows; the man can't say I ever piss him off really, I do everything he asks of me.

'You married her, your problem,' Carl said giving me a lovely side glance.

'She is your fucking stepmother so have some respect,' Stuart stood up and towered over his son.

'Do you hear me?' he shouts again.

'How can I take her seriously when she isn't much older than me?' Carl shouted back.

Stuart had to stop himself from slapping his son for his bare-faced cheek, and Stu never hit his kids. Lucy would get a small smack on her hand and sent to her room when she was naughty, but as a rule, he didn't agree with smacking his children even if they did deserve it. Carl deserved a slap that evening with the nasty things he was saying about me but instead he was ordered to spend the night in his room. That didn't bother Carl as he had his big TV, latest Xbox and everything else a teenage lad could want. After Carl went to his room, Stuart asked me if I was okay.

'Yes, but now he will hate me even more,' I stressed.

'No, he won't and if he does he will be out.'

'Come on Stu, we both know you would never kick him out, I just wish he treated me like he used to.'

Carl was lovely to me only a few months ago but because I was the one who must nag him to get up in the morning or even worse I was the one who had to tell him to go to bed at night when all he wanted to do was kill zombies all night. It was evident that I was going to become the enemy. I had asked Stu to wake his son up for me before he went to work, and he had agreed.

I had heard a rumour that Jody had, in fact, moved back to Ireland and was married and divorced within a matter of months, she hadn't returned any of my calls, so I am guessing she had changed her number.

Stuart had also just given up his job, so he could come and work at the market with me, he said it was because he knew that Christmas was going to be busy. I knew it was because he was becoming even more paranoid that I was going to run away with the first man who talked to me. I couldn't even go to the shop without him acting all weird for the first few minutes I got back home, it was like he honestly thought I was waiting for the first chance to run a mile. It was frustrating because I love him too bits, but this insecurity was starting to wear me down.

With no Jody and the girl, I met years ago through Stuart called Kelly, now banned from coming to ours, I just have Stuart and the kids. Stuart got funny when I had mentioned about only having him in my life like it was a personal insult in some way. He said I should be happy with what I had, which I was but that didn't stop me wanting to make friends. Last time I saw Kelly she had popped round for a coffee and a smoke on her way back home from work, she was excited and telling me about her works do, she met a man called James and was planning a date with him. When Kelly mentioned that it would be good to drag me out one evening, Stuart's mood turned, he went from being all bubbly and in an awesome mood to telling Kelly to leave and never return. After she had left, I did ask him what his problem was, and he said to me that he always knew she wanted to split us up. He was convinced that the whole three years we have been together that my friend had secretly hoped to get me away from him and find myself a better-looking man. Stu isn't an oil painting, but I love him regardless, and I spent the next few days sucking up to him and trying to make him feel loved. This constant reassurance was the only thing that seemed to keep him from sulking like a child. We must say we love each other at least five times a day.

UNHEALTHY RELATIONSHIPS...

Stuart and I had been married for over three years when we got our first scare. I hadn't been feeling myself lately, and I had been suffering from severe cramps and stabbing pains in my private parts. I was advised to have a smear, and when my result returns three weeks later I had a letter asking me to contact my specialist straight away; we both started to panic a bit. It turned out I had abnormal cells in and around my cervix. At the clinic, a lot of scary words were being thrown about the room like hysterectomies and cancers. Stuart was as white as a ghost as the doctor goes on to tell me that I needed to have a small operation to laser the cells away. I was taken to the next room while Stuart waited for me in the waiting area. It was all over quick enough, and within half an hour I was told I could go home. The doctor had given me painkillers that were far too big for me even to try and swallow and had warned me that I may experience a little pain in a few hours.

She wasn't joking either, that evening it felt like the worse period pain I had ever experienced. Stuart was doing an excellent job of looking after me and told me to stay in bed while he bathed the kids and got them both to bed. Harry was a little unsettled, but Stuart said it was just because he hadn't kissed his Mummy. I was in tears as Stu walked into our bedroom holding our son. Harry's smile when he saw me was enough to make me wipe my face and pretend I was okay. He wrapped his tiny arms around my neck as Stuart lowered him down for a kiss. I could tell he just wanted a big hug off Mummy, but I could hardly move. Stuart settled Harry in his cot before coming back into the bedroom with the painkillers.

'You know I can't swallow them,' I said.

'You can at least try.'

'Stuart honestly I will choke if I even try,' I was almost crying again.

He walked back into the kitchen looking somewhat frustrated with me and returned with two teaspoons.

'I will crush them for you,' he says smiling at me.

Within an hour Stuart was in bed beside me, and even though I was no longer in as much pain, the last thing I want to do was have sex. Stu had a hard on and kept grabbing my hand and using it to help please him.

'Please, Stuart you cannot expect me to want to do anything after the day I have had.'

'But I can't go to sleep without you doing your wifey duties,' he said with that childish voice he did. 'Your mouth still works.'

I could not believe him sometimes, but I agreed to please him before we turned over to go to sleep. It didn't take long, and a few minutes later I was rolling on my side and drift off to sleep.

It was a whole six weeks later when I was called back up for my check-up. It seemed like good news when I was sent home and told that I didn't need another check-up for six months. At least I had six months of not worrying.

Stuart had started getting ill lately too, he kept bleeding every time he went to the bathroom, and I had told him to go to the doctors about it, but the stubborn man wouldn't listen and told me that he didn't need a doctor he just needed his wife. I had had severe piles myself, so I know how painful it could be, but he insisted that it didn't hurt at all. He had started to put on a lot of weight these past few months as well, but I had tried to prepare healthier meals for him, much to his disgust at times. I had told him that he needed to try and be a little healthier when his angina started affecting him again. He kept getting a tight chest, but still, the stubborn pig would not take his medication. His tablets for high blood pressure and high cholesterol he took every evening before bed, but that was only because I put them in a shot glass beside his nightly drink of water and I refused to turn the lights out or do my wifey duties until they were gone. He needed his spray for the angina attack though and refused point blank to use it because it gave him a headache. I just wanted to shake him because I would prefer a sore head over a tight chest pains any day.

I was a bit of a hypocrite in that I just had my cervix removed, and I was still smoking, but Stuart was doing everything he could to kill himself off. Drinking every evening which had never bothered me before because he was a happy drunk ninety percent of the time, the worst thing he did was fall asleep in his chair and it took a good hour to wake up enough to push him up the stairs. He also ate so much junk, and I caught him putting my home cooked meals in the bin and nipping out to the Chinese while picking his kids up or heading to the shop. I know they say that you cannot help someone if they don't want help, but I had no choice but to try and get him to look after himself more.

'I refuse to buy you any more pork scratchings Stu,' I warned him while we were doing our weekly shop.

'I will just get them myself then,' he said all defiantly.

'they are pure fat, and surely really bad for you,' I was concerned he would cause himself a heart attack.

'I would rather live an unhealthy life I enjoy than be forced to eat crap food and drink water. I want steak and beer and that is what I am having.'

I knew not to argue with him, and I kind of agreed with what he was saying, but in the same breath, he wasn't doing himself favours. When we returned home, he told me that he had started bleeding again.

'Are you sure you are not secretly a woman, and this is just your monthly period?' I said making a joke about the situation.

I was starting to worry now and even more so when he told me that he would need to take a pair of boxers with him when he goes out just in case he leaks.

'You must be a woman,' I laugh.

'You are getting cheekier lately,' he said waving his finger at me.

'You are becoming more stubborn Stuart,' I waved my finger back at him.

'Stuart you do need to go to the doctors and get checked out,' I said in a serious tone.

'Please don't nag me, I didn't marry you because you are a nag, I married you for the opposite reason, so don't be a nagging wife.'

He had a cheek really as I never usually nag, but this was his health at the end of the day, I would never forgive myself if something happened and he ended up in a hospital all because I hadn't henpecked him. Least me telling him to go and get checked out, I knew I had done what I could to try and persuade him. He was a very stubborn man though.

That afternoon I ring my Mum and tell her about Stuart being so stubborn, she informed me that it could be more severe than piles and that it could be a sign of cancer. I worried because the last thing we needed was to both end up ill. If he didn't make himself an appointment with the doctors, then I would.

It took a little persuading to get him to go to his appointment, but he finally did after me going on at him for ages beforehand. When he got home he seemed a little annoyed, so I asked him if he had got any answers from the doctors, he just grunted at me and sat in his chair with his arms folded across his chest.

'Don't you think I have a right to know what is wrong with my husband?' I asked bringing him in a freshly made coffee.

'The knob-head said I should move out and leave my family.'

I don't believe him for one second and asked him to explain why his doctor would say that to him.

'He said I am at very high risk of having a stroke and stress could bring it on.'

'So, he told you to leave your family?' I asked confused.

'I was asked how many people lived in our house, about my job, and my relationship and the doctor said that being in a busy house could start it off, Sarah he said I have the blood pressure of an eighty-year-old man.'

I placed my arms around him as he sobbed into my arms.

'I will never move out you know,' he said lifting his face to mine 'I have no life without you and the kids.'

I kissed his forehead and asked if that was what the bleeding was about.

'No, I was too embarrassed to mention that.'

'Stuart that was the whole point of you going!' I was frustrated with him then.

'I know but turns out I am a time bomb, ready to pop at any moment,' he tried to make light of the situation, but it wasn't helping at all.

'Stuart, I think you need to go and have a full M.O.T at the hospital,' I warned.

'Sarah, please stop nagging me, I don't need any doctors I just need you.'

A few weeks later Stuart informed me that he felt terrific again as the bleeding had seemed to stop. I was guessing it was just a severe case of hermeroids and nothing too serious now. I still worry about him, but I daren't show it, Stuart does enough worrying about the both of us.

Now that my husband was feeling better it was almost inevitable that I was going to get ill again. I didn't know what was wrong with me, but I was feeling sick all the time lately. You can tell I was worn out because I had started to get spots on my chin. I never usually get spots, so I was a little annoyed; I didn't wear makeup anymore and looked after my skin better than I ever did in the past, but now my body waits until I am almost thirty to give me a teenager's complexion. Stuart kept taking the piss out of my big spot and said it doubled in size every time he looked at it. I had gotten bigger since this morning, but I refused to touch it. Most of my chin was red and just brushing over it slightly hurt.

The next morning, I woke up, and the spot on my chin had undoubtedly multiplied overnight. I thought I should go to the doctors and see if there was any medication I could take to speed up the healing process but even the thought of walking outside had me feeling a little apprehensive. It wasn't like the thing wasn't noticeable because the spot was now the size of my chin, and the pain of just the air getting to it, had tears forming in my eyes.

I was lucky to get get a cancellation appointment for later that afternoon and Stuart has asked my Mum to watch the kids for us. Talking about my Mum, she had informed us that she was moving to Cornwall to be closer to her sister Michelle. Mum had recently found out that her sister had cancer and had offered to move down to help if she could. To be honest, apart from me she hadn't got much keeping her here, and I thought the fresh start would do her a world of good. Stu told my Mum that he should take me to the doctors and made out that I was feeling worse than I was. Mum happily agreed to take Harry and Lucy for the day and told us that she would feed them for us. I was glad I didn't need to take them with me. Harry wasn't too bad and loved playing with the toys in the waiting room, but Lucy was eight now and got bored within minutes.

We dropped the kids off with Mum, and she gasped as she saw my swollen chin.

'I can see what you mean!' she said knowing Stuart had told her about my second head growing on my chin.

'It's really sore,' I tried to say but even moving my mouth set off the burning pain again.

'Anyway, we best get my wife to the doctors, will be back about six if that's okay?' Stu says giving my Mum a cuddle before getting back into the driver's seat.

'See you then, and hope you get sorted love.'

I just wave my hand as Stuart starts up the engine.

When I got into the doctor's surgery I started to panic a little, the doctor looked in my mouth and started poking at my chin which had me crying out in pain, he then told us to wait in the waiting room while he made a few phone calls.

'Sounds serious,' I said to Stuart who was now looking as worried as me.

'What do you think it is?' he asked me, but I just shrugged my shoulders.

'I honestly don't know but hope the doctor does.'

We were called back into the doctor's room a few minutes later, and he told me that I needed to go and have an x-ray. I asked if he meant our local hospital and he informed me that I needed to travel to the specialist hospital in the next town. That is where I have gone before when I have given birth. We were advised to go straight to the dental department and that the consultant would be waiting for me. Stuart was stressing and kept squeezing my hand; he looked like he was about to burst into tears at any moment.

'I love you more than anything in this world wifey,' he said as we got into the car, when I looked at him, tears were falling down his face.

'Stuart don't be stressing yourself, we don't even know what is wrong with me yet,' it hurts to talk, but I needed to reassure him.

'I am not going to be on this planet much longer; we need you to be healthy.' He was full blown crying, so I undid my seatbelt again and leaned over to pull him into me, I held him as he sobbed into my arms.

'Calm down Stu please, we need to get to the hospital.'

He sat back in his chair and wiped his tears with the back of his hands. Stuart then pumped out his chest, took a big breath and said.

'Let's get you fixed then.'

It took half an hour to get to the hospital, and our conversation on the journey was all about how Stuart would like his funeral. This had turned into a regular topic lately, and we usually had this talk at night when all the kids were settled. Stuart is wholly convinced that he was going to die in the next few years and because I had heard it so much, I could quickly just talk to him like I would any conversation. I felt a little guilty because he had talked about how I should live my life after he had gone and as much as I agreed I would never move on and I would never meet another man if Stuart died, part of me wonders how life would be without him around. I loved him so much, but his insecurities and paranoia were getting beyond a joke, and I was starting to feel a little suffocated with him. Stuart and I spent every single minute of the day together, and it even went as far to say that if I was sat in the bedroom reading a book, he would come in and sit on the bed talking to me until I would finally put my book down. If I was reading, I was not giving him my undivided attention. Sometimes I did wonder if I married a fully-grown child.

Once we got to the hospital waiting room, Stuart started to really try and convince me that everything would be okay and that we were in the best place. I knew he was right, but it doesn't stop my heart from jumping out of my chest as I was called into the x-ray room. Stuart stays outside but only because he isn't allowed in the room with me. I was asked to remove my necklace and earrings, so the x-ray could be taken. I hadn't taken this necklace off my neck in years, so I found the clasp very fidgety. I finally removed my jewellery, and the doctor asked me to open my mouth. It hurt as I felt the skin tightening around my swollen chin and burns even more when the doctor slid a big plastic rectangle in my mouth. It felt like it was cutting into me as my head was placed on a small shelf. My head was then strapped into place. The doctor then walked around the other side of a big screen and took my x-rays.

It is almost an hour when I was called back into a room with the doctor who had just done my x-ray. Stuart came with me, and I was glad to have hold of his hand as the doctor informed me that I needed an emergency operation. He went on to tell us that I had a growth and until they removed it they couldn't be sure that is wasn't cancer. I felt like I was about to be sick. It was only six months ago that I needed my cervix removed and now this. I had a hundred-thoughts running through my mind, and none of them were nice, but when Stuart asked if I was okay, I just smiled well as best as I could with a second chin and told him to stop worrying. I was booked in to have my operation at seven the next morning, and I was told not to eat anything and only to drink water for the rest of that evening.

Stuart left me at home while he went to pick up all the kids, Rachel and Elise were staying over that evening, and they had no idea about the crazy day we had had or about me having to go to the hospital the next morning. I was hoping he had already told them about it before they got here because it was getting even harder to talk as the day had gone on. I was scared about the hospital and really hoped that they would put me to sleep before they cut my mouth open. What was I going to look like with a massive scar on my chin? I was not going to be pretty after tomorrow anyway.

I was still crying when Stu returned, and he rallied around me all night, fussing about and making sure I was comfortable enough. All I wanted to do was go to sleep but at the same time as soon as I woke up I needed to go and be operated on, so I really shouldn't rush to go to bed. I stayed up a little longer but by ten o clock I was done in, and Stuart was carrying me into bed. He then whispered in my ear that I didn't have to do my wifey duties because my mouth was sore. I didn't respond because I was half asleep, but I still thought he had a fucking cheek to even mention it to me while I was like this. I hoped for his sake he was joking.

We are at the hospital for seven in the morning, but Stuart needs to rush off as soon as the doctor had been in to see me. Rachel was at home keeping an eye on the two little ones. Harry was okay and would happily play with the girls for hours, but Lucy had started to act out in jealousy lately, so I could understand why Stuart wanted to get home as soon as he could. He had told me that he would return once I was out of surgery, and I would get Debbie up to mind the kids when he came to see me later. I was laying in the hospital bed in my private room with only my phone to keep me occupied, and all I could do was play a few games. I, unlike the rest of the world, did not have social media. Stuart wouldn't allow it, even when I had told him it was a smart idea to have it to advertise our business he had refused point blank to hear me out. I was not the only person who thought it is a bit harsh that I was not allowed social media, but I knew how Stuart's mind worked and I could guarantee that he would have heart failure if I ever got a message or whatever you call it when people communicated online.

The doctor came into my room and told me that I would be going down for surgery in the next hour, he told me that they would be doing the incision in the inside of my mouth so that no visible scar would be left. He had warned me that they may have to take one of my teeth out to get at the growth better but that they would avoid it if they could. I texted Stuart to tell him what I had just been told and he responded telling me that the kids were good and that he would be back before I woke up if Debbie arrived on time. I just sent a reply saying okay with a few kisses and then got a text back telling me that he loved me and that I was not allowed to die on him. We were both in agreement that being rushed in for surgery did make it sound like the growth I had was cancerous. That was the last text I needed to hear before I got put under, but I just told him to stop worrying and that I would see him in a few hours.

After the surgery, I came round with a smashing headache, and I couldn't feel my face at all. I could just about see my reflection in the mirror opposite me, and my face looked three times the size it was before, even my eyes were all puffy. My tongue was numb, and I was unsure if I was even swallowing this saliva or just letting it build up in my mouth. Part of me was wishing I was still asleep as I was feeling very groggy above everything else. I could feel myself dipping in and out of sleep. When I woke up again, I heard Stuart talking to someone just outside my room. I didn't think I could speak and didn't really want to risk it, so I lay in my bed waiting for him to come in the room. I did think he had already been in to see me, but as soon as I saw his face, he had just got there himself.

'Oh my god wifey, what have they done to you?' he asked in pure horror.

I shook my head slightly and mouth the words I can't talk. Stuart sat on the chair beside my bed and started crying into my hand.

'They really did go to town on you,' he said sobbing still.

The doctor returned to my room within twenty minutes of me waking up, and he told us that they could remove the lump with not really any significant problems. He said that while I was having the lump removed, they had decided to take three of my wisdom teeth out as well.

'We were unsure what the lump was until we got the results back from the lab, but it had caused a lot of damage underneath your gum line.'

Stuart asked the doctor to explain more, and he said that the pressure of the growth caused an infection in my jawline which holds my teeth in place, he then told me that as my mouth heals, my teeth would start to shift, and I may be left with gaps in my teeth.

'Can't she get braces if that happens?' Stu asked.

'I am afraid not; you see the bone wouldn't cope with any extra pressure that the braces may cause.'

Well, I thought that a few crooked teeth were better than the big scar on my face that I imagined before. The doctor then asked me to try and speak and to move my tongue, so he could check there wasn't too much nerve damage.

'The main problem we did encounter was that we had no choice but to cut through one of your nerves. This will cause a bit of discomfort and or can paralyse that part of your mouth.'

I looked at the doctor shocked, and he told me that I could get feeling back on my lower lip as the time went on but that it was something that they couldn't guarantee.

'How long before I get my results back?' I asked.

'Will be about six to eight weeks,'

The doctor leaves me to get changed back into my regular clothes and told us that he would be back soon with my prescription as soon as he got it signed off. Once I had my medication, we made our way back home. Stuart told me that I was to go straight to bed and get some sleep and I was feeling that shitty at the minute, that there was no way I was going to disagree with him. We stopped off at the shop while Stu headed in to get me some soft foods to eat. The doctor did say it would be a good week before I could try and eat solid foods again, so I spent the next week eating bananas and soups. Stuart was terrific at looking after the kids and the market while I recovered for a few days in bed. By day three though I was going crazy with being stuck at home and I asked Stuart if I could go to the market with him.

The next day I was regretting going to the market, but Stuart had made me a bed at the back of the stall where no one could see me. He had no idea about half the stuff we sold and had said he needed me with him just in case he mispriced something, even if I was laying down at least he could keep an eye on me and not be worrying all day long that I was in the house on my own. I spent most of the day drifting in and out of sleep, and I was only woken a few times when Stuart had popped into the back of the unit to make us a cup of tea. I needed to let my tea go cold and use a straw to drink it, but it was better than drinking water which was all that I had swallowed for a few days. Stuart kissed me on the forehead and told me that he would be glad when we are no longer guessing what was wrong with me and finally got these results.

'Either way, good or bad we just need to know,' I said.

'It will be good news Sarah, we have told you, you are not allowed to die, and that is that' he smiled at me and went back to the till to serve one of our locals.

I could hear Stuart saying that I had been unwell hence why he was running the stall today. Stuart would never really serve anyone before and would just walk around the market talking to the other traders or hibernating out the back where I was. None of our customers could see you here, but you could hear every single word that was being said, so maybe that was why he liked hiding in here on a normal trading day.

HEALING OLD WOUNDS…

I knew my husband was an insecure, paranoid man but I also knew that half of it was down to him believing I was far too good for him. Our pillow talk was still the same as it ever had been, talking about what would happen when or if one of us died. I was thirty years old and talking to Stuart about how I would like a tree in my memory instead of a headstone. To anyone else, our nightly conversations probably seemed weird, but I was used to it by now. I reminded Stuart that it was his birthday next week and he ended up snapping at me and told me to stop nagging him.

'Just because I didn't celebrate my birthday this year, doesn't mean we can't celebrate your birthday Stu, you know the kids won't let us ignore it,' I state.

Stuart just turned over in bed and told me that he didn't think he would still be here next week. For a second, I thought he was saying that he was leaving me, but it transpired that he had been stressing since I was in the hospital about his own health and just didn't want to tell me. The bleeding had started again, and now he was always sweating. It was August, and even though it was the height of the summer, it hadn't been all that warm this year. I had got used to sleeping with the fan up to full, but I couldn't get used to his snoring and would end up at the bottom of the bed most mornings. Stu hated me sleeping upside-down and last time he woke me up just to argue with me because he believed I had got out of bed.

Stuart would have a dream about me being with someone else, and then it would take an entire day to convince him that it was all in his head. Some days, I would need to get Rachel or Carl to tell their Father how unreasonable he was being and then that got thrown in my face because his kids were siding with me. Stuart was not an easy man to live with, but I was far too easy going and let the man have his rants.

Stuart had said a few times that I was so easy to keep happy; he said that all he had to do was not hit me and I was the most relaxed wife to live with. Stu couldn't see how Greg would have wanted to beat me up and that even he knew all he needed to do was raise his voice and I did as I was told. That had not stopped going through my mind, and I was slightly annoyed at Stuart's observation of me. I just wanted a nice quiet life with no stress or drama so if that meant doing every single thing my husband asked me then so be it. It had turned him into the laziest man I had ever known though, and he even had me open and pour his can anytime he wanted a drink.

He was drinking a lot lately too but insisted that he wouldn't give up the things he liked to be healthier, he would rather be unfit and overweight and enjoy his life, than be imprisoned by rules and regulations of society. Who was I to judge, I still smoked weed as soon as the kids were in bed, it is my only vice and not one I am ashamed of at all. Besides most people, I have known are doing a hell of a lot worse than me. Yeah, I smoke weed, but I look after my home and my family and still manage to run my own business, I know I should quit smoking due to health reasons, but I haven't so I am not about to start on my husband for having the same mentality as me.

I still had over four weeks to wait for my results back from the hospital, but even though Stu is stressing big time about it all, I am not worried. I think that if they found out that it was cancerous that I would know sooner rather than later. I was still very bruised, and I could talk if I didn't move my mouth too fast. The main problem was my bottom lip was still numb, and I knew the doctor said that he had to cut through my nerve, I was kind of hoping that was his way of telling me the worse possible outcome. I didn't think I would still be numb two weeks later. I think this was what has set Stuart off on his whole death sentence speech lately, the waiting, I think was the worst of it.

Rachel had been staying over most evenings, and it turned out that she didn't want to live with her Mum. Debbie wasn't bad or anything, but being a schoolteacher, I don't think she knew how to turn the nag button off. Rachel was seventeen now and wanted a bit of freedom which she said she got when she was at ours. I did try and look after Stuart's kids as well as I did him and Rachel knew that she had it easy at ours. Now and again, we asked her to watch Lucy and Harry for an hour or so while we would nip to the shop, or if Stuart was picking me up at the market.

I had been down the market most of the afternoon sorting out the new stock and pricing it all. This was the part I enjoyed the most because Stuart really had no idea how much a customer was willing to spend, whereas I had years of experience now. We had had this business for just under six years now. Time does go quickly and as much as Stuart didn't want to celebrate his birthday that had just past I was hoping he remembered it was our six-year anniversary the next day, though he hadn't mentioned it and I had decided to be stubborn after him not even getting me a card for my thirtieth. I knew we didn't have much money, but I was still a little hurt by it. Had it been my twenty-ninth or thirty-first I'd be a bit less miffed about it all.

He had me a little worried too lately because not only was he forgetful which wasn't like Stu, but he seemed to have very little energy and he was out of breath a lot. I was sure his lifestyle choices held a crucial factor in this, but I still wished he would go and see a doctor. It was just gone five in the evening, and he was on his way to collect me, so I packed the last of the stock away in the back of the stall and pulled down the roller shutter.

Stuart looked tired when he pulled up in the car. He told me that he was hoping for a lay down as soon as I got home to take over the kids. Of course, I agreed and sent him upstairs as soon as we got in through the door.

'I will bring you a coffee up in two secs,' I said as both Harry and Lucy start fighting for my attention.

'Mummy! she pulled my hair.'

'He started it,' snapped Lucy.

I wished I had stayed at the market, at least the only person arguing was my own thought in my head. I settled the kids down with Rachel and the TV while I headed upstairs to Stuart. He looked at me with a half-smile, the sweat beads dripping down his head.

'You need to see a doctor,' I said worried.

He is the most frustratingly stubborn man I had ever met, and he sent me down the stairs feeling like a proper nagging wife.

'I wish your Dad would stop being so pig-headed at times,' I said to Rachel as I sit to roll a smoke.

'He was struggling to breathe when we were making that deal on the bed, he said it was because he was too hot, but he does seem ill,' she gave me a pitiful look.

'He won't listen to me,' I sighed.

'Sarah if he won't listen to you, then no one has a hope of getting him to the doctor.'

She had a point, and all he kept repeating was that he just needed his wife, it would seem sweet if he just had a cold or something, but he had been like this for a week now and not getting any better. I walked into the kitchen to fetch my lighter and I found myself just standing looking out onto the garden. It was nice at the start of the holidays, but with all Carl's half bikes scattered all over the place and the spray-paint on the shed from last weekend, I found myself crying at the sight. I was sure everything was just getting too me lately, so I made myself a coffee and headed into the unsightly garden to have my smoke. Rachel joined me and had a few drags on my smoke too. Stuart did say she was seventeen and could smoke if she wanted but I still felt like a bad influence on her.

It was just gone nine in the evening when Stuart came into the living room. I was sat in his chair where I always sat when he wasn't there, which was very rarely lately. He just looked at me with sad puppy dog eyes as I got up off the chair, he placed his head on my shoulder and asked me to get him a beer.

'Okay, but I am sure it won't make you feel any better,' I warned.

'Won't make me feel any worse.'

The next morning, I headed to the market on my own, the past week had been slower than usual, and I was guessing the fact that my face was still yellow and brown from the bruising was playing a factor in it. Stuart had messaged to say that he would be down as soon as Rachel's bed had been delivered. I replied telling him that it was a slow day and not to rush. I was enjoying the peacefulness and had been taking the advantage to get some reading done. I thought Stuart was winding me up at first, but it turned out that he did not like me reading, maybe it was the type of books I chose which was the real problem. I had just read a book about a boy who was wrongly mistreated growing up by his mother. Even though the boy in the book suffered no sexual abuse, I could relate to it a lot. Stuart knew about my past or at least the main outline. Anytime I had wanted to talk or even mention it, Stu fell apart. The thought of someone hurting me so badly was too much for him to handle, so I was glad he didn't know if I am honest. Stuart said the books I read would mess with my head, but in fact, I think it had the opposite effect. It is kind of nice to know that I am not the only person who went through what I did. It is even nicer to know that they survived it just like me.

I think now that I am older I can say that I have put my past behind me in a lot of respects. Even though I have forgiven my mentally ill Father, I will never forget what he has done to me. Reading books with similarities to my own childhood is just a reminder to me, of how strong I am. If he couldn't break me, then nothing ever will, and with Stuart and the kids and the love they all have for me I could never have asked for more. I have gone through so much in my life so far, and I am only thirty years old, and whether it was my Dad, my cousin or Greg, not one of them have broken me.

In the dead of night…

Stuart met me at the market as planned, but he only stayed for ten minutes before he had a paranoid moment that Rachel would try and put up her new bed by herself, he was worried that Harry might get hurt, so he headed home to make the bed. I told him I would get the bus home, but he insisted on picking me up. I managed to finish reading my book which I was pleased with, and I had just been to the bookman next door to get a new read for the next day. I had told Stuart to stay at home tomorrow as we had the Sky man coming around and Stu had made it clear that I was not allowed in the house on my own with a man. I had told him how unreasonable his paranoid mind was but as far as he was concerned, every man on this planet wanted to take his wife away from him. I hadn't said this to him, and I never would be so cruel, but I felt like he was trying to push me away with all his insecurities.

I started to pack up just as Stuart turned the corner, he smiled as soon as he saw me, but I noticed his face was all red and the sweat was pouring from him again. He looked weak, so I told him to sit down while I finished packing all the dreamcatchers and windchimes away.

'I am fine just a little out of breath,' he said trying to convince me.

'Told you that you needed to go to the doctors Stuart, you are worrying me.'

'I will let you make me an appointment tomorrow,' he sighed.

I knew he felt like he had lost some battle, but he needed to see a doctor, even if Stuart ended up divorcing me for being a nag, which he had light-heartedly said to me a few times recently. I was glad he was finally listening to me, and with any luck, the doctors would give him some antibiotics, and he would be back to my big childish bear. This poorly and ill Stuart was like having ten sick children all at once, but I think I did a decent job of looking after him.

'We needed to go to Tesco's before we headed home' he said trying to lift himself from the seat.

'Getting old,' I joked putting out my hand to help him to his feet. I knew it was because he wasn't well, but I couldn't resist a quick little line now and again.

'Cheeky,' he had just turned forty-one.

We needed to pick up some bedding for Rachel's new bed and some pizza for dinner tonight. I grabbed the pizza and told Stuart that I would meet him in the bedding aisle once I am done. He was walking slowly with his head down. I wished I could make him better, and as much as I bitch in my head about him, I loved this man to bits. It was hurting me seeing him this run down. I decided to go for a chili chicken pizza for me, and Rachel and Stu and the kids were having meat feast. Sorted and after this long day, I was glad I didn't have to cook a big dinner.

When I get to the bedding I saw Stuart leaning up against the shelves; he looked like he was about to pass out, so I rushed to his side.

'I am just a bit lightheaded,' he said trying to stand up straight.

'We need to get you to the hospital never mind doctors,' the colour had completely drained from his face, and I was starting to worry.

'Not a chance, I just need an early night.'

I could have just shaken him!

'Will you pick up the bedding and I will meet you in the car?' he asked.

Stuart made his way slowly towards the front of the shop while I picked out a butterfly bedding set, a ten-tog quilt, and some pillows, I was trying to be quick as I could, so I could get my husband home, but the tills were on the go slow. I hated these self-serve tills and even more so when the stupid thing was telling me there was an unexpected item in the bagging area. Like it is fucking magical and knows what to expect. I wouldn't mind but the only thing that fits in the bagging area was the quilt anyway, and he hasn't given me a chance to scan anything else through. The cashier was too busy chatting with her colleague to even notice me standing there so after a few moments I walked over to ask for her assistance. The silly bitch rolled her eyes at me for interrupting her natter. Hello blondie this is what you get paid for. That wasn't what I said to her, but the urge was there. Instead, I just smiled and thanked her, a slightly sarcastic thank you but one just the same.

Stuart was sat in the car and didn't look any better.

'Did you get everything?' he asked.

I quickly showed him the pattern of his daughter's new quilt cover, and he told me that he thought she would love it, I knew she would because it was like the one she pointed out in the Argos book.

When we got home, Stuart headed upstairs to get his head down for an hour. I helped Rachel make her bed before pre-heating the oven for the pizzas.

'I got us extra spicy chicken.'

Rachel smiled at me and told me that I was too good for her, I was never too good for anyone I just knew what pizza her favourite and I pointed this fact out.

'I know, but every time Mum buys pizza she refuses to get spice because both Carl and Elise are girls,' she laughs.

'Elise is a girl, and well Carl is debatable,' that's cruel, but the boy does spend hours in the bathroom getting ready, making sure every single hair is in place. Then he puts a helmet on and heads to the BMX park, made no sense to me.

I didn't wake Stuart up when the pizza was cooked because I was guessing he needed a good sleep, plus he loved cold pizza. Personally, I didn't see the appeal, but each to their own I guess. He came down the stairs at just gone eleven at night; I was just about to head to bed after I had placed this order for the new stock.

'Shit, love you look ill,' I said concerned more than ever.

'Do you want your spray?' I asked.

He was holding his chest as he came into the living room, so I could tell his angina was playing up again.

'No' he said sitting in his chair.

'It was meant to be for when you get pains like this, and you said it does work?' why wouldn't he bloody take his spray?

I got up from my chair and headed to the medicine cupboard to get his spay anyway.

'I know you don't like it, but you need to take it,' I begged him.

He was looking at me with bulging, tear-drenched eyes, trying his hardest to conceal the pain he was in, he then took a deep breath.

'I am fine, tell me what stock you ordered to take my mind off this shit,' he sat tall and placed his hands like a steeple on his stomach.

I started to list off all the things that I had ordered so far, and he seemed pleased enough with what I was getting.

'What about the plaques?' he asked.

Stuart had seen some lovely grave pieces on the wholesaler's site which were seventy percent off, and with us selling a lot of angels and cherubs lately he thought he was onto something. I did have to remind him that we were a mythological gift shop and not a memorial store, he said he knew, but I was thinking otherwise with all his suggestions so far.

It was just coming up to one in the morning when we said goodnight to Rachel and left her watching TV downstairs, Carl had been in for a while now and was watching a movie in his bedroom, Harry and Lucy were fast asleep, so it was time to get my uncomfortable husband back to bed. He wasn't helping at all, and I tried with all my strength to peel him from the chair. He could move, but he thought it was funny watching me struggle. We finally got upstairs a whole ten minutes later. Stuart went to the bathroom, locked the door as usual while I lit the candles in the bedroom and closed the curtains properly.

Stuart had been in the bathroom ages now, and I needed to pee, so I knocked on the bathroom door quietly. When he opened the door, he placed his arms around me and started to squeeze me.

'I will wet myself if you don't move,' I warned.

He let go of me and sulked into the bedroom when I return he was laying on his back looking up at the darkened ceiling. I climbed in beside him, and he told me that I was not going straight to sleep.

'Really?' I asked, 'You are clearly in pain and somehow I don't think me sucking you off is going to help!' I sat back up.

'At least I will go with a smile on my face,' he grinned.

I could tell he was still in a lot of pain and his breathing was already erratic, but my husband wanted to be pleased before he went to sleep and who was I to change our routine on him? Almost every evening without fail he asked me to at least perform oral on him, if he was horny enough, then he would please me back. I got on my knees and start ed massaging him with my mouth; he then asked me to climb on top. I was not feeling it tonight, and you could tell as I tried and lower myself on him.

'Fuck me wifey; you are tight tonight.'

I think the word he meant was dry. He was inside me for a few minutes when I climbed back off him.

'Stuart, you are in far too much pain for me to do this.'

I was expecting him to get moody, but he agreed and rolled over onto his side, so I could tickle his neck, it always sent him straight to sleep, but tonight he wasn't drifting off. Stuart then got out of bed and opened the bedroom window, the fan was already on full speed, and I understood that he was three times bigger than me, but I was starting to feel the chill, so I got myself under the covers before asking if my husband if he was okay. He said he was, but I didn't believe him and started to mention the hospital.

'Please for the life of me Sarah, stop nagging.'

'I am only nagging because you won't listen!' I explained.

'If I wanted a nagging wife I would have married Debbie!'

Stu then made his way to the bathroom and told me he was fine he just needed five minutes. The light may have been off in the room, but I could see by his face how much pain he was in, and he couldn't have any more painkillers for at least an hour.

'I know you aren't meant to, but do you want more painkillers love?' I asked.

'I just need five minutes, honestly,' I thought he was trying to convince himself.

Stuart went into the bathroom, but I didn't hear him lock the door this time, so I was guessing he wasn't in the toilet. Stuart always locked the door for fear of Lucy or his girls walking in on him.

I must have drifted to sleep because I was woken by an almighty crash, stunned and confused I looked at the clock, and it was twenty-two minutes past two. Shit, I looked to see Stuart, but he hadn't returned to bed, and I realised the sound had come from the bathroom. I jumped out of bed quicker than I ever have done in my life and ran to the bathroom door, it was open, but Stuart was on the floor, and it looked like he was trying to be sick, I couldn't get the door open, so I kept pushing it harder. I shouted his name, but he didn't respond and then I realised he was having a fit, not being sick. I had never seen anyone having a fit and I panicked. I found the strength from somewhere to squeeze myself into our tiny bathroom.

I didn't know what the fuck to do. Stuart was trying to stand himself back up, but I thought he needed to lay down. There was no fucking room in this stupid bathroom, but I managed to roll him over onto his back.

As soon as I saw his face I could tell something serious was wrong with him, Stuart wasn't acknowledging me at all, his eyes were darted forwards and looked like they were about to pop out of his head, and he was biting down on his tongue. I had heard about people choking on their tongues whilst having a fit, so I tried and force his mouth open. He was like a dog with a locked jaw. I couldn't do this on my own. I turned him onto his side I placed him in the recovery position, and his body was still jolting, he needed medical help and fast, so I reassured Stuart that I would be back in a second.

I ran into my bedroom to retrieve my phone, but I couldn't see it anywhere, I then crashed into Carl's room shouting for him to wake up, he told me to fuck off, so I ripped his covers off him and screamed that we needed his phone to ring an ambulance.

'What the fuck?' he shouted sitting up.

'It is your Dad Carl. We need to get him to the hospital; he is having a fit!' I panicked.

Carl jumped out of bed and pushed past me.

'He is in the bathroom!' I shouted as he ran into mine and his Dad's bedroom.

'Stupid bitch, leaving him on his own!' he snapped.

I glanced at Carl's phone, but it was also dead and wouldn't charge lately.

'Stay with him,' I shouted as I ran down the stairs to Rachel. She was awake and heard something going on, but thought it was just her brother arguing so stayed in her room.

'I need your phone, quick,' I begged.

Rachel doesn't say a word she just passed me her phone while I rang the emergency services.

After what seemed like forever I asked if my husband was still breathing. I was stood on the landing when Carl started to shout my name. As I ran into the bathroom I could see that he wasn't breathing anymore, the tips of his ears were blue, and his mouth was starting to turn blue, I passed Carl the phone as the paramedics on the other end were telling me to open Stuarts' mouth. It wouldn't open no matter what I tried, so Carl tried to take over. I was asked to place my unconscious husband on his back, and I was told how to do CPR on him. I was pushing on his chest counting in time with the person on the other end of the phone for over twenty minutes before Rachel shouted to say the paramedics were here. Stuart was already dead. That cold stare had no life in it at all, but even though I knew he was gone, I wouldn't stop pounding at his chest, one, two, three and a big push on four. One, two three and a big push on four. I was lifted from my husband's chest by one of the paramedics who told me that they would take over from here.

'He might have had a stroke,' I said remembering what the doctor had told him.

'We will take it from here mam,' the taller paramedic said.

Rachel was in the bedroom opposite with Harry and Lucy, and I was asked if I could get them down the stairs and out of the way, so they could bring Stuart onto the landing to have more room. Rachel and Carl took the kids down the stairs. Harry was still half asleep so didn't seem to notice anything happening around him, but Lucy was wide awake and could see her stepfather on the bathroom floor.

'What's wrong with daddy?' I hear her say as she is carried down the stairs.

'Dad has just slipped on water and banged his head,' Carl told her 'He will be fine.'

'He will have a headache,' Lucy replied.

I was in floods of silent tears, dripping from my chin and I honestly felt like I was about to faint, so I sat on the top step hearing the urgency in the paramedic's voices. I think I must have zoned out a little for a second until I was asked to go down the stairs by one of the paramedics, I remember looking at him and thinking God you're tall. Then the fear sank in.

I was sat on the sofa, while Rachel and Carl took my two to their Mum's house and explained what had happened. I was on my own when the paramedic informed me that there was nothing they could do to save my husband and that they would wait with me until the police arrived. Police, shit did they think I had done this to him? They could see my concern and informed me that it was protocol in sudden deaths. My husband was laying on my landing dead, and I panicked and turned to run, up the stairs. One of the paramedics was still stood at the top of the landing.

'Please he will be scared if he is on his own,' I begged the man to move out of my way.

'I am sorry too miss, but you need to go down, I know it's hard,' he looked at me as I fell into a pile on the floor.

I could hear my Mum now in the living room. Carl must have run across the road to get her for me. As soon as she saw me, she wrapped her arms around me. I wanted to tell her what happened, but I couldn't speak.

I was sat on the sofa with my Mum when the police arrived. They asked me to explain what had happened and when I tried to tell them, it dawned on me that I could have saved his life if I had only stayed awake. I had drifted off to sleep for no longer than twenty minutes, but I could have saved his life at that time. I was told that Stuart would have an autopsy to determine the cause of his death, but I couldn't help but think that if I had got him to go to the doctor sooner, then he could still be here now.

I was thirty years old and thought I had finally found my happy ending when Stuart and I got married. I knew he talked about death a lot, but I didn't believe for one second that I would be a widowed parent at such an early age.

Stuart didn't deserve to be dead; he was far from the easiest man to cope with at times, but he was the most loving Father I had ever met. Harry was going to grow up wishing his Dad was still here, whereas I was just filled with even more hatred for my own Dad. Why did Stuart have to leave me? Why was he not here for us? Why was it the men in my life who deserve to be dead are just happily getting on with their lives when my husband is lying dead on my floor.

The paramedics left, and the tall one told the female police officer who has just interviewing me that the undertakers had been called and would be here as soon as they could. I looked up at the clock, and it was almost six in the morning already. I had been asked by the officer if I wanted her to ring anyone, but I told her that I would do it myself when everyone was awake. My Mum rang my brother Daniel who was looking after my little sister to tell him what had happened. She was in floods of tears, and it hit me how close she was to my husband.

Rachel returned to the house just before seven with her Mum. Debbie was a mess and couldn't even come into my house. I think knowing Stuart was still upstairs was just too much to handle. Seeing how cut up she was, made me feel a little guilty. Debbie and Stuart were together for thirteen years and had three kids together. She had known him for most of her life, and there was me who only shared seven years of my life with him. Seeing how cut up her and Rachel were I think is what was upsetting me the most.

I was angrier than I had ever been in my life and hurting more than I thought was possible while my Father was enjoying his new life, god knows where. I might not have been able to tell my story before, but that day had proved that you can lose everything in one single heartbeat. I could die any minute, and I won't leave this earth regretting not saying anything. Stuart was no longer here to protect me which I know sounds childish and immature, but he was my hero, he saved me from Greg, and I felt like my past couldn't touch me when I was with him, now that he had gone what was I meant to do?

The undertakers came through my back gate, and I was ushered into Rachel's bedroom while the police escorted the undertaker upstairs. Rachel was in floods of tears but the anger I think had stopped me crying. That made me even more annoyed that I couldn't cry. I was fucked up or what? I knew it was all going to hit me soon, but I was grateful that for now I could hold myself together for everyone else. I knew I said I was now a widow at the age of thirty, but those poor kids had just lost their Father. Rachel was almost eighteen, and I heard every young woman needs her Daddy. I wouldn't know of course. Carl was only just turned seventeen and Elise was about to become sixteen in a few months. These kids were far too young to lose their Dad. I started to cry again when I think of Harry growing up without his Dad. He turned six in two weeks, and I knew Stuart had something planned, but he had kept it from me as he said it was a surprise for me as well. Now we would never know what he had planned, but I needed to make sure my son didn't suffer even though we knew it was going to be hard. He was too young I think to realize fully what was going on. Lucy, on the other hand, I was not looking forward to telling her that her Daddy was gone. She had already lost one parent when Simon moved away and stopped bothering with her, now Stuart was gone as well,

I was wondering how she would cope. How would any of us cope?

The police said their goodbyes and Mum had to get back to my brother and sister, so Rachel and I were sat in the living room in silence for ages. I then made my way up to the bathroom, and I was left with the blanket they used to cover him and blood stains on my towel. The paramedics said they put an incision into his throat to try and unblock his airway, so I was guessing that was where the blood had come from. I sat on the bathroom floor and cried silently for over half an hour. I then walked into the bedroom and saw Stuart's wedding ring on the bedside cabinet. He would take it off every night because his fingers used to swell up in the evening, though I used to wind him up and say he took it off, so he could pretend he was single. He never liked me talking about him being unfaithful, even if it was all in a joking sense he would still take offense and go moody. I broke down again realising that I would never see his sulky face again, or his big smile when I walked into a room, or even be cursing him for snoring all night long. The realisation that he wasn't going to walk through that bedroom door again was too much for me to handle and I felt like my heart was going to explode as I tried to hold the tears in.

I had no idea what I was meant to do next. I had never organised a bloody funeral before, and I didn't know where to start. First thing was first, I needed to ring Stuart's Dad and tell him that his son had died. I can't even see the screen as I try and find his Dads number through the tears escaping me.

It was surreal that just a few hours ago he had made a joke about dying with a smile on his face. That was no smile, the fear in his eyes, and the panic on his face as if he knew it was the end. I was unsure if that image would ever leave my mind.

I was scared, how was I meant to tell a Father, that his son was dead? The phone started to ring......

TO MY READERS

Thank you so much for reading this story. First of all, I want to say that I understand this story hasn't gone the way you might have hoped. I can tell you I feel this same frustration a hundred times over, after all, it is my life you have just read.

When I met Simon, I was too young to have a family and settle down, but I craved the love I never received as a child and at the time Simon gave that to me. I never had a childhood so to become a mum myself so young affected me in ways I didn't realise at the time, and this resulted in the end of our family unit.

Meeting Greg, I thought was amazing at the start but soon my fear for him would lead me to make the worst decision in my life, letting my son move in with his Father. Now, I know that would have annoyed you as the reader, but I want you to understand that I still beat myself up about that, to this day. Mark, on the other hand, loves living with his dad and is a very bright happy young man who I am so proud of. We see him as often as we can and every phone call he tells me how well he is doing at school and life in general. Mark is happy living with his Father, and it may not be the ideal family set up, but it worked for us as a family unit, and that is all that matters.

Stuart was the most playful loving man I could have ever met and yes at the start it took me an awfully long time to trust him and even to love the man, but he worshipped me regardless. Stuart knew I had a past, but he never wanted to know the full story because he said it would rip him apart and I believe had he known, it would have. Life seemed perfect and yes, he was a controlling man through his fear of losing me, but I let him be that way. I changed myself for him and from the arrogant man I first met at my cousin's flat all those years ago to the loving father I found in him, we have both come such a long way together. When I was recently asked how I cope with the loss of Stuart I always say I don't know, but the truth is; losing the man I loved after years of pillow talk about his death made it easier to deal with. Also given the fact that I have never had it easy in life, leads me to think that I was born to deal with so much pain and heartache.

Since I can remember, I have had to deal with it all, and a lot of my life hasn't gone into these stories so far. I believe I was designed to take the stresses of life to help others with their own. Abuse happens everywhere and can follow you into adulthood if you let it.

I have worked with many women who themselves have had similar situations where they find themselves leaving one abusive relationship and falling straight back into another one. This happens all too often, and we need people not to sit and judge us, but to support us even if we are or have made the wrong decisions. It is hard to think with a clear head when fear is controlling you, and I think some forget that unless they have been through it themselves.

As for my Father, well he moved away, and even though the family are all still on talking terms with him, I am not. Nothing has needed to be said, I told my story, and unfortunately, I wasn't believed, and I am still not believed by most to this day. I hear he is very mentally ill and causes himself enough paranoia that he is his own prisoner in his own mind, and as much as I have thought about pressing charges, I refuse to put my children and my family through all that. I at least want to wait till my children are grown up so that they don't need to be dragged into it all.

Life hasn't been easy, but I promise there is a light at the end of all this and I hope you get the chance to see where my life takes me. The third and final book to this story is available on Amazon now and titled Where will my journey end?

SR xx

www.ingramcontent.com/pod-product-compliance
Lightning Source LLC
La Vergne TN
LVHW051622080426
835511LV00016B/2121